822.912 OCA

CAERLEON COLLEGE
OF EDUCATION.

BOOK No.

D0719277

013551

COLLECTED PLAYS

SEAN O'CASEY

COLLECTED PLAYS

Volume Three

PURPLE DUST
RED ROSES FOR ME
HALL OF HEALING

CAERLEON COLLEGE
OF EDUCATION, LIBRARY

LONDON
MACMILLAN & CO LTD
NEW YORK · ST MARTIN'S PRESS
1962

013551

*This book is copyright in all countries which
are signatories to the Berne Convention*

—

First Edition 1951
Reprinted 1958, 1962

MACMILLAN AND COMPANY LIMITED
*St Martin's Street London WC*2
also Bombay Calcutta Madras Melbourne

THE MACMILLAN COMPANY OF CANADA LIMITED
Toronto

ST MARTIN'S PRESS INC
New York

PRINTED IN GREAT BRITAIN

CONTENTS

▼

PURPLE DUST

A Wayward Comedy in Three Acts

TO

SHIVAUN

CHARACTERS IN THE PLAY

CYRIL POGES
BASIL STOKE
SOUHAUN, *Cyril's mistress*
AVRIL, *Basil's mistress*
BARNEY, *their manservant*
CLOYNE, *their maidservant*
O'KILLIGAIN, *a foreman stonemason*
1ST WORKMAN
2ND WORKMAN
3RD WORKMAN
REVEREND GEORGE CANON CHREEHEWEL,
   P.P. of Clune na Geera
POSTMASTER
YELLOW-BEARDED MAN
THE FIGURE
THE BULL

SCENES

ACT I.—A room in an old Tudor mansion
          in Clune na Geera.
ACT II.—The same.
ACT III.—The same.

TIME.—The present.

ACT I

SCENE : *A wide, deep, gloomy room that was once part of the assembly or living room of a Tudor-Elizabethan mansion. The floor is paved with broad black and dull red flagstones. The walls are timbered with oak beams, and beams of the same wood criss-cross each other, forming the roof, so that the room looks somewhat like a gigantic cage. The beams are painted, alternately, black and white so as to show they are there and to draw attention to their beauty ; but the paint makes them too conspicuous and, therefore, ugly.*

On the right is a huge open fireplace, overhung by a huge hood. In the centre of the fireplace is a big iron arm with a swinging cross-piece thrust out like a crane ; from this cross-piece hangs a thick chain to which a big shining copper kettle is attached. At the back are two rather narrow arched doorways, one towards the right, the other towards the left. Between these are two long, deep, mullioned windows. At the right, nearly opposite the fireplace, is a wider arched doorway leading to the entrance hall. Near the fireplace are two straight-backed seats, like infantile church pews, each big enough only to hold one person. A small Elizabethan or Jacobean table is somewhere near the centre of the room. On this table is a vase in which are a collection of violets and primroses, mostly primroses.

It is about seven o'clock of an autumn morning, fine, crisp, and fair.

Three workmen are seen in the room, two with shovels and one with a pickaxe. One with a shovel and the one with the pickaxe are standing near the archway leading to the entrance hall ; the other, with a shovel, is beside the wide fireplace, looking curiously at it. The 1st Workman is a tall, lean man

3

*with a foxy face; the 2nd Workman is tall too, and strongly
built; he has a dreamy look, and has a dark trim beard faintly
touched with grey; the 3rd Workman is stouter than the others,
and not so tall. They are all roughly dressed in soiled clothes,
and wear high rubber boots.*

1st Workman [*near the fireplace*]. Well, of all th' wondhers,
to come to live in a house that's half down and it's
wanin' over. Thrickin' th' rotten beams into a look
o' sturdiness with a coat o' white and black paint, an'
they for long a dismal dwellin', even for the gnawin'
beetle an' th' borin' worm.

3rd Workman [*with the pickaxe*]. They like that sort of
thing.

1st Workman. An' th' maid was tellin' me they're goin'
to invest in hins an' cows, an' make th' place self-
supportin'.

3rd Workman. An' th' two o' them business men, rollin'
in money.

1st Workman. Women you're not married to cost a lot
to keep; an' th' two with them'll dip deep into the
oul' men's revenue. Goin' over to London done them
a world o' good.

3rd Workman. Irish, too, an' not a bit ashamed o'
themselves.

1st Workman. Ashamed is it? Isn't th' oulder one
proclaimin' she's straight derived from th' Duke of
Ormond?

3rd Workman. An' we knowin' th' two o' them well as
kids with patched petticoats an' broken shoes, runnin'
round th' lanes o' Killnageera.

1st Workman. God be good to her, anyway, for bringin' a bit o' th' doddherers' money to where it's needed.

3rd Workman. Th' two poor English omadhauns won't have much when th' lasses decide it's time for partin'.

2nd Workman [*who has been silently leaning on his shovel, looking dreamily ahead of him*]. That day'll hasten, for God is good. Our poets of old have said it often : time'll see th' Irish again with wine an' ale on th' table before them ; an' th' English, barefoot, beggin' a crust in a lonely sthreet, an' th' weather frosty.

1st Workman. Afther a reckless life, they need th' peace o' th' country.

3rd Workman [*assuming a listening attitude*]. They're stirrin'.
  [*Mr. Cyril Poges, Souhaun, and Barney come in by one entrance at the back; Avril, Basil Stoke, and Cloyne from the other; they dance in what they think to be a country style, and meet in the centre, throwing their legs about while they sing. Avril has a garland of moonfaced daisies round her neck and carries a dainty little shepherd's crook in her hand; Cyril Poges, a little wooden rake with a gaily-coloured handle; Souhaun has a little hoe, garlanded with ribbons; Cloyne, a dainty little hayfork; Barney, a little reaping-hook; and Basil Stoke, a slim-handled little spade. Each wears a white smock having on it the stylised picture of an animal; on Poges's, a pig; on Basil's, a hen; on Souhaun's, a cow; on Avril's, a duck; on Cloyne's, a sheep; on Barney's, a cock.*
  [*Poges is a man of sixty-five years of age. He was, when young, a rather good-looking man, but age has altered him a lot. He is now inclined to be too stout, with a*

broad chest and too prominent belly; his face is a little
too broad, too ruddy, and there are perceptible bags of
flesh under his eyes. He has a large head; getting bald
in front; though behind and over his ears the hair is long,
fairly thick, and tinged with grey. He has a fussy
manner, all business over little things; wants his own
way at all times; and persuades himself that whatever
he thinks of doing must be for the best, and expects
everyone else to agree with him. He is apt to lose his
temper easily, and to shout in the belief that that is the
only way to make other people fall in with his opinions.
He has now persuaded himself that in the country peace
and goodwill are to be found; and expects that everyone
else should find them there too. Under the smock he is
dressed in morning clothes, and he wears a tall hat.

[Basil Stoke is a long, thin man of thirty, with a rather
gloomy face which he thinks betokens dignity, made
gloomier still by believing that he is something of a
philosopher. His cheeks are thin and their upper bones
are as sharp as a hatchet. He is clean-shaven, and the
thin hair on his half-bald head is trimly brushed back
from his forehead. His eyes are covered with a pair of
large horn-rimmed glasses. Under the smock he is dressed
in jacket, plus-fours, and he wears a cap.

[Souhaun is a woman of thirty-three years of age. She
must have been a very handsome girl and she is still
very good-looking, in a more matronly way. She has
the fine figure of her young friend Avril, but her arms
and her legs have grown a little plumper. She is still
attractive enough to find attention from a good many men,
when her young friend is out of the way. She wears,
under the smock, what a lady would usually wear in the
morning.

[Cloyne is a stoutly-built, fine-looking girl of twenty-six or

*so, and wears the servant's dress under her smock, and
has a smart servant's cap on her head.*

[*Barney is a middle-aged man with a discontented face and
a muttering manner. Under his smock he wears the usual
dress of a butler.*

[*Avril is dressed, under her smock, in gay pyjamas.*

Poges [*singing*] :

>   Rural scenes are now our joy :
>   Farmer's boy,
>   Milkmaid coy,
>   Each like a newly-painted toy,

All :

>   In the bosky countrie !

Avril [*singing*] :

>   By poor little man the town was made,
>   To degrade
>   Man and maid ;
>   God's green thought in a little green shade
>   Made the bosky countrie !

All [*chorus*] :

>   Hey, hey, the country's here,
>   The country's there,
>   It's everywhere !
>   We'll have it, now, last thing at night,
>   And the very first thing in the morning !

Basil [*singing*] :

>   Our music, now, is the cow's sweet moo,
>   The pigeon's coo,
>   The lark's song too,
>   And the cock's shrill cock-a-doodle-doo,

All :

> In the bosky countrie !
>> [*chorus*]
> Hey, hey, the country's here,
> The country's there,
> It's everywhere !
> We'll have it, now, last thing at night,
> And the very first thing in the morning !

[*As they are singing the last lines of the chorus for the second time, those who have come in by the left entrance go out by the right one ; and those who have come in by the right entrance go out by the left one. The workmen stand silent for a few moments, watching the places where the singers disappeared.*

1st Workman. Well, God help the poor omadhauns ! It's a bad sign to see people actin' like that, an' they sober.

3rd Workman. A sthrange crowd, they are, to come gallivantin' outa the city to a lonely an' inconsiderate place like this.

1st Workman. At home, now, they'd be sinkin' into their first sleep ; but because they're in the counthry they think the thing to do is to get up at the crack o' dawn.

3rd Workman. An' they killin' themselves thryin' to look as if the counthry loved them all their life.

1st Workman. With the young heifer gaddin' round with next to nothin' on, goadin' the decency an' circumspection of the place.

3rd Workman. An' her eyes wiltin' when she sees what she calls her husband, an' widenin' wondherfully whenever they happen to light on O'Killigain.

1st Workman. A handsome, hefty young sthripling, with a big seam in his arm that he got from a bullet fired in Spain.

3rd Workman. For ever fillin' the place with reckless talk against the composure of the Church in the midst of the way things are now.

2nd Workman. Ay, an' right he is, if ears didn't shut when his mind was speakin'.

1st Workman [*to 2nd Workman*]. If I was you I'd be dumb as well, for Canon Chreehewel's mad to dhrive him outa th' place, with all who hear him.

2nd Workman [*fervently*]. There's ne'er another man to be found as thrue or as clever as him till you touch a city's centre ; an' if he goes, I'll go too.

1st Workman [*a little derisively*]. Me brave fella.

3rd Workman. It's what but they're thryin' to be something else beside themselves.

1st Workman. They'd plunge through any hardship to make themselves believe they are what they never can become.

2nd Workman [*dolorously*]. An' to think of two such soilifyin' females bein' born in Ireland, an' denizenin' themselves here among decent people !

3rd Workman. Whissht ; here's the boss, O'Killigain.

[*O'Killigain comes in from the side entrance, with a short straight-edge in his hand. He is a tall, fair young man twenty-five or twenty-six years old. He has a rough, clearly-cut face ; dogged-looking when he is roused, and handsome when he is in a good humour, which is often enough. He is clean-shaven, showing rather thick but*

*finely-formed lips. His hair, though cut short, is thick
and striking. When he speaks of something interesting
him, his hands make graceful gestures. He has had a
pretty rough life, which has given him a great confidence
in himself; and wide reading has strengthened that
confidence considerably. He is dressed in blue dungarees
and wears a deep yellow muffler, marked with blue
decoration, round his neck. He is humming a tune as he
comes in, and goes over towards the men.*

O'Killigain [*lilting, as he comes in*] :
   They may rail at this life, from the hour I began it,
   I found it a life full of kindness and bliss ;
   And until they can show me some happier planet,
   More social and bright, I'll content me with this.

   [*To the men*] 'Morra, boys.

All the Men. 'Morra, Jack.

O'Killigain [*with a gesture pointing to where he thinks the
   people of the house may be*]. Up yet ?

1st Workman. Up is it ? Ay, an' dancin' all about the
   place.

O'Killigain. Bright colours, in cloth and paint, th' ladies
   want, they say ; jazz pattherns, if possible, say the two
   dear young ladies : well, they'll want pretty bright
   colours to cheer up this morgue.

3rd Workman. It's a strange thing, now, that a man with
   money would like to live in a place lonesome an' cold
   enough to send a shiver through a year-old dead man !

O'Killigain. Because they think it has what they call a
   history. Everything old is sacred in every country.
   Give a house a history, weave a legend round it, let

some titled tomfool live or die in it — and some fool
mind will see loveliness in rottenness and ruin.

1st Workman. A nephew of the Duke of Ormond, they
say, dhrank himself to death in it, and the super-
numary wife of the older codger says she's a direct
descendant of the nephew ; and she says they've come
from the darkness an' danger of England to settle down
in what is really their proper home.

O'Killigain. And they're goin' to have the spoons and
forks an' knives done with what they say is the
Ormond crest ; Ormond's motto will shine out from
their notepaper ; and this tumble-down oul' shack is
to be christened Ormond Manor.

2nd Workman [*savagely*]. The English gett, hurryin' off
with the ensign privilege of an Irish gentleman !

3rd Workman. Isn't it sthrange how many'll fall for a
mere name ? Remember oul' Miss MacWilliam who
used to faint with ecstasy the times she told the story
of sittin' for a second in the King o' Denmark's chair ;
an' oul' Tom Mulligan who swaggered round for years
afther the son o' the Earl of Skibbereen had accidentally
spit in his eye !

O'Killigain. Well, men, we'd better make a start.

1st Workman [*warningly*]. Shush ! Here's the flower o'
Finea !

> [*Avril comes in from the left entrance. She is a pretty girl
> of twenty-one or so, inclined, at times, to be a little
> romantic, and is very much aware of her good looks. She
> is far from being unintelligent, but does little and cares
> less about developing her natural talents. Her eyes are
> large and expressive, but sometimes sink into a hardened*

lustre.   She is inclined to think that every good-looking
young fellow, rich or poor, should fall for her pretty face
and figure, and is a little worried if one of them doesn't.
She adopts a free-and-easy and very unnatural attitude
when she is talking to workmen.   She is dressed now in
gay scarlet trousers, widening at the ends, and very tight
around her hips and bottom ; low-cut black silk bodice,
slashed with crimson, half hidden by a red-and-white
striped scarf thrown carelessly round her shoulders — and
black shoes.   She trips over in a slow dancing way to
where the workmen are standing, and as she comes in she
lilts the first verse of The Maid of Bunclody.

Avril [*close to the workmen*]. Top o' the mornin', boys !

O'Killigain [*humouring her*]. Same to you, miss, an' many
of them, each of them fairer an' finer than the finest
of all that ever brought the soft light o' the dawn at
the peep o' day into your openin' eyes.

Avril. It's meself that hopes you like the lovely house
you're renovatin' ?

O'Killigain. An' tell me who wouldn't like the lovely
house we're renovatin' ?   It's a dark man he'd be,
without a stim o' light, an' destitute o' feelin'.

1st Workman [*enthusiastically*]. Sure, miss, it's dumb with
many wondhers we've all been for years that no one o'
the well-to-do laid hands suddenly on the house to
give it the glory again that musta been here throughout
the jewel'd days of the times gone by !

Avril. When it's thoroughly restored it'll be a pleasure
an' a pride to the whole district.

O'Killigain [*with just a touch of sarcasm in his voice*]. Sure,
when we're done with it wouldn't it be fit for the

shelther an' ayse an' comfort of Nuad of the Silver
Hand, were he with us now, or of the great Fergus
himself of the bright bronze chariots ?

Avril. Or even the nephew of Ormond's great Duke, the
warlike ancestor of my very own friend an' distant
cousin ?

O'Killigain. An' all the people here who are anything'll
be mad with envy that they hadn't seized holt of it
to make it what it'll soon be shown to be ! [*Avril lilts
a reel and dances lightly about the room. The 1st and 3rd
Workmen join in the lilting of the air. As she is passing
O'Killigain he catches her excitedly and whirls her recklessly
round the room till she is breathless, while the two men
quicken the time of the lilting. To Avril while she stands
breathlessly before him*] Bow to your partner. [*Avril bows
to him and he bows to her. Indicating the two men who
lilted the tune of the reel*] Bow, bow to the bards.
  [*She bows to the two men, and when she has bent to the
  bow, O'Killigain gives her a sharp skelp on the behind.
  She straightens herself with a little squeal of pain and
  a sharp cry of indignation, and faces him angrily.*

Avril [*indignantly*]. You low fellow, what did you dare
do that for ! How dare you lay your dirty hands on
a real lady ! That's the danger of being friendly with
a guttersnipe ! Wait till you hear what Mr. Basil
Stoke'll say when he hears what you've done. Get
out of the room, get out of the house — go away, and
never let your ugly face be seen here again !

O'Killigain [*with some mockery in his voice*]. Sure, I meant
no harm, miss ; it was simply done in the excitement
of the game. [*To 1st Workman*] Wasn't it, now, Bill ?

3rd Workman. Ay was it, miss. Sure, th' poor man lost his caution in the gaiety and the gayer tune.

O'Killigain. I did it all in play ; I thought you'd like it.

Avril [*sarcastically*]. Oh, did you ? Well, I didn't like it, and I don't allow anyone to take advantage of any effort I make to treat workmen as human beings.

2nd Workman [*maliciously*]. If I was asked anything, I'd say I saw a spark of pleasure in the flame of pain that came into her eyes when she was hot !

Avril [*furiously — to the men*]. Be off, you, and let me speak alone to this young man ! I don't require any explanation from such as you ; so be off, and I'll deal with this fellow ! [*The three workmen slide away out of the scene. With a gentler tone in her voice*] Never, never do a thing like that again, young man.

O'Killigain [*with mocking earnestness*]. Never again, young lady. You looked so handsome, gay, and young that my thoughts became as jaunty an' hilarious as your little dancin' feet.

Avril. Never again, mind you — especially when others are here to stand and gape. [*She goes over and feels the muscle of his arm.*] There's too much power in that arm to give a safe and gentle blow to a poor young girl.

O'Killigain. Ashamed I am of the force that sent a hand to hit a girl of grace, fit to find herself walkin' beside all the beauty that ever shone before the eyes o' man since Helen herself unbound her thresses to dance her wild an' willin' way through the sthreets o' Throy !

Avril. It's I that know the truth is only in the shine o' the words you shower on me, as ready to you as the

wild flowers a love-shaken, innocent girl would pick in
a hurry outa the hedges, an' she on her way to Mass.

O'Killigain. Is it afther tellin' me that you are, an' your
own words dancin' out as fair an' fine as the best o'
mine ?

Avril. An' why wouldn't they, now, an' me that sang
me song, first runnin' me years in, an' runnin' them
out, in th' fields an' roads that skirted the threes an'
hills o' Killnageera ? But is there an Irishman goin'
who hasn't a dint o' wondher in his talkin' ?

O'Killigain. I never met many who had it ; but I got the
touch of makin' a song from me mother, who —
[*proudly*] — once won a grand gold medal at a Feis for a
song of her own, put together between the times of
bringin' up six children an' puttin' an odd flower on
the grave of the one that died.

Avril. You must sing me a few of your songs sometime.

O'Killigain. Now, if you'd like to listen, an' you think
that the time is handy.

Avril. Not now ; we might be disturbed ; but some
evening, somewhere away from here.

O'Killigain. I will, an' welcome ; some of them, too,
that have been set in a little book, lookin' gay an'
grand, for all the world to see. Come ; listen — [*in a
mocking whisper*] — and brave the wrath of the gouty,
doughty Basil Stoke.

Avril [*with a toss of her head*]. That thing ! [*With bitter
contempt*] A toddler thricking with a woman's legs ; a
thief without the power to thieve the thing he covets ;
a louse burrowing in a young lioness's belly ; a

perjurer in passion ; a gutted soldier bee whose job
is done, and still hangs on to life !

O'Killigain [*embracing her tightly*]. Tonight, or tomorrow
night, then, beside the blasted thorn three.

Avril [*with fright in her voice*]. The blasted thorn tree !
Oh, not there, not there — for evil things sit high, sit
low in its twisty branches ; and lovers, long ago, who
leaned against it lost their love or died. No, no, not
there : a saint himself would shudder if he had to
pass it on a dusky night, with only a sly chit of a
moon in the sky to show the way.

O'Killigain. Oh, foolish girl, there never can be evil
things where love is living. Between the evil things
an' us we'll make the sign of the rosy cross, an' it's
blossomin' again the dead an' dhry thing will be, an'
fruit will follow. We are no' saints, and so can abide
by things that wither, without shudder or sigh, let
the night be dark or dusky. It is for us to make dying
things live once more, and things that wither, leaf and
bloom again. Fix your arm in mine, young and fair
one, and face for life.

Avril [*after a little hesitation*]. Undher the thorn three
then, with you.
    [*As the sound of voices is heard he holds her tight for a*
    few moments, kisses her several times, then lets her go.
    He goes over and examines a wall where a telephone is
    evidently being put in.
    [*Avril, all demure, stands at the other end of the room*
    watching him.
    [*Souhaun, followed by Poges and Basil, comes into the room.*
    She is carrying a large two-handled earthenware jug in
    her right hand, and two coloured cushions under her left

arm. Cyril Poges is carrying a large coloured picture of himself in a gold frame ; and Basil Stoke too is bearing a picture of himself in a silver frame ; he has a hammer sticking out of his side pocket. Cloyne follows them in with a six-step A ladder. Poges and Stokes are wearing gum-boots reaching to their thighs, and bright scarves round their necks.

[Poges and Basil rest the pictures against a wall.

Souhaun [to Avril]. Oh, here you are, with Mr. O'Killigain. We were wondering where you were. We've a lot to do, dear, before we can get the house comfortable, so don't keep Mr. O'Killigain from his work. *[She leaves the jug down in a corner.]* Filled with gay flowers, Cyril, this jug'll be just the thing on your quattrocento desk-bureau.

Poges. Lovely, darling. *[To O'Killigain]* We've been for a run over the fields, O'Killigain ; lovely ; feel as fresh as a daisy after it. *[Indicating the boots]* Great comfort, these boots, in the long damp grass. Saw a swarm of rabbits — quaint creatures.

Basil. With these and rubber hats and rubber coats, we'll be able to weather anything. I've got the hammer. Have you got the nails ?

Poges. I forgot them. I'll get them now.

Basil. And I'll get the string.

[One goes out left, and the other right.

Souhaun [to Cloyne]. Hold this curtain stuff end, Cloyne, till we see its width.

[Cloyne holds one end of the stuff while Souhaun holds the other. O'Killigain, pretending to be interested, bends over Cloyne and, stretching out a hand to handle the stuff,

half puts his arm around Cloyne's neck, who is very well pleased.

O'Killigain. Finely woven as a plover's wing, it is. No way odd it ud look as a cloak for the lovely Emer ; an', if it hung from th' sturdy shouldhers of Queen Maev herself, she'd find a second glory !

Souhaun [*displeased at his covert attention to Cloyne*]. Over here, Cloyne, please ; hold this end.
    [*Souhaun and Cloyne change places, and O'Killigain bends over Souhaun.*

Avril [*to O'Killigain*]. I must have a chat with that man working for you who knows everything worth knowing about Ireland's past and present, Mr. O'Killigain.

O'Killigain [*very seriously*]. And please, miss, don't try to make fun of him. Touch him not with a jibe, for he's a wandherin' king holdin' th' ages be th' hand.

Souhaun. How could a common worker be a king, O'Killigain ?

O'Killigain. Easier than for a king to be a common worker. Th' king o' a world that doesn't exist was a carpenter.

Avril. Where is the real world to be found, then ?

O'Killigain. Where I have found it often, an' seek to find it still.

Avril. And where's that place to be found ?

O'Killigain. With the bittherness an' joy blendin' in a pretty woman's hand ; with the pity in her breast ; in th' battlin' beauty of her claspin' arms ; an' rest beside her when th' heart is tired.

Cloyne. Sure, it's only makin' fun of us all he is.

O'Killigain. Softer an' safer than St. Patrick's breastplate
is a woman's breast to save a man from the slings of
life. [*Singing softly, moving a little away. Slyly towards
the women :*]

Come in, or go out, or just stay at the door,
With a girl on each arm an' one standin' before ;
Sure, the more that I have, the more I adore,
For there's life with the lasses,
Says Rory O'More !

Oh, courtin's an illigant, gorgeous affray,
When it's done in the night, or just done in the day ;
When joy has been spent, sure, there's joy still in store ;
For there's life with the lasses,
Says Rory O'More !

When all has been done, though nothin's been said,
Deep in the green grass, or at home in the bed ;
To ev'ry brave effort we'll yield an encore ;
For there's life with the lasses,
Says Rory O'More !

[*As he ends his song, Poges and Basil return, the one with
the nails, the other with the string-wire.*

Poges [*to O'Killigain — briskly*]. The garage is well in
hand, isn't it, O'Killigain ?

O'Killigain [*who has tapped the wall, and is shaking his head*].
Yes, well in hands.

Poges [*enthusiastically*]. Good man ; when it's done I'll
get a first-class artist over from London to paint and
make it exactly like a little Tudor dwelling, so that
it won't in any way distort the beauty of the fine old

house. What do you say, O'Killigain ? [*O'Killigain is
silent.*] Eh ?

O'Killigain. I didn't speak.

Basil [*who has moved over, and is looking ecstatically up at an
end wall*]. Early Tudor, I think ; yes, Early Tudor, I'll
swear. A great period, a great period. Full of flow,
energy, colour, power, imagination, and hilarity.

O'Killigain [*tapping the wall beside him — ironically*]. And
this is Middle Tudor — not a doubt about it.

Poges [*looking ecstatically at the other end wall*]. Late Tudor
this one, I'm sure. Ah, England had no equal then.
Look at the Lionheart, eh ? Smashed the infidel,
smashed him out of Jerusalem into the desert places.
What was his name, follower of the Prophet ? You
remember, Hegira, the white stone, or was it a black
stone ? — oh, what was the bounder's name ?

Souhaun [*helpfully*]. Tuttuttankamen, dear ?

Poges [*scornfully*]. Tuttuttankamen ! My God, woman,
he was only the other day !

Avril [*more helpfully*]. The Mahdi, dear ?

Poges [*more scornfully*]. The Mahdi ! [*Plaintively*] Is there
no one here knows a line of the history of his country !

Basil [*with complacent confidence*]. Genghis Khan.

Poges [*emphatically*]. Genghis Khan ! That was the name
of the bounder driven from Jerusalem by the Lion-
hearted Richard. A warrior, a hero. And maybe he
was actually in this very house. It's all very moving.
[*To O'Killigain*] I imagine I hear the clank, clank, clank
of armour when I walk the rooms, and see the banners

and banneroles, with their quaint designs, fluttering
from the walls ! Don't you feel the lovely sensation
of — er — er — er — old, unhappy, far-off things, and
battles long ago ? [*O'Killigain is silent.*] [*Insistently*]
Don't you feel something of all that, O'Killigain, eh ?

O'Killigain [*quietly*]. I let the dead bury their dead.

Souhaun. Oh, don't worry Mr. O'Killigain, Cyril ; he's
a workaday worker, and neither understands nor takes
an interest in these things.

Poges. Nonsense ; O'Killigain's an intelligent man, and
is only too glad to learn a little about the finer things
of life ; and to think of great things past and gone is
good — isn't that so ?

O'Killigain. Occasionally, perhaps ; but not to live
among them. Life as it is, and will be, moves me more.

Poges. Come, come ; we mustn't be always brooding
upon the present and the future. Life is too much
with us, O'Killigain ; late and soon, getting and
spending, we lay waste our powers. But you've never
read good old Wordsworth, I suppose ?

O'Killigain. As a matter of fact, I have.

Poges. You have ? Well, that promotes a fellowship
between us, eh ? Great man, great man ; but a
greater poet, eh ?

O'Killigain [*with some vehemence*]. A tired-out oul' blatherer ;
a tumble-down thinker ; a man who made a hiding-
place of his own life ; a shadow parading about as the
sun ; a poet, sensitive to everything but man ; a
bladder blown that sometimes gave a note of music ;
a fool who thought the womb of the world was

Wordsworth ; a poet who jailed the striving of man
in a moral lullaby ; a snail to whom God gave the
gleam of the glowworm ; a poet singing the song of
safety first !

Poges [*irritated*]. Oh ! Is that the result of the new
schooling ? I'm afraid very few will agree with you,
my friend. Well, well, we've more to do than discuss
the merit of a poet ; so hasten on the work of building
the garage, like a good man.

O'Killigain [*bowing ironically*]. I go, sir.   [*He goes out.*

Poges [*to the others*]. Isn't that a shocking example of bad
taste and ignorance ? [*To Souhaun*] There's one of your
fine countrymen for you, dear.

Souhaun. Well, Cyril dear, you know you were just
trying to show off to him. A few little quotations,
drummed into you at school, is all you know of
Wordsworth. You're never tired of saying that poetry
isn't your cup of tea.

Poges [*angry*]. Modern poetry, modern poetry isn't my
cup of tea ; and I don't care who knows it. But I
don't deny the past. Tradition — that is our strength
in time of trouble ; tradition, follow the traditions,
the only things that count in a cultured man's life.
Keep as close as we can to the beauties of the past —
the, the glory that was Rome and the grandeur that
was Greece — Shakespeare knew what he was talking
about when he said that.

Basil. Well, by living in this old historic house we're
keeping close to the old traditions.

Souhaun [*dubiously*]. It's beginning to feel a little cold and
damp to me.

Poges [*astonished and indignant*]. Cold ? What are you talking about ? Damp ? Nonsense. Were it warmer, it would begin to feel uncomfortable. What do you say, Cloyne ?

Cloyne [*who has been dusting the walls with a long-handled duster*]. I feel quite cosy, sir ; though there is a bit of a breeze blowing down the chimney.

Poges [*shivering a little*]. Eh ? Cosy, eh ? Of course you do ; we all do. Think, too, of the loveliness all round us : river, lake, valley, and hill. [*Lilting*] Angels, often pausing here, doubt if Eden were more fair. Here we have the peace of Eden.

Souhaun. And you must admit, dear, that we Irish are a simple, hearty, honest, and obliging people.

Basil [*enthusiastically*]. They're dears. All I've met of them are dears ; so quaint and charming — they are sweet. They need control, though ; they need control.

Poges. I agree. All the Irish are the same. Bit backward perhaps, like all primitive peoples, especially now, for they're missing the example and influence of the gentry ; but delightful people all the same. They need control, though ; oh yes, they need it badly.

Basil. We must get to really know the country ; it's one thing to be sensitive about the country scene, and quite another to understand it.

Poges [*heartily*]. Quite right, Basil. We must get to know the country so that everything in it is natural to us. [*Lilting*] To plough and to sow, to reap and to mow, and to be a farmer's boy-oy-oy. The different trees, for example, to call them by their names the instant we see them.

Avril. In winter or summer.

Poges. Quite. In the summer by their fruits.

Avril. Trees don't have fruits, Cyril.

Poges. Of course not. I mean barks and branches. It will be a joy to say to some ignorant visitor from the city : That tree ? Oh, that's just an oak ; and that one there by the river is a — a——

Avril. Gooseberry tree, Cyril.

Poges. A lilac, or something. [*To Avril*] Don't be funny. This is a serious matter.

Cloyne. We mustn't forget the hens, either, sir.

Poges. Hens ? Yes, of course — the hens. A fine idea. Yes, we'll have to have hens ; a first-class strain, though : nothing else would be of any use.

Cloyne. A first-class strain, of course.

Poges. And a cow as well.

Avril. A cow might be dangerous.

Poges. Dangerous ? Nonsense ; if he was, then we'd simply have to keep him in a cage. [*He sets up the step-ladder, mounts it, and holds up his picture against the wall.*] How does that look ?

Souhaun [*taking no notice*]. First of all, we must get to know the nature and names of all the wild flowers of the district.

Poges [*letting the picture rest on the ground, and turning to the rest*]. Especially the wild flowers that Shakespeare loved — the — the — er — er — [*his eye catches sight of primroses in a little vase on the table*] — the primrose, for instance ; you know — the primrose by the river's brim, a yellow primrose was to him, but it was nothing more ; though we all actually know all there is to be known about the little primrose.

Basil [*letting his picture rest on the ground, leaning over the top so that he at one end of the room and Poges at the other look like preachers in pulpits, panelled with their own portraits*]. That's just ignorant complacency, Cyril. Of course, if we regard, assume, or look at the plant purely as a single entity, then a primrose is a primrose, and there's nothing more to be said about it.

Poges. Well, you can't assume or regard the primrose as an elm tree, can you, old boy ?

Basil [*quickly*]. Don't interrupt me for a minute, please. If we take the primrose, however, into our synthetical consideration, as a whole, or, *a priori*, as a part, with the rest of the whole of natural objects or phenomena, then there is, or may be, or can be a possibility of thinking of the flower as of above the status, or substance, or quality of a fragment ; and, consequently, correlating it with the whole, so that, to a rational thinker, or logical mind, the simple primrose is, or may become, what we may venture to call a universal. See ?

Poges [*bewildered*]. Eh ? Oh yes, yes ; no, no ; yes, yes : eh, what ?

Souhaun [*to Cloyne*]. Cloyne, you'd better go and look after the fires in our room.

[*Cloyne rises and goes out.*

Avril [*with mockery in her voice*]. Hush, listen all — great men are speaking !

Poges [*to Basil*]. Eh, what the devil are you trying to say, man ?

Avril [*with triumphant mockery*]. Ah, Cyril, you're caught !

Poges [*indignantly*]. Caught ? Who's caught ? Me ? Nonsense, girl. He has simply compounded a fact with a fallacy. Can I see ? Have I eyes ? Yes. Very well, then. I see a flower with a root, leaves, and a blossom ; I ask myself, What is it ? I answer, A flower ; I ask, What is it called ? I answer, A primrose.

Basil [*languidly*]. So you say, sir.

Poges [*vehemently*]. So everyone says, sir !

Basil [*leaning forward towards Poges*]. And what is a flower, sir ?

Poges [*furiously*]. A flower ? Good God, sir, a plant ; a contrivance springing out of the earth ; a vegetating combination of root, leaves, and blossom.

Souhaun. Calmly, Cyril, calmly.

Basil [*leaning back and closing his eyes wearily*]. I knew you'd just say that, sir. Words ; you're merely using words. Try to think, sir, of a primrose, not as a primrose, but as a simple object, and as a substance outside of yourself.

Poges [*half frantic*]. Damn it, man, don't I know that a primrose isn't a substance inside of myself ! Tell us how a man is to think of a primrose except as a primrose. He can't think of it as the dear little, sweet little shamrock of Ireland, can he ? It is indeed a pitiful humiliation to have to listen to a half-educated fool !

Basil [*angry at last — setting the picture aside and taking a threatening step towards Poges, Avril stepping in front to restrain him*]. A fool ! Do you say I am a fool, sir ? Is a man versed in all the philosophies of the world to be called a fool !

Avril. Basil, dear !

Souhaun [*getting in front of Poges*]. Cyril, darling, do remember that we are having just a little friendly discussion about a common country flower !

Avril [*ironically*]. Basil is only trying to share his great knowledge with us.

Poges. He calls that knowledge, does he ?

Souhaun. We must remember that Basil passed through Oxford, dear.

Poges. I don't care if he crept under it or flew over it ; he's not going to punish me with what he picked up there.

Basil [*a little tearfully*]. Considering that I have read every word written by Hume, Spinoza, Aristotle, Locke, Bacon, Plato, Socrates, and Kant, among others, I think my views ought to receive some respect from an ignorant man.

Poges [*boastfully*]. I was reared any old how ; and here I am today, a money'd man, able to say to almost any man, come, and he cometh, and to almost any other man, go, and he goeth — and quick too ; able to shake hands with lords and earls, and call them by their Christian names. This — [*he touches his forehead*] — and these — [*he holds out his hands*] — did it all, without an inherited penny to help ! [*He looks bale-*

C.P.—III   C

fully at Basil.]   And that's more than some of them
can say.   And I never passed through Oxford !

Souhaun [*soothingly — to Basil*]. Come, now, go away for
a few minutes, till he's calm again.

Basil [*tearfully and wrathfully*]. Souhaun and you can see,
Avril, that the virtue of respect and ready veneration
that every right-minded Englishman has for the classic
colleges has gone completely out of him.

Souhaun [*soothingly*]. There now, there now ; it'll all
come back soon.

Basil [*almost weeping*]. Whenever he got the chance he
hurried me down to Oxford to meet this professor
and that doctor, itching all over to obtain a degree
honoris causa, in any faculty of Divinity, Science,
Literature, Medicine, or Law !

Poges [*scornfully*]. And most of them anxious for tips from
the Stock Exchange.   Go away, man, and weep in
silence.   [*He lifts his picture up against the wall.*]   We
have something else to do.   Here, how does that look
there ?

Souhaun [*gently pushing Basil out of the room*]. There, go,
dear, till you recover yourself.

Basil [*going out — loudly*]. *Quisabit grunniodem expectio
porcum* — what can one expect from a pig but a grunt ?

Poges [*with the picture against the wall*]. There, how does
that look here ? [*Pityingly*] Poor fool ; juvenile mind,
Souhaun, juvenile mind.   But snappy enough, when
he likes, and I, by cunning investment, having doubled
his income for him.   Ingratitude.   [*Impatiently*] Well,
how does this look here ?

Souhaun. I think the opposite wall would be more suitable, dear.

Avril. Where it is, is best, mother.

Poges. Make up your minds, make up your minds!

Souhaun. Where it is, dear.

Poges. How is it for height?

Souhaun. A little higher.

Avril. A little lower.

Poges. One of you, one of you!

Souhaun. A little to the right, now.

Avril. A little to the left, now.

Poges [*lowering the picture to the ground*]. Which is it? How is it? What is it!

> [*Cloyne comes in with a newspaper in her hand.*

Cloyne [*to Poges*]. Your newspaper, sir — the *Financial Universe.*

> [*She leaves it on the table, and goes out again. Poges breaks open his paper, and is about to look at it when Barney appears at the left entrance. A sound of cackling is heard outside, and the loud lowing of a cow, and the crowing of cocks.*

Poges [*with the paper half spread before him*]. What the hell's that?

Barney. There's a man outside wants to know if you want any entherprisin' hins?

Poges. Any what?

Barney. Any hins, entherprisin' hins?

Poges [*impatiently*]. What the devil would I want with hins enterprising or unenterprising ?

Barney. He says it's all over the counthry that you're searchin' high an' low for entherprisin' hins.

Cloyne [*appearing at the right entrance*]. There's two men here wantin' to know if you'd buy some prime an' startlin' cocks, goin' cheap ?

1st Workman [*appearing beside Barney, and shoving him aside to get in front*]. Excuse me, sir, but there's a friend o' mine just arrived with a cow that ud do any man good to see ; a baste with a skin on her as shiny an' soft as the down on a first-class angel's wing ; an' uddhers that'll make any man hard put to it to fetch enough pails to get the milk she gives !

Poges. Hins, cocks, and cows ! [*To 1st Workman*] What the hell do you take me for — a farmer's boy, or what ?

Souhaun. It's all out of what you said about having hens and a cow in the place. [*To Cloyne*] And you, you little fool, must have gossiped it all over the district !

Cloyne. The only one I mentioned it to was Mr. O'Killigain.

1st Workman [*coming over to Poges*]. Listen, sir, whisper, now : Sthrike for th' honour of St. Patrick, while the iron's hot, for the cow. An' whisper, don't, for the love o' God, have anything to do with the hins an' cocks they're thryin' to palm off on you — there isn't one o' them that isn't th' essence of a false pretendher !

Souhaun [*angrily — to Cloyne*]. I won't have you gossiping to O'Killigain, spending time with him you ought to give getting the house in shape ! The idea of discussing our private affairs with O'Killigain ! If you think that O'Killigain has taken a fancy to you, you never made a bigger mistake, my girl.

Cloyne [*indignantly*]. Indeed, ma'am ? Well, if Mr. O'Killigain bids me the time o' day, I'll do the same, without any permission from you, ma'am !

Barney [*impatiently*]. An' what am I goin' to say to the man who's brought th' entherprisin' hins ?

Poges [*shouting*]. Pack him off about his business !

[*Barney goes out.*

[*To Cloyne*] And you do the same to the man who brought the startling cocks !

Souhaun [*to Cloyne*]. And no more trespassing on the good nature of O'Killigain, either !

Cloyne [*turning and facing Souhaun swiftly as she is going out*]. There's a withering old woman, not a hundred miles from where I am, who ought to take her own advice, an' keep from thryin' her well-faded thricks of charm on poor Mr. O'Killigain herself ! [*She goes out.*

Poges [*loudly and complainingly*]. Oh, stop these unseemly disputes in a house that ought to know only peace and dignity ! Can't you try to act as the *les grand dames* and the *les grander monsieurs* must have acted when they moved about here in this beautiful Tudor house. While we're in it, let us forget the vile world and all its ways. [*Angrily — to 1st Workman, who has been tugging at his sleeve for the last few moments*] What the hell do you want, man ?

1st Workman [*earnestly, almost into Poges' ear*]. Listen, whisper, sir ; take the bull be th' horns, an' get the cow, before she's gone. An' as for entherprisin' hins,

or cocks that'll do you credit, leave it to me, sir, an'
you'll go about with a hilarious look in your eyes !

Poges [*catching 1st Workman by the shoulders, in a rage, and
pushing him out of the room, and down the passage*]. Get out,
get out, you fool, with your hins and cocks and cows !

Souhaun [*quickly — to Avril, when Poges has disappeared round
the entrance*]. Go on up, and flatter and comfort your
old fool by ridiculing my old fool ; and, when he's
half himself again, wanting still more comfort and
flattery, wheedle a cheque out of the old prattler.

Avril [*jumping up*]. Splendid idea !   [*She runs off out.*

Souhaun [*calling after her*]. A good one, mind you !
        [*Poges comes back fuming, and brushing his coat where it
        touched the 1st Workman.*

Poges. Are we to have no peace down here where peace
was born ? [*He takes up the paper again and begins to
read it.*] Uum. Ha, tin shares up again. Good. [*He
buries his face in the paper.*] If it weren't for the damned
taxes.
        [*1st and 3rd Workmen peer around corner of the left
        entrance ; then they come over quickly and smoothly to
        where Poges is buried in his paper, the 1st Workman
        standing on his left hand and the 3rd Workman on his
        right.*

1st Workman [*persuasively — towards Poges' paper*]. Listen,
here, sir : if it's genuine poulthry you want, that lay
with pride an' animation, an' not poor, insignificant
fowls that set about th' business o' layin' like a
member o' Doyle Eireann makin' his maiden speech,
I have a sthrain o' pullets that'll give you eggs as if
you were gettin' them be steam !

Poges [*angrily — glancing over the top of his paper*]. Go away, go away, man, and don't be driving me mad !

3rd Workman [*towards Poges' paper*]. Oh, the lies that some can tell to gain their own ends ! Sure, sir, everyone knows that his poor hins are harmless ; only venturin' to lay when heavy thundher frightens them into a hasty sign o' life ! But it's meself can give you what you want, with a few lively cocks thrown in, to help them on with the work of furnishing nourishment to the whole world.

Poges. Go away ; when I want poultry, I'll get into touch with the experts in the Department of Agriculture.

1st Workman [*horrified — partly to Poges and partly to Souhaun*]. Oh, listen to that, now ! Didja hear that, ma'am ? The Department of Agriculture, is it ? Wisha, God help your innocence, sir. Sure, it's only a tiny time ago that the same Department sent down a special sthrong covey o' cocks to improve the sthrain, an' only afther a short probation, didn't they give the hins hysterics ?

Poges. Hysterics ? Good God !

3rd Workman. Ay, an' hadn't the frightened farmers to bring guns to bear on the cocks when they found their hins scatthered over hill an' dale, lyin' on their backs with their legs in the air, givin' their last gasp, an' glad to get outa the world they knew so well ! The few mighty ones who survived were that stunned that there wasn't an egg in th' place for years !

Poges [*good-humouredly catching the men by the arm and leading them to the left entrance*]. Now, now, men, I'm busy ;

I've some very important business to think about and can't be bothered with hins !

1st Workman [*as they go out*]. Another time, sir ; but don't think of the Department in this important matther : they'll send you hins'll paralyse the cocks, or cocks that'll paralyse the hins !   [*They go out.*

Poges [*returning, and reading the paper*]. Childlike people, the Irish, aren't they ? Hysterical hins ! Dr. What's-his-name, the fellow who said all man is moved by streams of thought that never enter his head — well, he'd find something to study down here. Well, it's delightful to be in a lovely house, in a lovely country, with nothing to think of but hysterical hins ! [*He suddenly concentrates on something in the paper.*] I must have some of those shares. [*He runs to the telephone and joggles and shakes it.*] What can be the matter with this Exchange ? — I can't hear a sound ! [*To Souhaun*] Call one of the workmen, will you ? I must get through to London at once.

[*Souhaun runs out to call a workman. In a moment or two the 2nd Workman comes into the room.*

2nd Workman. Is it me you want, sir ?

Poges. Not you especially ; I just want to know if you know, or anyone in the county knows, why I can't connect with the Exchange ?

2nd Workman. Oh, is that all, sir ?

Poges [*snappily*]. Is that all ! Isn't it enough, fool !

2nd Workman [*sharply*]. Who th' hell are you callin' a fool to ?

Poges [*placatingly but with some impatience*]. My good man, please let me know if you can say why the Exchange doesn't answer my call.

2nd Workman. Ask anyone from one end o' the counthry to the other, or even O'Killigain himself, if Philib O'Dempsey's a fool, an' see what they'll say. A sound mind, armed with a firm education for seven long years in a steady school, an' now well fit to stand his ground in any argument, barrin' th' highest philosophies of the greatest minds mendin' th' world !

Poges. My good man, I only asked you a simple question.

2nd Workman [*ignoring the remark*]. Comin' over here, thinkin' that all the glory an' grandeur of the world, an' all the might of man, was stuffed into a bulgin' purse, an' stickin' their tongue out at a race that's oldher than themselves by a little like a thousand years, greater in their beginnin' than they are in their prime ; with us speakin' with ayse the mighty languages o' the world when they could barely gurgle a few sounds, sayin' the rest in the movement of their fingers.

Poges [*shouting in rage*]. Go to the devil, man, and learn manners !

2nd Workman [*going on vehemently, but moving slowly to one of the entrances*]. Hammerin' out handsome golden orna- ments for flowin' cloak an' tidy tunic we were, while you were busy gatherin' dhried grass, an' dyin' it blue, to hide the consternation of your middle parts ; decoratin' eminent books with glowin' colour an' audacious beauty were we, as O'Killigain himself will tell you, when you were still a hundhred score o' years away from even hearin' of the alphabet. [*Beside the entrance.*] Fool ? It's yourself's the fool, I'm sayin',

settlin' down in a place that's only fit for the housin'
o' dead men ! Settlin' here, are you ? Wait till God
sends the heavy rain, and the floods come !

[*He goes out.*

Poges [*to Souhaun*]. There's Erin, the tear and the smile
in her eye for you ! The unmannerly ruffian !
Venomous, too — wanting me to wait till the floods
come ! Cheeking me up to my very face !

Souhaun. Well, it's not a royal face, is it ? You'll have
to learn to be respectful to the people if you want
them to be respectful to you.

Poges [*sarcastically*]. I'll be most deferential in the future.
[*Stormily — to 1st Workman appearing at the entrance*] Well,
what do you want ?

1st Workman. Excuse, but I sailed in, hearin' you were in
a difficulty, an' I wanted to see if I could help.

Poges. Well, I want to know where's the man who is
responsible for putting in this 'phone ?

1st Workman. Why, is there anything wrong with it, sir ?

Poges [*stormily*]. Everything's wrong with it, man ! I
can't get on to the Exchange.

1st Workman. Sure, that's aysily explained : it's not
connected yet.

Poges. It was to be connected first thing this morning.
When will it be connected ?

1st Workman [*cautiously*]. Oh, now, that depends, sir.

Poges. Depends ? Depends on what ?

1st Workman. On how long it'll take to get the sthrame o'

sound from here flowin' safely to whatever other end
there may be fixed for it to be heard in.

Poges [*impatiently*]. Get O'Killigain, get him to come here
at once.

1st Workman. Sure, that's the Postmaster's job — Mr.
O'Killigain has nothing to do with it.

Poges [*shouting*]. Then get me the man that has something
to do with it !

Souhaun [*who has been looking at the coloured curtain stuff and
spreading it out*]. Now, Cyril, see what you think : Is
the red with the green stripe or the green with the red
stripe the most suitable to go with the walls ?
    [*The sound of horses trotting is heard outside, becoming
    plainer, till the sound ceases somewhere close to the house.*

Poges [*to Souhaun — with irritation*]. For goodness' sake,
one thing at a time. [*To 1st Workman*] Go and get the
man that's doing this job.

1st Workman. I'm afraid you'll have to thravel a long way
if you want to get him, sir ; you see, he had to go to
pay his last respects to a dead cousin ; but never fear,
he won't be gone beyond a couple of hours, unless
something out o' the ordinary keeps him away the
whole o' the evenin' an' th' strongest part o' th' night.
    [*Poges sinks down on one of the seats, silent and confounded.*

Cloyne [*appearing at back entrance*]. Th' horses are here
now, sir.

Poges [*sitting up*]. Horses ? What horses ?

Cloyne. The horses Mr. Basil an' Miss Avril ordhered to
come here.

Souhaun. Basil and Avril are going out for a little canter, Cyril.

Poges [*peevishly*]. But this is not the time to be thinking of amusement ; we have to get the house into some shape. Ask O'Killigain to come here.

Souhaun [*to Cloyne*]. Yes, get O'Killigain, Cloyne ; he has a good eye, and will be able to judge which of these curtain stuffs should go on the windows.
     [*Cloyne goes. O'Killigain appears at the left entrance with an anxious look on his face.*

O'Killigain. Who's going to ride these horses that are outside ?

Souhaun [*haughtily*]. Miss Avril and her friend Mr. Basil Stoke are going to ride them.

O'Killigain. I suppose you know these horses are mettle-some creatures, and need riders at home in the saddle ?

Souhaun [*more haughtily still*]. Miss Avril and her friend learned the art in a London riding-school, and exercised frequently in Richmond Park ; so your kind solicitude is unnecessary, sir.

O'Killigain [*viciously*]. Richmond Park isn't Clune na Geera, ma'am. The horses there are animals ; the horses here are horses. [*Avril comes tripping in, dressed in jersey and jodhpurs, and is followed by Basil, dressed in a dark-green kind of hunting coat, buckskin breeches, and big gleaming top-boots with spurs ; he carries a whip in his hand, and a high, handsome, shining tall hat on his head. With a frightened look at Basil*] Good God !
     [*He turns on his heel and walks out again.*

Basil [*with complacent conceit — to Souhaun*]. The old ways coming back again to the old house, Souhaun.

Souhaun [*rapturously*]. Isn't it grand, dear ? Don't forget to go through the village.

Avril [*joyously*]. Basil has been so kind, Souhaun, dear ; he has given me a grand cheque.

Souhaun [*giving Basil a kiss and winking at Avril*]. Basil, you're a darling !

Poges [*grumpily*]. Be careful how you handle those horses.

Basil [*haughtily — to Poges*]. Did you say anything, sir ?

Poges [*with some heat*]. I said be careful how you handle those horses !

Basil [*with a mocking bow*]. Thank you, sir ; we'll do our best. [*To Avril*] Come, darling.
[*Avril trips out, and Basil follows her in a way that he deems to be stately.*

Poges. I hope they'll do no damage, now.

Souhaun. Oh, never fear ; Basil sits the saddle like a centaur.
[*The movement of horses' hooves is heard, then a trot, getting fainter till it dies away.*

Poges [*exasperated*]. God send he doesn't frighten the horse. More decent of him had he remained here to get this telephone going. They all seem to be determined here to keep us away from every semblance of civilisation ! [*To Souhaun — stormily*] Will you, for God's sake, try to get O'Killigain to do something to get this thing in order ? [*He goes over to where Souhaun is busy with the curtains and pulls the curtains out of her hands, then flings them on the floor.*] D'ye hear, d'ye hear what I'm saying to you, woman ?

Souhaun [*losing patience and seizing him, and shaking him roughly*]. What d'ye think you're doing, you old dim-eyed, old half-dead old fool ! I'll disconnect you as well as the telephone if you don't learn to behave yourself ! You settled on coming here, and you'll put up with the annoyances !

Poges [*protestingly*]. Eh, eh, there ! It was you who per-suaded me to come to this god-forsaken hole !

Souhaun [*shaking him more fiercely*]. You're a liar, I didn't ! It was you yourself who were always pining to see the little squirrels jigging about on the trees, and see the violets and primroses dreaming in the budding stir of spring ! [*She pushes him violently from her.*] Another snarly sound out of you, and I'm off to live alone.

Poges [*gloomily*]. You can well afford to be independent now, since, like a fool, I settled five hundred a year on you.

[*During this contest Cloyne has appeared at the left entrance and now gives a judicious cough.*

Souhaun [*quickly — to cover dispute from Cloyne*]. We'll decide on this stuff, then, for the curtains, Cyril, dear.

Poges. It'll look delightful, darling. [*Pretending to see Cloyne for the first time.*] Oh, what do you want ?

Cloyne. Canon Creehewel's outside an' would like to have a few words with you, if you're not too busy.

Poges [*showing irritation*]. Oh, these priests, these priests ! Thick as weeds in this poor country. Opposed to every decent thought that happens not to have come from

them. Ever on guard to keep the people from growing
out of infancy. No one should give them the slightest
encouragement. Oh, if the misguided people would
only go back to the veneration of the old Celtic gods,
what a stir we'd have here ! To the delightful, if
legendary, loveliness of — er — er — er — what's his
name, what's her name, what's their name ? I have so
often said it, so often in my mind, the chief, or one of
the chief gods of the ancient Celts ?

Souhaun. Was it Gog or Magog, dear ?

Poges [*with fierce scorn*]. Oh, no, no, no ; try to think a
little, if you really want to assist me. Can't you
remember that Gog and Magog were two Philistinian
giants killed by David, or Jonathan, or Joshua, or
Joab, or Samson, or someone ? It's the old Celtic god
I have in mind, the one — what was his name ?

Souhaun. Gulliver ?

Poges. Oh no ; not Gulliver !

Souhaun. Well, I don't know the hell who it was.

Poges [*slapping his thigh exultantly*]. Brobdingnag ! That
was the fellow — the fellow that ate the nine nuts — or
was it seven ? — plucked from the tree hanging over
the well near the world's end.

Cloyne. What am I to say to the Canon, sir ?

Poges. What does he want ; did you ask him what he
wants ?

Cloyne. He says he just wants to drop a word or two of
thanks for the fifty pounds you sent him.
    [*A murmur of voices is heard outside. It comes nearer
    and the sound seems excited.*

Poges [*listening*]. What's that, now ?

1st Workman's Voice [*outside*]. Keep his head up.

3rd Workman's Voice [*outside*]. You're home, sir, you're
home now.

> [*They come in supporting Basil by the arms, followed by
> the 2nd Workman, holding Basil's coat-tail. Basil is
> pale, and has a frightened look on his face. His lovely
> coat is spattered with mud and, in some places, torn.
> The 1st Workman is carrying the tall hat, now looking
> like a battered concertina.*

Poges [*anxiously*]. What's this ; what's happened ?

1st Workman [*soothingly*]. He's all right, sir ; just a little
shock. We seen him crawling towards the house an'
went to his help. His horse flung him. [*Whispering to
Poges*] He shouldn't be let on anything more mettle-
some than a rocking-horse, sir.

Souhaun [*running to Basil*]. Are you much hurt, Basil,
dear ?

Basil [*brokenly*]. Bruised, bruised from head to foot.

Poges [*with irritation*]. Well, why the hell didn't you stay
here and help me to get the telephone fixed ?

Basil. Why didn't you hold me back by force ? Oh,
why did you let me go !

Souhaun [*anxiously*]. Where's Avril ?

Basil [*ignoring her query*]. Oh, I should never have ven-
tured upon an Irish horse ! Irresponsible, irresponsible,
like the people. When he wouldn't go, I gave him just
a little jab with the spur — [*moaningly*] — and the brute
behaved like a wild animal, just like a wild animal !

1st Workman [*soothingly — to Souhaun*]. He's not hurt much, ma'am ; came down in th' grass on his poor bum.

Souhaun. But where's Avril ? [*Shaking Basil's shoulder*] Where's Avril ?

Basil. Gone !

Souhaun. Gone ?

Basil. Away with O'Killigain. He came bounding up to help Avril and abused me for falling off. Then they cantered away together. [*Loudly and a little shrilly*] Naked and unashamed, the vixen went away with O'Killigain !
> [*Plaster falls and a hole appears in the ceiling, almost directly over the fireplace ; then a thin rope, with a bulb attached to its end, comes dangling down, followed by the face of a heavily Yellow-bearded Man, who thrusts his head as far as it can go through the hole.*

Yellow-bearded Man [*to those below*]. Hay, hay there ; is this where yous want the light to go ?

Poges [*with a vexatious yell when he sees where the rope hangs*]. No it isn't, no it isn't, you fool ! [*Indicating a place near the centre and towards the back*] There, there's where it's wanted ! Where my desk will be ! Oh, they're knocking down more than they're building up !

Yellow-bearded Man [*soothingly*]. Don't worry ; just a little mistake in measurement, sir. Never fear, we'll hit th' right spot one o' these days ! The one thing to do, sir, is to keep cool.
> [*He takes his head out of the hole and disappears, leaving Poges furious.*

C.P.—III   D

Poges [*shouting up at the hole*]. Who are you to order me to keep cool ? I won't keep cool. I refuse to keep cool !

Souhaun [*to Poges*]. Here, help me in with poor Basil till he drinks some brandy and lies down for a little.
　[*Poges takes one arm, Souhaun takes the other, and they lead Basil out of the room.*

Poges [*to Basil — helping him out*]. I hope you realise the sterling trouble you give people by your damned refusal to recognise your limitations !

Basil [*petulantly*]. Carry me out, man ; carry me out !

Cloyne [*as they pass*]. What am I to do with the Canon, sir ?

Poges [*ferociously*]. Tell him I'll give him another cheque if he gets the telephone fixed for me before the night is out !
　[*Basil, Souhaun, and Poges go out by the left entrance ; Cloyne by that on the right, leaving the men standing together in a corner of the room.*

2nd Workman [*pensively*]. Th' spirit of th' Grey o' Macha's in our Irish horses yet !

1st Workman [*excitedly*]. Did yous hear that, eh ? Did yous hear what he just let dhrop ? That the lassie o' th' house went off with O'Killigain riding naked through the locality !

2nd Workman. Stark naked she was, too. Didn't I know well be th' cut of her jib that she was a hop, step, an' lep of a lassie ! An' right well she looked too !

1st Workman. Th' sight near left me eyes when I seen her go prancin' out without as much as a garther on her to keep her modesty from catchin' cold.

3rd Workman. This'll denude the disthrict of all its self-denyin' decency.

1st Workman [*excitedly jumping upon a seat to get nearer to the hole in the ceiling*]. Cornelius, eh, there, Cornelius !
[*The yellow-bearded head is thrust through the hole again.*

Yellow-bearded Man. What's up ?

1st Workman. Didja hear th' terrible thing that's afther happenin' ?

Yellow-bearded Man. No ; what terrible thing ?

1st Workman. The lassie o' th' house's gone careerin' all over th' counthry on horseback with only her skin as a coverin' !

Yellow-bearded Man [*horrified*]. G'way !

3rd Workman [*up to him*]. An' th' poor men workin' in th' fields had to flee to th' ditches to save th' sight of their eyes from th' shock o' seein' her !

Yellow-bearded Man [*with aggravated anguish in his voice*]. Oh, isn't it like me to be up here outa sight o' th' world, an' great things happenin' !

CURTAIN

Act II

The same as in the preceding Act.

The two portraits, one of Stoke, the other of Poges, are now hanging on the wall at back, between the windows. Bright-green curtains, broadly striped with red, are on the windows. A Jacobean armchair has been added to the two stiff pew-like seats beside the fireplace. The table is to the left, so that two mattresses, one beside the other, can be seen, with their heads against the wall and their feet towards the front. On these, wrapped round with rugs and blankets, are Poges and Stoke. Some thick rolled-up floor rugs are lying against the wall. A bunch of pampas grass is in the earthenware jug standing on the table. The rejected crimson curtain stuff is lying over one of the pew-like seats. A walking-stick — Basil's — is leaning against the wall, near to where he is lying.

It is about half-past seven on a cold and misty morning. A few misty beams of sunlight are coming in through the windows, paling the light of a lighted lantern standing between the two beds.

The two men are twisting about uneasily on the mattresses; when Poges twists to the right, Basil twists to the left, and vice versa. Then Poges, wearing a blue beret with a black bow at the side, lifts his head a little and glances over at Basil. He is in that drowsy state felt by a man who has spent long hours of the night trying to get to sleep and failing to do so.

Before the scene is disclosed, the hooting of owls is heard first; then the faint lowing of cattle, grunting of swine, crowing of cocks, bleating of sheep; then, vigorously from various directions the whistling of the chorus of *The Farmer's Boy.*

Poges [*after he has twisted about several times — half to himself, half to Basil*]. Good God, isn't it cold ! [*Basil is silent.*] Eh, Basil, are you awake ? How d'ye feel now ?

Basil [*with a faint groan*]. Stiff as hell still ! It's a mercy I'm alive. And, on the top of it, Avril to make a laughing-stock of me by enjoying herself with O'Killigain.

Poges [*sympathetically*]. It was damned mean of her, Basil. She's inclined that way, I'm afraid. You'll have to keep a strong hand over her, my boy.

Basil [*with a deep groan*]. I can't — now.

Poges. Why can't you, man ?

Basil. A month before we came here I did a very foolish thing.

Poges. Oh ?

Basil [*mournfully*]. Settled five hundred a year on her for life.

Poges. Oh ! [*A fairly long pause.*] Basil, Basil, I did the same to Souhaun !

Basil. We're done for, Cyril.

Poges [*in a sprightly way*]. No, no ; a month in the country'll make us young again. We'll be as lively as goats in no time. Besides, we can always cautiously hint at an increase in the settlement.

Basil [*gloomily*]. With the workers always striking for higher wages, it'll have to remain a hint.

Poges [*as gloomily*]. It's damnable, Basil. If much more is given to them, how's a poor man to live ? [*He sinks*

back on the mattress and pulls the clothes over his head.
Outside a cock crows loudly, followed by the call of a cuckoo.
Clicking his tongue exasperatedly — from under the clothes.]
Dtch, dtch, dtch ! Isn't it a good thing those birds
aren't in the house ! [*The cock crows again, much louder*
this time, and the cuckoo calls again. Popping his head from
under the clothes.] Damn that cock and cuckoo ! Did
you hear that cock crowing, Basil, and the cuckoo
calling ?

Basil. Deafening, aren't they ! And the owls, too, all
the night. Jungle noises !

Poges. The country's not going to be so quiet as I
thought. Still, I'm glad we came.

Basil. So am I, really. These sounds are just part of the
country's attractions — pleasant and homely.

Poges. And stimulating, Basil, stimulating. Look at the
sunlight coming in through the windows — another
dawn, Basil ; another life. Every day in the country
brings another chance of living a new life.

Basil [*enthusiastically*]. And we're going to live it, eh,
what, Cyril ?

Poges [*enthusiastically*]. Oh, boy, ay !
  [*Souhaun appears at the back entrance, left, and Avril at*
  entrance to the right. Both are wearing fur coats over
  their night-dresses, and shiver a little.

Souhaun [*plaintively*]. For goodness' sake, will you two
men get up and do something. Cloyne's fallen down in
a dark passage and hurt her wrist, and she can't do
much.

Poges. Oh ?

Avril. And something will have to be done to heat the rooms — we were almost frozen last night.

Poges. Ah ! Well, we weren't scorched with the heat either.

Souhaun. Well, stir yourselves, and you'll soon get warm. O'Killigain and his men are already at work, and will want to be coming in and out of here.

> [*The cock crows louder than ever, and is joined by many more, a few of them at a great distance, so that the sounds are heard but faintly ; these are mingled with the barking of dogs, the lowing of cattle, the bleating of sheep, the twittering of birds, the grunting of pigs, and the cackling of hens.*

Avril. There, you hear ; everything's alive but you two.

Poges. Well, we'll be in the midst of them all in a second.

> [*The two women withdraw. Basil and Poges, with the clothes wrapped round them, sit up, and dive down again. After a second or two they sit bolt-upright again, and again dive down.*

Poges [*shivering*]. Ooooh, Basil, cold !

Basil [*shivering*]. Bitter, bitter ! What would I not give now for a cosy flat ; a cosier bed ; and a blazing hot-water bottle !   [*They lie quiet for a short time.*

Poges. There's nothing for it but to plunge out of the summer into the black and bitter winter.

Basil. You say the word.

Poges. Ready ! Steady ! Go !

> [*They climb laboriously out of the beds. When they get out, it can be seen that they have been fully dressed, even*

to their heavy topcoats and scarves wound round their necks.

Poges [*blowing on to his hands and rubbing them*]. Ooooh, crisp, isn't it? Healthy, though. Ooooh! Where the hell's that Barney, that he hasn't a fire lighted for us? Oooh! One would want to be on his tail all day. [*Shouting*] Barney, Barney! [*Barney comes in holding some logs in the crook of his right arm, and a lantern in his left hand. Cloyne follows, with some paper and a bellows. Her left wrist is bandaged. Barney is wearing a topcoat, and has a muffler round his neck. Cloyne, too, is wearing a heavy coat. They both go over to the fireplace. As they come in*] Ah, here we are. Bit nippy, Barney; sharp, but beneficial. [*To Cloyne*] You'll have to be more careful with the steps and passages. Mind your feet coming in, mind your head going out. Oooooh! [*To Basil*] You better slip off, and give the others any help you can. [*As Basil is going*] What about your walking-stick?

Basil [*moving stiffly*]. I must try to do without it—about the house, anyway.

[*He takes the lantern that is beside his bed, and goes out, limping a little.*

Poges [*to the other two*]. Well, what do the pair of you think of the country, eh? And the house? Better than any your old Kings of Tarara had, eh?

Cloyne [*effusively*]. I'm sure it'll be lovely, sir, when we settle down.

[*Poges has been jerking his arms about in an effort to drive the cold from his body. Cloyne begins to fold the clothes on the beds, and tidy them up.*

Poges. Of course it will. We'll enjoy it all; we'll feel

younger ; we will *be* younger. The air, fresh air,
pure air, exhilarating air, will be able to get at us.
[*He sucks in his breath and blows it out again.*] Ooooh !
Soon we won't know ourselves. We'll eat better,
sleep better ; flabby muscles will become firm, and
we'll realise that we are alive, alive, alive-O. Think of
the walks we'll have ; so much to see, so much to hear,
so much to smell ; and then to come back, nicely
tired, to such a lovely house. A life for the gods !

Cloyne. Wondherful, wondherful, sir.

Poges. Now I must be off to swallow down a cup of tea,
for there's a lot to be done, a lot to be done yet.
                              [*He hurries off out of the room.*

Cloyne. The poor oul' codger !

Barney. Comin' down to this back o' God-speed place
for rest an' quietness ! Afther all that science has
thried to do for us, goin' back to lantherns an' candles.
Th' only electric light he'll allow in a Tudor house is
one over his own desk ! Runnin' in the face o' God
Almighty's goodness — that's what it is.

Cloyne. They'll get tired of it before us.

Barney. I can tell you, I'm tired of it already. Looka the
place we're livin' in : doors everywhere shaped like
doors o' dungeons ; passages dark as hell when it was
first formed ; crackin' your head when you're goin' in,
and breakin' your toe when you're goin' out ; an' I'm
tellin' you, it's only beginnin'.

Cloyne. It might be worse.

Barney [*striking a match to light the paper*]. We're goin' to be
worse, I'm tellin' you.

Cloyne. We can't be worse than we are.

Barney [*as the flames of the paper die down*]. There's no chance o' kindlin' here. Why did you say, then, that we might be worse ?

Cloyne. Well, so, indeed, an' we might.

Barney. How can we be worse, woman, when we're as bad as we can be ?

Cloyne. Simply be bein' worse than we were.

Barney. How can we be worse than we were, when we're as bad as we can be, now.

Cloyne. You'll see we'll be worse before we're betther.

Barney. Damn these logs ! Isn't that what I'm sthrivin' to dhrive into your head ?

Cloyne. What are you sthrivin' to dhrive into me head ?

Barney. That we'll be worse than we were before we're as bad as we are now, an' in a week's time we'll be lookin' back with a sigh to a time, bad as it could be then, that was betther than the worst that was on top of us now.
  [*Poges bustles in again. The heavy topcoat is gone and he is now dressed in bright-blue shorts, emerald-green jersey, brown shoes, and the scarf is still round his neck. He has a cup of tea in his hand, and he is sipping it as he comes into the room. He is miserably cold, but he puts on a brisk air, sorting it out in his mind that to be cold in the country is natural, to be ignored as far as possible, and to be countered by a smiling face, a brisk manner, and the wearing of brilliant clothes denoting freedom of movement and utter disregard of the common rules of convention. He is feeling far from comfortable, but*

thinks this shouldn't be shown ; for the colder you are, and the more uncomfortable you feel, the brisker you must be, and the hardier you'll get.

Poges. Here we are again ! Ready for anything now. [*Losing his gay attitude when he sees that the fire isn't lighted.*] Isn't the fire lighted yet ? What are you doing, Barney ? Being in the country's no reason why we should be frozen to death.

Barney. I can't get a spark out of it, afther all me sthrivin'.

Poges [*testily*]. You can't light logs with a bit of paper, man. Oh, use your brains, Barney, use your brains.

Barney. An' what else have I got to light them with ?

Poges. Small sticks, man ; put some small sticks under them.

Barney. An' will you tell me where I'm goin' to get the small sticks ? Isn't the nearest shop a dozen miles away ?

Poges. Well, if there's no sticks, sprinkle a little paraffin on them.

Barney [*sarcastically*]. An' where am I goin' to get the paraffin ? There's no oil wells knockin' about here.

Poges [*severely*]. Don't be funny. You've got to remember you're in the country now.

Barney. Isn't it meself that's gettin' to know it well !

Poges. We've got to do things for ourselves : there's no chance of pushing a button to get things done here.

Barney. Sure, I'm beginnin' to think you're right.

Poges. Can't you see that those logs are too big ?

Barney, I think I do, unless me sight's goin' curious.

Poges [*hotly*]. Well, then, why don't you do it !

Barney. Arra, do what ?

Poges [*loudly*]. Make them smaller, man !

Barney [*calmly and sarcastically*]. An' how ?

Poges. And how ? Why, with an axe, of course.

Barney [*losing his temper — loudly*]. An' where's the axe, an' where's the axe ?

Poges. There must be an axe knocking about somewhere.

Barney. There's nothin' knockin' about here but a bitther breeze whirlin' through the passages that ud make the very legs of a nun numb !

Cloyne [*trying to mollify things*]. Sure, the poor man's back-broken an' heart-broken thryin' to kindle it, sir.

Poges [*who has been waving his arms and stamping his feet while his teeth chatter — turning fiercely on Cloyne*]. You mind your own business, girl ! [*Seeing her putting the mattresses by the wall.*] Have we got to sleep down here again tonight ?

Cloyne. Ay, an' yous have. Th' other rooms are too damp still. Sure, Mr. O'Killigain says that it'll take a month of fierce fires to dhry them out.

Poges [*testily*]. Mr. O'Killigain says this, and Mr. O'Killigain says that ! I'm getting tired of what Mr. O'Killigain says. If we have to sleep here, you or Barney'll have to stay up all night keeping the fire going, or we'll be frozen in our sleep. [*His eye catches*

*sight of the telephone. He goes over to it and lifts the
receiver.*] Not a sound ! No, oh no ; not a bit of a
hurry. [*Angrily to Cloyne*] Go out, girl, and send in the
boy who's working at this telephone. [*With a low moan*]
Ireland !

> [*Cloyne goes out by the doorway on the right leading to the
> entrance hall. After a few seconds the loud lowing of a
> cow is heard, followed by a scream from Cloyne, who
> rushes frantically back into the room, pale and trembling.*

Cloyne [*breathlessly rushing back into the room, falling on the
floor, and catching Poges wildly by the legs*]. Save me !
Stuck his head into me face, th' minute I opened the
door. Mother o' God, I'll never see th' light of
another day with th' fright I got !

Poges [*alarmed*]. What is it, what is it, woman ?

Cloyne [*almost incoherent*]. A bull, a wild bull, out in th'
enthrance hall !

Barney [*frantically*]. A wild bull ! We're all desthroyed.

Poges [*trying to release himself from Cloyne's hold*]. Let me go,
girl ! Let me go, or I can't defend myself. If he
comes in here, the whole of us'll be horned !

Cloyne [*frantically*]. My legs have given undher me. Let
me hold on to you, sir — it's me only hope !

Poges [*to Barney*]. Put the table to the doorway, man, and
help to bar him out — quick, quick, man ! And a
mattress. [*To Cloyne while Barney is pushing the table and
a mattress to the door*] Why didn't you clap the door in
his face, you fool ?

Cloyne. Wasn't he half into the hall before I'd the door

half open ! Oh, sir, what are we goin' to do ? Oh,
please go, sir, an' thry an' shove him out !

[*The bellow of the animal is heard outside in the hall.*

Poges [*half dead with panic*]. My God, woman, you can't
shove bullocks about ! [*Shouting*] Souhaun, there's a
wild bull in the house ! Help, O'Killigain, help.
[*To Barney*] Run, run, man, and get Mr. Stoke to bring
down the gun. Oh, go quick, man ! An' keep well
out of range. [*Barney runs off. Shouting*] O'Killigain,
help ! Can't you let me go, girl ?

Cloyne [*still clinging to him*]. Carry me off, sir, please.
Don't leave me here to die alone ! Maybe he won't
be able to climb the stairs afther us. Oh, when I
came to th' counthry, I never thought there'd be wild
animals on th' door-step !

[*Basil appears at one of the entrances at the back ; he moves
forward stealthily and extends a gun to Poges.*

Basil [*nervous*]. What is it, what is it ?

Poges. A bull, out in the hall.

Basil. Who let him in ? Damn it, such carelessness !
You must be on guard in the country, you know.
Here, take the gun, man.

Poges [*angrily — to Basil*]. Come out, come out in the
open, man, and be ready to use the gun if he comes
into the room ! [*Shoving the gun from him.*] You use it,
man ; weren't you an A.R.P. man ?

Basil [*indignantly*]. I never did anything more than clay-
pigeon shooting ! Let whoever let the damned
animal in, let the damned animal out ! [*He pokes
Poges with the gun.*] Here, take this, and down him —
you're nearer the bull than I am.

Poges [*angrily*]. I'm not a toreador, am I ? And don't point, don't point the gun at me ! Lower the barrel, man ; oh, lower the barrel ! D'ye want me to die two deaths at once ? What's the advantage of your passing through Oxford if you can't face a bull with a gun in your hand ? Be a man, man, and not a mouse.

Basil [*keeping well in the passage, and only showing his nose*]. Telephone the police, the fire brigade, or something.

Poges [*violently*]. Don't you know the kind of a country we're in ! There's no police, no fire brigade, no telephone ! Come here, if you won't use the gun, and help me carry this girl away out of danger.
  [*The cow puts a stylised head, with long curving horns, over the barricade and lets out a loud bellow. Cloyne spasmodically tugs the legs of Poges, making him lose his balance so that he topples to the floor, after a frantic effort to save himself.*

Cloyne. Oooh, sir, save me !

Poges [*with a wild shout as he is falling*]. My God, he's on top of us ! We're done for ! Help !
  [*Basil throws the gun into the room and runs for his life.*

Barney [*in the far distance*]. Sing out, sir, if you want any assistance !
  [*Someone is heard stirring outside where the animal is; this stir is followed by the voice of the 1st Workman shooing the cow out of the hall. After a few moments, Poges slowly sits up and listens.*

1st Workman [*shouting outside*]. Eh, oick, oick, eh, yeh gett ; ay, ay, oick oick !
  [*Poges gets up on to his feet, shaking a little, and going over, picks up the gun and, steadying himself on it, stands over*

the prostrate Cloyne, who is almost in a faint, bundled up on the floor, with her face hidden in her hands. Shortly after, the 1st Workman appears at the entrance with a bucket of coal and some sticks. He looks over the table, astonished to see the prostrate Cloyne, and Poges standing near with a gun in his hand.

Poges [*stormily*]. Where the hell did that bull come from ? who owns her ? who let that bull come tearing into a private house ?

1st Workman. Bull, sir ? Oh, that wasn't a bull, sir. [*He pushes the table back to its place.*] Jest a harmless innocent cow, sir. Frightened the poor girl, now, did it ? [*Cunningly*] But I see it didn't frighten you, sir.

Poges [*flattered*]. No, no, not me. [*To Cloyne*] Here, girl, get up on your feet. [*Loudly*] It wasn't a bull ; I knew it couldn't be a bull ! and it's gone, so get up. [*Putting down the gun.*] Get up ! [*With the help of the 1st Workman and Poges, Cloyne gets up on her feet.*] There now, be off with you. Get Miss Avril to give you a stiff glass of whiskey, and you'll be all right. And take this gun back to Mr. Basil.
   [*He picks up the gun and hands it to the shaking Cloyne.*

Cloyne. Oh, sir, this place is worse than a jungle in th' desert !

Poges. Go on, go on ! I thought you Irish were a brave people.
   [*He is shaky himself, but he stiffens himself to conceal the tremors.*

Cloyne [*going out with the gun*]. For ages now, it's bulls I'll be dhreamin' of, an' there's ne-er a lock on me door either !

Poges. Fainting, shouting, screaming, and running about for nothing ! No nerves, no nerves, no spirit ; no coolness in a crisis.

1st Workman [craftily]. An' did they all think it was a bull, sir ? An' you stood your ground. Looka that now. Prepared for anything, sir.

Poges [taking it all in]. The other fellow, Mr. Basil, ran for his life ; think of that — ran for his life !

1st Workman. Did he, now ?

Poges. British, too, think of that ; surprising and disappointing, very. [*Briskly and a little anxiously*] Still, I must acquaint the police. I can't have cows or bulls wandering about the rooms of Ormond Manor.

1st Workman [who has started to light the fire]. One o' th' ladies sent me in to light a fire for you. [*Placatingly*] Sure, sir, she was only the cow me friend brought this mornin' so that, when you had a minute, you could run out an' look her over. A fine animal, sir. She got loose an' wandhered in when she found th' door open. She's betther than th' best that was in th' cattle raid o' Cooley.
  [*Souhaun comes in by a back entrance followed by Avril. She is carrying a black vase, striped with blue, and has a jazzy overall on one of her arms. Avril carries a blue bowl, striped with black. They are carrying them very carefully, as if they were very precious indeed.*

Souhaun. What's all this commotion about a bull ? We had to stop Basil from trying to throw himself out of a window !

Avril. And Barney got out on top of the roof.

C.P.—III   E

Poges. Oh, nothing, nothing at all ; a stray cow in the garden mooed, and Basil lost his head and Cloyne lost her feet.

Avril. But Barney, when he was rushing past, said that you were out here roaring for help !

1st Workman. Roarin' for help, is it ? Indeed an' he wasn't, for I can testify to that, but standin' here, cool as you like, he was, waitin' for the worst.

Souhaun. Well, if we're to stay in the country, we'll have to get used to all kinds of animals, big and small.

Poges [*shaking his head*]. I'm convinced now that poor Basil can't be wholly English. There's a weak joint some- where.

Souhaun [*leaving the overall on a seat*]. There's your overall, dear, to wear when you're working, and we're taking your precious Annamese vase and Cambodian bowl to our room for safety, till everything's straight.

Poges. Oh, that's right, if anything happened to either of them, I'd pass out. Lift the vase up, dear, till I see it a second. [*She lifts it up.*] Oh, Lord, isn't it lovely ? [*To Avril*] The Cambodian bowl too. [*She lifts it over her head.*] A little too high, dear; just go down on one knee. [*She does so.*] Aaah ! Precious, precious ! The chaste form, the tender planes, the refined colouring ; the exquisite design, the *tout ensemble* — they go down into the undiscoverable deeps of the heart !

1st Workman. Arra, be God, indeed an' they do, sir.

Avril [*languishingly*]. A background of eau-de-nil would set them off to their full advantage.

Souhaun [*cocking her eye at them*]. Oh no, Avril ; Chinese white's the pure and proper background for them.

Avril. Eau-de-nil.

Souhaun. Chinese white, dear.

Poges. Neither. Chrome yellow's the tone. A warm and pure cloak, as it were, for the chaste bodies of the vase and the bowl. [*He goes over and touches them tenderly.*] My darling treasures ! Take them off, and lay them down with circumspection. Mind the step going out.

[*Souhaun and Avril go slowly and stately out, carrying the vase and the bowl as if they were precious relics.*

1st Workman [*to Poges who has come over to the fireplace where a fine fire is blazing now*]. There y'are, sir ; a fire that'll warm y' up an' make your mind easy.

Poges [*stretching out his hands to the fire*]. Good, great, grand ! Are you the workman who knows all the stories and legends of Ireland since the world began ?

1st Workman. No, no, not me, sir ; it's Philib you mean — th' powerful man with th' powerful beard. [*Touching his forehead.*] Some say he isn't all there, but a wondherful man, ay, indeed, is Philib. Does a man good to talk to him.

Poges. I'll have a chat with him, the first chance I get.

1st Workman [*looking round the room with a ravishing air*]. This is a wondherful house, so it is. It's an honour to be workin' in it. Afther hundhreds o' years standin' in frost, rain, an' snow, frontin' th' winds o' the world, it's a marvel it isn't flat on its face, furnishin' only an odd shelther for a sthray fox ; but here it stands, an' we all waitin' for a windy winther ud stagger it an' send it tottherin' down.

Poges [*indignantly*]. Tottherin' down ! What d'ye mean, tottherin' down ? The place is as firm as a lighthouse. Tottherin' down, indeed !

1st Workman [*repelling the idea that he thought of such a thing*]. Tottherin' down, is it ? Now who, in th' name o' God, save a sure an' safe fool ud think it was tottherin' down ? Not me, now ; oh no, not me. Tottherin' down me neck ! Isn't the grand oul' house goin' to show, soon an' sudden, a sign of what a fine residence it was when the quality harnessed their horses for a hunt be the risin' rim o' th' dawn, or sat down in their silks an' satins to their evenin' meal in the shadowy shine o' th' golden candles !

Poges. Purple nights and golden days, my friend. [*He sighs.*] Aah !

1st Workman [*with a long, deep, imitative sigh*]. Aah ! We'll never set eyes on the like o' them again, sir ; th' sparklin' carriages comin' an' goin', th' steeds throttin' nicely an' neatly, or movin' at a gallop, always elegant, on a visit to me lord here, or me lady there, with th' sky above in a fair swoon o' pride for th' fine things movin' about below ; an' they full o' grace, an' decked out in the grandeur o' th' West Indies an' th' East Indies, sobered down a thrifle for use in a Christian counthry, the women's bosoms asway with jewels, like a tendher evenin' sky, alive with stars. An' th' gentlemen, just a dim step down, but elegant too, in finery fair, with ruffles an' lace, with cutaway coats an' vests embroidhered, each holdin' a cane to keep them steady, an' all halo'd with scents to ring them round from th' smell o' th' poor an' dingier world at work or play !

Poges [*enthusiastically*]. Those were handsome days. [*He fixes a plume of pampas grass in his beret.*] When shall we look upon their like again ? [*He folds the crimson curtain stuff round him as if it were a cavalier's cloak.*] The lawns and ramparts still are here, and we shall be the men! [*He snatches up Basil's walking-stick.*] The plume in the hat, the velvet cloak over the shoulder, the tapering rapier in the hand ! [*He makes a vicious lunge at the 1st Workman, who narrowly dodges the pass.*] Die, varlet !

1st Workman [*remonstratively*]. Eh, eh, there ; careful, sir, be careful ! Be careful how yeh prod !

Poges [*leaning on the stick as if it were a sword — sorrowfully*]. Where are the kings and queens and warriors now ? Gone with all their glory ! The present day and present men ? Paltry, mean, tight, and tedious. [*Disgustedly*] Bah !

1st Workman. What are we now, what are we all, but a tired thribe thryin' to do nothin' in th' shortest possible time ? Worn away we are, I'm sayin', to shreds and shaddas mouldin' machines to do everything for us. Tired, is it ? Ay, tired an' thremblin' towards th' edge of th' end of a life hardly worth livin' !

Poges [*gloomily pacing up and down*]. Not worth living, not worth living.

1st Workman [*with greater energy*]. Time ago, an' we gave a ready ear to one speakin' his faith in God an' his neighbour ; but now, there's so many gabbers goin' that there's hardly a listener left. Sure, that in itself is as sharp a punishment as a lease o' hell for a long vacation. It's meself is sayin' ourselves came late, but soon enough to see the finery fade to purple dust, an' the glow o' th' quality turn to murmurin' ashes.

Poges [*striking the attitude of a clumsy cavalier*]. We won't let them perish completely ! We'll keep the stern old walls standing. We'll walk where they walked, sit where they sat, and sleep where they slept !

1st Workman. An' talk as they talked too.

Poges [*wildly*]. Our pride shall be their pride, our elegance their elegance, and the banner of the Ormonds shall fly from the battlements again ! The King, the King, God bless him !

1st Workman [*warningly*]. I wouldn't say too much about the King, sir ; we're a little touchy about kings down here in Clune na Geera.

> [*From outside is heard a scream from Souhaun and a squeal from Avril ; then the sound of running feet, and the crash of breaking chinaware. After a moment or so, Souhaun pitches into the room from the left entrance at back, and Avril from the right one. Souhaun is holding the top rim of the vase in her hand, and Avril the butt of the bowl. When he sees the damage, the 1st Workman slinks off.*

Poges [*furiously*]. What the hell's all this ?

Avril [*breathlessly*]. Rats !

Souhaun [*breathlessly*]. Gigantic creatures !

Avril. Here.

Souhaun. There.

Both [*together*]. Everywhere !

Poges [*in anguish*]. Oh, look at what's left of my Annamese vase and Cambodian bowl ! A hundred pounds of the best for each, and then only when I happened to catch

the cunning Keeper drunk in the Bazaar of Singapore.
What the hell were the pair of you thinking of?

Souhaun. Rats.

Avril. Here, there, and everywhere.

Poges [*wildly*]. You evil-handed dolts to destroy my two
best treasures! You'll pay for them, you'll pay for
them!

Avril [*scornfully*]. We'd look well thinking of them, and
we running for our lives.

Souhaun. You can imagine what it was when Basil is up
there now on guard with the gun.

Poges [*mockingly*]. Oh, he's the boy to shoot down wild
animals. [*Imploringly*] For God's sake go up and take
the gun off him or he'll send a bullet through the body
of some human being! And for the future, you and
your friend keep your awkward hands off any treasures
I may have left.

Souhaun [*scornfully*]. Treasures! Who told you that the
Annamese vase and your old Cambodian bowl were
treasures?

Poges. Everyone who saw them, woman!

Souhaun. Ay, to humour you. Well, let me tell you they
weren't more valuable than a second-hand vase or
bowl bought at a Woolworth sale. That's the fact,
and it's best to know it.

Poges [*with quiet emphasis*]. And who gave you that in-
formation?

Avril. Couldn't anyone, not a fool, see what they were
the minute they saw them?

Souhaun. The minute Mr. O'Killigain set eyes on them, he said that they went from Derby in thousands to Singapore and Saigon for suckers to buy them !

Poges [*with furious scorn*]. Oh, indeed, did he ? Oh, an authority on what kind of art d'ye call it in Clune na Geera ? I'll test them. I'll send them to the Curator of the Wallace Collection. We'll see. Mr. O'Killigain — good God !
  [*He takes the pieces from Avril and Souhaun and puts them on the table. Cloyne appears at an entrance at back with a troubled look on her face.*

Cloyne. Here, they've gone and dumped the garden tools an' the roller right in front of the hall door ! And the roller's so close that when you want to go out or come in you have to climb over it.

Poges. Tell whoever brought them to bring them to the back and put them in the shed, fool !

Cloyne. How can I tell him when him an' the lorry's gone ?

Poges [*furiously*]. And why didn't you tell him before he went ?

Cloyne. An' didn't I now ? He just said that the back was threnched be the workmen an' he hadn't time to build pontoon bridges.

Poges. What a country ! What a people ! [*Viciously — to Souhaun*] And you encourage them, because you and your friend Avril are Irish too !

Souhaun. If you ask me, you're not such a shining paragon of goodness yourself.

Poges [*explosively*]. I believe in efficiency ! I demand efficiency from myself, from everyone. Do the thing thoroughly and do it well : that's English. The word given, and the word kept : that's English. [*Roaring*] And I'm an Englishman !

Souhaun. You are indeed, God help you !

Cloyne. An' what are we goin' to do about the garden tools an' th' roller ?

Souhaun [*in a bustling and dominant way, catching up the jazz-patterned overall and putting it on Poges*]. Here, if we waste any more time talking, the house will never be ready to live in. Put this on, and go and bring the roller from the front door through here, out of the way, to the back. When you've done that, bring the garden tools to the back too, and let us see your grand English efficiency at work while I and Avril do some of the hundred things remaining to be done.
[*She gives him a push from her, and she and Avril hurry away out by one of the back entrances.*

Cloyne [*warningly*]. It seems a heavy roller, sir, so mind you don't sthrain yourself when you're pullin' it.

Poges [*testily*]. Go away, go away, girl ; I'm not an invalid. [*Cloyne goes. Poges moves over to the blazing fire and stretches out his hands to the flame. The 2nd Workman comes in by left entrance at back wheeling a barrow filled with bricks. He is a powerful man of fifty, with gleaming eyes and wide and strong beard. As he comes nearer, Poges turns to give him greeting. Warmly*] Good day, good sir ; it's a cold day that's in it, surely.

2nd Workman [*eyeing Poges curiously*]. Ay is it, for them who has to brave it, an' can't stand all day in front of a sturdy fire like a kingly Pharaoh.

Poges [*a little nonplussed*]. Quite, yes, yes, quite. Everyone tells me the place round here is a rich storehouse of history, legend, and myth?

2nd Workman [*with a little scorn in his voice*]. It's a little they know an' little they care about those things. But the place has her share o' histhory an' her share o' wondhers.

Poges [*flatteringly*]. And I'm told you have a rare stock of them yourself.

2nd Workman. Ay, indeed, I have me share o' wondhers, new an' old.

Poges [*trying to be Irish*]. Looka that, now. Arra, whisht, an' amn't I told it's strange stories you do be tellin' of the noble things done by your fathers in their days, and in the old time before them.

2nd Workman [*sinking into a meditative mood*]. When less than a score of the Fianna brought back the King of England prisoner, invaded Hindostan, an' fixed as subjects the men of all counthries between our Bay o' Dublin and the holy river that gave to holy John the holy wather to baptize our Lord.

Poges [*astonished*]. I never heard that one before.

2nd Workman [*with murmuring scorn*]. An' where would th' like o' you hear it, man? That was in the days o' Finn Mac Coole, before his hair was scarred with a hint o' grey; the mighty Finn, I'm sayin', who stood as still as a stone in th' heart of a hill to hear the cry of a curlew over th' cliffs o' Erris, the song of the blackbird, the cry o' the hounds hotfoot afther a boundin' deer, the steady wail o' the waves tumblin' in on a lonely shore ; the mighty Finn who'd surrendher an emperor's pomp for a place with the bards, and the gold o' the King o' Greece for a night asleep be the sthream of Assaroe !

Poges [*solemnly*]. A great man, a great man, surely ; a great man gone for ever.

2nd Workman [*sharply*]. He's here for ever ! His halloo can be heard on the hills outside ; his spear can be seen with its point in the stars ; but not with an eye that can see no further than the well-fashioned edge of a golden coin.

Poges [*moving back a step — a little awed*]. You see these things, do you ?

2nd Workman. I hear sthrange things be day, an' see sthrange things be night when I'm touched be the feel of the touch of the long-handed Lugh. When the Dagda makes a gong o' the moon, an' the' Sword o' Light shows the way to all who see it.

Poges. Aah !

2nd Workman. Then every rib o' grass grows into a burnished fighter that throws a spear, or waves a sword, an' flings a shield before him. Then Ireland crinkles into a camp, an' kings an' sages, queens an' heroes, saints an' harpers stare me in the face, an' bow, an' pass, an' cry out blessing an' vict'ry too, for Heber's children, with the branch of greatness waving in their hands !

Poges [*sadly*]. And there it ends !

2nd Workman [*giving Poges a drowsy glance*]. I'm thinkin' it
might have been well for some if the end an' all was
there ; but it sthretches out to the sight of a big dim
ship with a followin' fleet in the great dim distance,
with a stern-fac'd man in the blue-gold coat of the
French Armee, standin' alone on th' bridge of the
big dim ship, his eyes fixed fast on the shore that was
fallin' undher the high-headed, rough-tumblin' waves
o' the sea !

Poges [*awed into interest — murmuringly*]. A big dim ship
and a following fleet, carrying a man in the blue-gold
coat of the French Armee — who was he, and when
was that, now ?

2nd Workman. Th' man was Wolfe Tone, and the time was
yestherday.

Poges. Yesterday !

2nd Workman. The man was there, but the fleet was a
golden dhream, always comin' in an' ever goin' out o'
th' Bay o' Banthry !
   [*O'Killigain has come in at the commencement of the 2nd
   Workman's musing, unnoticed by the dreaming worker,
   and barely noticed by the interested Poges, listening
   intently to what is being said, and a little awed by the
   influence of the 2nd Workman. O'Killigain comes
   softly over, and stands a little behind but close to the
   dreaming workman.*

Poges [*bending towards the 2nd Workman*]. And who was
the man in the blue-gold coat of the French Armee ?

2nd Workman. He was a great Irish soldier and a great
Irish friend to the people of no property in Ireland.

O'Killigain [*very softly*]. And there are others.

2nd Workman [*softly too, but not so softly*]. And there are
others ; for through the roads of the four green fields
goes Shane the Proud, with his fine head hidden,
waving away his more venturesome friends from the
horns of a bull, the hoofs of a horse, the snarl of a dog,
an' th' smile of an Englishman.

Poges [*going back a step*]. The smile of an Englishman !

2nd Workman [*unheeding the interruption*]. An' in the midst
of them all is Parnell standing still ; unheeding he
stands with a hand on his breast, his white face fixed
on the East, with his wine-coloured eyes flashin'
hathred to England !

O'Killigain [*very softly*]. And there are others.

2nd Workman [*with a glance at O'Killigain*]. They came
later, an' haven't wandhered fully back to where they
cleared a way for a gropin' people, but they will come,
an' stare us into the will to take our own again.

Poges [*detaching himself from the spell*]. And do none other
of those you know, good man, see the things that you
see ?

2nd Workman. Barrin' a few an' O'Killigain there, they
see these things only as a little cloud o' purple dust
blown before the wind.

Poges. That's very sad.

2nd Workman. Barrin' O'Killigain there an' a few, what
is it all now but a bitther noise of cadgin' mercy from
heaven, an' a sour handlin' o' life for a cushion'd seat
in a corner ? There is no shout in it ; no sound of a
slap of a spear in a body ; no song ; no sturdy winecup
in a sturdy hand ; no liftin' of a mighty arm to push

back the tumblin' waters from a ship just sthrikin' a
storm. Them that fight now fight in a daze o' thradin' ;
for buyin' an' sellin', for whores an' holiness, for th'
image o' God on a golden coin ; while th' men o'
peace are little men now, writin' dead words with
their tiny pens, seekin' a tidy an' tendher way to the
end. Respectable lodgers with life they are, behind
solid doors with knockers on them, an' curtained glass
to keep the stars from starin' !

[*The 2nd Workman stoops, lifts the shafts of the barrow,
and is about to go out.*

Poges [*to 2nd Workman — placatingly*]. My own great-grand-
father was Irish, I'm told, and my grandmother was a
kind of a Scotswoman.

2nd Workman [*going out with the barrow slowly*]. That's not
such a lot, an' you're not sure of any of it either.

Poges. What a strange, odd man ! I couldn't get half of
what he was trying to say. Are there many like him ?

O'Killigain. Millions of them, though few of them have
tongues so musical.

Poges. He rather took to me, I think, and looks upon me
as a friend.

O'Killigain [*ironically*]. He looks upon you, and all
Englishmen, as a rascal, a thief, and a big-pulsed
hypocrite.

Poges [*indignantly*]. Good God, but that's pure ignorance.
Where would the world be without us ?

O'Killigain. The giddy globe would wobble, slow down,
stand still, and death would come quick to us all.

Poges [*a little puzzled by this remark*]. Eh ? Quite. Well,

no, not so bad as that, you know, but near it, damned
near it.

> [*Souhaun runs in with a look of dark annoyance on her
> face.*

Souhaun. Oh, look at you standing here still, and so much
to be done — [*her voice rises*] — so much to be done, so
much to be done ! I asked you to get the roller away
from the door an hour ago, and here's Barney after
twisting his wrist trying to climb over it standing in
the same old place ! [*She catches him by the overall.*]
Come, for God's sake, and take the damn thing out of
the way !

Poges [*pulling her hand away from the overall — angrily*].
Oh, have some decency, order, and dignity, woman !
Can't you see I'm having a serious discussion with
O'Killigain ? [*He turns swiftly on O'Killigain.*] We,
sir, are a liberty-loving people, and have always striven
to preserve perfect — perfect, mind you — freedom of
thought, not only in our own land, but throughout the
whole world ; but that anyone should be permitted to
hold opinions such as are held by that lunatic just gone
out, and are apparently held by you, sir, too, is a
perfect scandal and disgrace !

Souhaun. Oh, there's no use of you trying to ride your
high horse here in Clune na Geera !

Poges [*stormily*]. I'm not trying to ride my high horse here
in Clune na Geera ! What is said in Clune na Geera is
a matter of very little importance indeed. But every
right-minded man the world over knows, or ought to
know, that wherever we have gone, progress, civilisation, truth, justice, honour, humanity, righteousness,
and peace have followed at our heels. In the Press, in

the Parliament, in the pulpit, or on the battlefield, no
lie has ever been uttered by us, no false claim made,
no right of man infringed, no law of God ignored, no
human law, national or international, broken.

O'Killigain [*very quietly*]. Oh, for God's sake, man, don't
be pratin' like a pantaloon priest !

Souhaun [*trying to push Poges from the room — impatiently*].
Go out and get the garden roller !

Poges [*loudly*]. I say, sir, that Justice is England's old
nurse ; Righteousness and Peace sit together in her
common-room, and the porter at her gate is Truth !

O'Killigain [*quietly, but sarcastically*]. An' God Himself is
England's butler !

Poges [*roaring with rage*]. That's a vile slander, sir !

O'Killigain. Whether it is or no doesn't matter much,
for in a generation or so the English Empire will be
remembered only as a half-forgotten nursery rhyme !

Poges [*fiercely as Souhaun is pushing him out*]. An opinion
like that deserves the jail !

Souhaun [*giving him a last strong push out into one of the back
entrances*]. Oh, go on ! [*She goes over towards O'Killigain
and stands looking shyly and a little archly at him.*] What
a naughty man you are to provoke him into such a
tantrum ! [*After a slight pause.*] I hear terrible things
about you, Mr. O'Killigain.

O'Killigain. Oh ?

Souhaun. That you are a great man for the girls !

O'Killigain. A pretty girl shows me a sign that God is
smilin'.

Souhaun [*archly*]. It's well I need the gay an' youthful gloss of pretty Avril, or it's shelterless I'd be from all your stormy moods !

O'Killigain [*gallantly*]. When I look at you close I see you a week or two oldher than your younger friend, an' when you go as bright about the house, an' dhress as gay as she does, you look like an earlier summer kissin' a tardy spring goodbye.

Souhaun. More than twenty years younger than the old fool Poges I am of course. It's ridiculous for me to be with him. I have a nice little income of my own now, and it's like a young bird I feel that has just got command of its restless wings. [*She pauses for a moment.*] You really do believe that I am as pretty as Avril ? You're not just teasing me, are you ?

O'Killigain. Not I. You are one o' th' fine sights of this world. [*He lilts :*]

There are many fair things in this world as it goes,
The blue skies of summer, th' flushing red rose,
But of all th' fair, blossoming things that men see,
A comely-built lass is th' nearest to me,
A comely-built lass is th' dearest to me !

And you are a comely-built lass.

Souhaun [*coming near to him and stroking his arm*]. Your poor arm, wounded for the sake of others. What's your name ?

O'Killigain. My name ? O'Killigain, of course.

Souhaun. No, no, your more familiar name ; the name your girl would call you by ?

O'Killigain. Jack.

C.P.—III   F

Souhaun [*lingering over it*]. Jack. What a dear name, Jack!
What a dear name — [*she suddenly stands on tiptoe and
kisses him*] — Jack!

> [*She is running out by the entrance on the right when she
> bumps into Poges laboriously pulling in a gigantic roller
> as high in diameter as he is tall. The heavy iron side-
> discs are vividly painted in panels of red, white, blue,
> green, and yellow. When the roller is pulled into the
> room, it can be seen that the 1st Workman is pushing it
> behind.*

Poges [*angrily, as Souhaun bumps into him*]. Eh, eh, there,
look where you are going, can't you?

Souhaun [*amazed at the size of the roller*]. God bless us,
Cyril, what on earth's that you're carting into the
house?

Poges [*petulantly*]. Can't you see what it is? The roller
you told me to bring through here to the back. The
roller, the roller I bought to roll the lawn.

Souhaun. But it's too big, man.

Poges. No, it isn't too big. The man who sold it to me
said that the bigger it was, the more effective it would
be.

Souhaun. But you'll never be able to pull a mighty thing
like that.

Poges. And what's to prevent me from pulling it?
Amn't I pulling it now? A child of ten could pull it,
the man said; well-balanced, you know, the man said.
Easy to pull, and easier to propel, the man said.

Souhaun. You've just been taken in, Cyril. The thing's
altogether too big. [*To the 1st Workman*] Isn't it?

1st Workman. It looks a size too large to me, ma'am.

Poges. The grass in this district needed a special big roller to level it, the man said, and this was the roller to level it.

1st Workman. Sure, that roller ud level a hill.

O'Killigain. The grass'll give way undher that, right enough.

Souhaun. The cheek of declaring that a child of ten could pull it like a toy.

1st Workman. G'way, ma'am, an' did he really say that now ?

Poges. One pull over the lawn with that roller would be enough for the season, the man said.

O'Killigain. An', faith, so it would, an' for every season afther too.

1st Workman. Sure, an' wouldn't a specially powerful horse himself wilt undher a thing like that ! Whoever gave you that, man, musta taken it off an oul' steam-roller.

  [*The 3rd Workman appears at entrance to right and proceeds to take an enjoyable interest in what is happening.*

3rd Workman. Mother o' God, looka what he's after buyin' be th' name of a roller ! Isn't it a shame, now, to have imposed on a poor, simple, inoffensive man with a vehicle like that !

Poges [*defiantly*]. It's a bargain, I know it's a bargain ; the man said it's a bargain.

Souhaun [*mockingly*]. The man said, the man said — ay, and you swallowed everything the man said.

O'Killigain [*to 1st Workman*]. Give Mr. Poges a hand to take this machine out of the sight of mortal men.

Poges [*obstinately*]. I'll take it myself, thank you all. Once you got the knack of balancing it, the man said, you could turn it with your little finger, and I believe what the man said.

O'Killigain [*to 3rd Workman*]. Here, you go on back to your work ; go on, off you go !
    [*He follows the 3rd Workman out of the room. Poges gives a mighty push to the roller, propelling it slowly to one of the entrances at the back. The 1st Workman goes over and helps him to push it.*

Poges [*fiercely — to 1st Workman*]. Let go, you ! I'll manœuvre it myself. Let go, I tell you !

1st Workman [*as fiercely — to Poges*]. Can't you see, man, the declivity runnin' down the passage that'll lead you, if the roller once gets outa hand, into God knows where ?

Poges [*with a roar into the face of the 1st Workman*]. Let go !
    [*The 1st Workman, startled, suddenly lets go his hold on the roller and the roller shoots forward down the declivity, Poges going with it, like a flash of lightning. Heard as he is careering down the passage — with anguish in his voice*] Help !
    [*There is a pause of a few moments, then a thud is heard, followed by a rumbling crash of falling bricks and mortar ; then silence again.*

Souhaun [*with vehement rage — running out*]. The blasted fool ! He has rocked the house and killed himself and hasn't made his will !

1st Workman [*staring down the passage*]. Right through the wall he's gone ! [*He runs to where the hole is in the ceiling,*

gets a seat and stands on it. Calling up to the hole] Eh,
Cornelius, eh, quick !
    [*The face of the Yellow-bearded Man appears at the hole,
    and he thrusts down his head as far as it will go.*

Yellow-bearded Man. Well, what's up now ?

1st Workman [*excitedly*]. The oul' man, the oul' fool, has
gone right through the wall with the roller, an' shook
the house — bang !

Yellow-bearded Man. Didn't I think it was an earthquake !
[*Testily*] An' don't be tellin' me these things while
I'm up here. Can't you wait till I'm down in th' world
o' men, and can enjoy these things happenin' !
    [*He angrily takes his head out of the hole. The 1st Workman
    gets down from the seat and runs out by entrance on right.*

1st Workman [*running out*]. Mr. O'Killigain, Jack, eh,
Jack !
    [*Souhaun returns, followed by Cloyne and Barney leading in
    the frightened Poges, powdered with the dust of the falling
    mortar. Souhaun arranges a mattress for him on which
    he squats, supported by pillows.*

Souhaun. You were warned, you were warned, and you
would have your own way. It's fortunate you are,
indeed, that none of your bones is broken.

Poges [*moaningly*]. Brandy, get me some brandy. [*Barney
goes out and comes back with a glass, brandy, and soda-water.
He fills out a glassful and gives it to Poges. After he has drunk
the brandy — to Cloyne and Barney*] Go way, you two, and
don't stand there gaping at me ! [*They go. Musingly*]
What a rascal that man must be who sold me the roller !
In this simple country, among a simple people, where

the very air is redolent with fairy lore, that such a dangerous and materialistic mind should be lurking !

Souhaun. For God's sake, man, talk sense.

Poges [*shaking his head sorrowfully*]. A gay and charming people, but irresponsible, utterly irresponsible.
   [*O'Killigain appears at the right entrance with a cloudy look on his face.*]

O'Killigain. Look here, that Basil of yours is goin' about the grounds carrying a fully-cocked gun at a dangerous angle. He'll do harm. Send someone to take it off him, or I'll twist it out of his hands myself ! And you'll want to be more careful yourself, or you'll have th' oul' house down !

Poges [*indignantly*]. Oh, what a conceited fool that fellow is — going about to do dangerous damage for want of a little common sense and caution. I don't believe he ever fired a gun in his life. [*To Souhaun*] Go out, dear, and take it off him, before he shoots somebody — and go quick ! [*Souhaun runs out by the entrance on the right, and O'Killigain is following her when Poges speaks to him, and halts him at the entrance.*] Oh yes, Mr. O'Killigain, a word please. [*He drinks some more brandy.*] Er, just a word. People are saying — there's a rumour going about that you and — and Miss Avril are — are, well, seen together at times.

O'Killigain. Well ?

Poges. Well ? Damn it, man, she's a lady, Mr. Stoke's a gentleman, and you're only a — a tradesman !

O'Killigain. Well ?

Poges. Well ? Oh, don't be welling me ! The week she was away from here was bad enough, and very

suspicious. She had the damned cheek to say she was
with you.

O'Killigain. So she was.

Poges. So she was, was she ? Well, it's dishonourable,
and it will have to stop.

O'Killigain. And who'll stop it ?

Poges [*firmly*]. I and Mr. Stoke will stop it.

O'Killigain [*quietly*]. You pair of miserable, old, hypo-
critical, wizened old getts, I'd like to see you trying !

Poges [*choking with rage*]. Get out of the house, and come
here no more ! I'll write to your parish priest !
I'll—— [*A shot rings out in the grounds outside.*] Good
God, the fool has shot somebody !
  [*O'Killigain goes off in a hurry. There is a pause. Then
  the yellow-bearded face is thrust through the hole in the
  ceiling as far as it can go, and shouts down at Poges
  sitting like Buddha on the mattress :*

Yellow-bearded Man [*down to Poges*]. He's shot her, shot her
dead, the poor little innocent creature ! Th' charmin'
little thing full o' gaiety an' go !

Poges [*very frightened, up to the Yellow-bearded Man*]. Shot
who, shot who, man ? Is it the young lass ?

Yellow-bearded Man. Without warnin' he done it, without
a flicker of an eyelid he sent her into the unknown !

Poges [*murmuring in agony*]. Avril ! Oh, my God, little
Avril. The curse of the Irish thorn-tree is on us !
The little lass gone. [*Near swooning*] Cut down like a
coloured bubble ! The fairies must be manœuvring,
and they'll get me next, maybe. Sweet little Avril the
first to go !

Yellow-bearded Man [*savagely*]. Twenty-five pounds, an' not a penny less, he'll pay for it, or I'll have the heavy law on him. I'd ha' let you have her at first for the twenty, but in some compensation for th' agony of seein' the poor thing sink down into death, I'll have to get the other five, or I'll have the heavy law on him !

Poges [*sitting up suddenly*]. What are you talking about, man ? What's shot, who's killed ?

Yellow-bearded Man. Be th' way, you don't know that that lean, skulkin' friend o' yours has shot dead me poor little innocent, poor little cow ! [*Sarcastically*] He thought it was a bull !

Poges [*bewildered*]. Oh, what a terrible country to have anything to do with ! My precious vase is gone, my beautiful bowl is broken ; a wall's demolished, and an innocent animal's shot dead : what an awful country to be living in ! A no-man's land ; a waste land ; a wilderness !

CURTAIN

ACT III

Before the room appears, the sounds of falling rain and swishing winds are heard; and these go on, at intervals, throughout the scene.

The same as in the preceding Act; but some more articles of furniture have been added to the room. Between the entrance to the right at the back, and the right wall, stands what is said to be a Jacobean china-cabinet, filled with old pieces of china. At each side of the larger entrance on the right stands an armoured figure, comical-looking things, with long sharp points pro-truding where the man's nose (if a man were inside the suit) would certainly be; each figure, standing stiff, holds a long halberd well out from his body. Over these are, crossed, pennons, green and blue, fixed on the wall.

A blazing fire is in the fireplace. No one is in the room. After a moment Poges, dressed in his jazz-patterned overall, with a paper in his hand, runs in and rushes over to the telephone.

Poges [*into the mouthpiece — hurriedly*]. Get me — Oh, good evening, good evening. This is Mr. Poges, Ormond Manor. Get me St. Paul, London : 123. The house is getting on all right, thank you. Be quick, please. [*Warmly*] There's no — seems — in it ; I am in a hurry. Oh, the ladies are quite well, sir. No, no, no ; I don't want to go to an all-night dance to hear Irish songs sung ! I want St. Paul ! Eh ? No, St. Peter won't do ; please don't try to be funny ; I am on very serious business. Get me the number I want at once ! [*He takes the mouthpiece from his mouth and gives vent to a roaring growl of anger.*] Whether it won't matter a hundred years from now isn't the point, sir. [*Shouting*] Damn it, get me St. Paul ! [*Bursting with rage*] No

wonder I use bad language. Is this the way business
is done here? No wonder this country's as it is.
What's wrong with it? [*Roaring*] Everything's wrong
with it! You what? You hope my stay here will
help to civilise me a little! [*He looks stupefied; then he slams
the receiver on the hook. Almost instantly the 'phone rings.
He whips off the receiver again and puts it to his ear.*] What
the hell does this — Eh? Who are you? St. Paul?
Good God! This is Poges, Bradford. Oh, it's an
awful place. People helpless, superstitious, and
ignorant. I want you to get me five hundred shares
in the Welldonian Cement Co.; shares are bound to
jump, the minute the bombing starts seriously. They
have jumped? Ah. What, a fiver a share, now?
Well, get me two fifty. What? Not one to be had?
[*Clicking his tongue*] Dtch, dtch. Run on them, eh?
One wouldn't imagine there'd be so many trying to
cash in on splintered bodies. The world, the world,
Bradford! Yes, yes, of course; if there's any going,
snap them up. Righto. Goodbye.

> [*He hangs up the receiver. Barney appears at the entrance
> on the right.*

Barney. Canon Creehewel would like to speak to you, sir.

Poges. Right; send the Canon in to me.

> [*Barney goes; and, in a second or so, the Canon comes in.
> He is inclined to be portly, has rather a hard face, head
> bald at the front, with bushy greying hair at the back of
> his head and over his ears. He is wearing a soft hat,
> sodden with rain, which he puts on the end of the table
> when he comes in; and a long dark cloak, glistening with
> rain too. He comes over eager — to Poges, with a smile
> on his face, and outstretched hand.*

Canon. Ah, my dear friend, I'm so glad to have a chance

of a word with you. How are you liking Clune na Geera ?

Poges. Splendid, though the weather has been cold and very wet. Take your cloak off.

Canon [*taking off his cloak. When his cloak is off, it can be seen that his clothes fit nicely*]. Isn't it a nuisance ; and we're in for more of it, by all accounts. If it goes on much more, the district will be a dismal swamp.

Poges [*indicating a seat*]. Sit down, Canon, sit down. Glass of sherry ?
    [*The Canon sits, and Poges sits too, opposite the Canon.*

Canon. No, thanks. I drink rarely. [*Apologetically*] Good example, you know. Well, welcome, my dear sir, to our district. You have a very beautiful house here. An old house, but a fine one. It is almost a sacred thing to keep an old thing from dying, sir ; for whatsoever things are just, whatsoever things are honest, whatsoever things are pure, whatsoever things are lovely and of good report, are invariably found close to, and, sometimes, intimately enclosed in the life and being of ages that have passed, and in the life of men and women who have gone away before us.

Poges [*gratified*]. I wholeheartedly agree with you, reverend sir. I feel it, I know it.

Canon. With all its frills, its frivolities, its studied ceremonial, however gaily-coloured its leisure may have been, the past had in it the core of virtue ; while the present swirl of young life, I'm saying, with its feverish sthrut of pretended bravery, its tawdry carelessness about the relation and rule of religion to man,

with all its frantic sthretching of pleasure into every
second of life, contains within it a tawny core of fear
that is turning darker with every chime of the passing
hours !   [*The rain and wind are plainly heard.*

Poges [*leaning towards the Canon — eagerly*]. We must
lengthen our arm back to the past and pluck back some
of the good things that haven't gone away as far from
us as the dead who knew them.

Canon. A worthy enterprise, dear sir, and I hope you and
your good people will be a help to us here to bring
some of the slow movement of the past into the reckless
and Godless speed of the present. [*He leans over
towards Poges till their heads nearly touch.*] You and yours
can do much to assist the clergy to keep a sensible
check on the lower inclinations of the people, a work
which should be near the heart of every sensible and
responsible man with a stake in the country.

Poges. I'll do all I can. [*Leans back with an air of business
importance.*] From the practical point of view, how am
I to help ?

Canon [*dropping a little into the idiom of the district*]. Help us
to curtail th' damned activity of the devilish dance
halls ! Open a dance hall, and in a month or less the
innocent disthrict becomes worse than your Leicester
Square in London when the night has fallen. If the
dance halls are allowed to go ahead without the
conthrol of the clergy an' responsible people, God will
go from Clune na Geera !

Poges [*shocked*]. Good God ! Such a condition of things
among a simple, charming, and pastoral people amazes
me.

Canon [*warming to it*]. Arra, wouldn't it sicken you, when the hot days come, to see fools of oul' men an' fools of oul' women too, settin' a bad example, goin' about nearly naked, in their coloured shorts, an' brazen-fac'd lasses mixed among them in low-cut bodices, defiant short skirts, or shorter trousers, murdherin' modesty with a restless an' a reckless hand !

Poges. A lamentable state of affairs entirely, sir.

Canon [*rising and going over close to Poges — intensely*]. An' like Eden, sir, we've a snake in our garden too !

Poges. Oh !

Canon. O'Killigain !

Poges. Ah !   [*The wind and the rain are plainly heard.*

Canon. Guard your womenfolk from him, for no woman is safe with that man. He publicly defends the wearing of low-necked blouses by brazen hussies ; he stands be the practice of courting couples walking the highways and byways be night. Why, one moonlight night, meetin' my curate dhrivin' home a lasciviously-minded girl, O'Killgain tore the stick from the curate's hand an' smashed it into pieces ! A dangerous man, my dear sir, a most dangerous man.

Poges [*a little nervously*]. I'm what you'd call a foreigner down here, and so couldn't interfere with O'Killigain personally ; but what I can do to help you, I certainly will, in any other way.

Canon. Thank you — I guessed you would. Your fifty pounds have helped a lot already. And now I've taken up a lot of your time and must go. [*He takes up his hat.*] By the way, how's the workman I sent you getting along ?

Poges. Which one ?

Canon. The one doing your electric light — a yellow-bearded fellow.

Poges [*emphatically*]. Oh, he's getting along splendidly !

Canon. I'm glad to hear it.   A good fellow — a Knight of St. Columbus.

Poges. Well, now, I never knew Columbus was a saint.

Canon [*smiling indulgently*]. Oh yes indeed ; a great Irish saint.

Poges. I always thought he was an American.

Canon. An American ; who ?

Poges. Christopher Columbus.

Canon [*smiling*]. Oh, there were two Columbuses, one Irish and the other — er — American.

> [*As the Canon is about to move away, Avril, followed by Souhaun, dances into the room from an entrance at the back. She is dressed in a low-cut blouse, short tailor-made skirt, and soft leather high boots moulded to her calves and reaching to just below her knees; and looks, indeed, a very tempting and desirable young hussy. She has a mackintosh over her arm. Souhaun, too, is dressed in very short shorts of a vivid crimson and a black V-necked jersey, looking as enticing, in a more mature way, as young Avril herself. Poges is a little embarrassed, but the good Canon does not flicker an eyelid. Souhaun whips off Poges' overall and shows him in a green jersey and brown shorts.*

Souhaun. You mustn't receive the Canon, dear, in an overall !

Avril. I say, Cyril, old boy, when are we going to get that damned bathroom ? It's a bit thick trying to have a bath in a basin.
              [*She sees the Canon and stops to gaze at him.*

Poges [*introducing her*]. Mr. Stoke's — er — wife — Miss Avril, Canon. [*Introducing Souhaun*] My — er — wife, Miss Souhaun.

Canon [*bowing graciously — to Avril*]. My dear young lady. [*To Souhaun*] Madam, I'm very pleased to know you.

Avril [*nodding to Canon — to Poges*]. Well, when are we going to have a decent bathroom, old cock o' th' walk ?

Poges [*deprecatingly*]. The Canon's here, Avril.

Canon [*jovially*]. Youthful spirits, sir, youthful spirits.

Poges. We'll have a bathroom if we can fit one in without injuring the harmony of the old house. The Tudor period never saw a bathroom. This generation's getting soft, Canon ; we want hardening.

Avril. Bunkum !

Poges [*indignantly*]. It's anything but bunkum ! Shakespeare had to do without one.

Souhaun. But surely, dear, you must know that the Tudor people knew nothing about the use of steam ?
              [*Basil now appears at an entrance at the back, and when he sees the company, he stays there and listens. He is dressed in a yellow jersey and black shorts. No one notices him.*

Poges [*petulantly*]. Steam ! We stand here, in the centre, not of a house, but of a great civilisation, and you mention steam !

Souhaun. In the centre of a hot bath, dear, I can remain in the centre of your civilisation.

Basil [*joining in — looking like a statue in the doorway*]. Not precisely, Souhaun, for it would require, or at least postulate, a full and concentrated retirement through the avenues of thought back to the time of which the visible surroundings are vividly, but quiescently reminiscent.   The conception of the conscious thoughts, interrelating with the — with the outward and inward action and reaction of all — or most of the bodily senses, incorporating the outward vision of sight with the inward vision of the inward conception of the — of the fragmentary stumuli — er — stimuli, into a perfect and harmonious whole ; a thing, if I may be allowed to say so, if not impossible, is at least improbable, sitting down, or indeed even standing up, in the middle of a hot bath.

Avril [*with mock enthusiasm*]. Hooray !

Poges [*to the Canon*]. Mr. Stoke, Canon ; cousin to the uncle of a K.G., and passed through Oxford.

Canon. Really ? Well, well, remarkable connections. [*In the far distance a faint clap of thunder is heard; the Canon cocks his ear to listen.*] I must be off. Bad sign. The soft rain that's falling may change to a downpour, and I've a long way to go.
[*Canon puts on his cloak.   Barney and Cloyne come in carrying a heavy Jacobean chair between them.*

Souhaun. Ah, the Jacobin chair. [*Indicating the way*] Out in the entrance hall, Barney.

Poges. Let's look at it a second. [*Barney and Cloyne pause.*]
Ah, Canon, old things take a lot of beating.

Canon. They do, they do, sir. Well, I must go now.

Poges [*halting him*]. One second, sir. [*He goes to the table,
writes a cheque, and hands it to the Canon.*] Another little
trifle to keep things going, Canon.

Canon. Twenty-five pounds ! Oh, thank you, and God
bless you, my very dear sir.

Souhaun. You must come to dinner some night.

Canon. I will, I will, with pleasure ; goodbye all.
              [*Midst a murmur of goodbyes the Canon goes out.*

Poges [*indignantly*]. Never showed the slightest interest
in the Jacobin chair. Ignorance ; Irish ignorance !
[*Angrily — to Cloyne and Barney, who are holding the chair
like a salesman displaying a piece of silk*] Bring the damned
thing into the entrance hall, will you, and don't stand
there like fools !
    [*Cloyne, in her hurry, jerks the chair from Barney's hold and
    it bumps to the floor.*

Poges. Oh, butter-fingers, d'ye want to destroy it ?
That's a Jacobin chair, man, a Jacobin chair !

Barney [*with a yell as he carries out the chair with Cloyne*].
Well, if I let a damned chair fall, I didn't knock a
wall down !

Poges. Impudent rascal. The more you do for them the
less they think of you ! [*He bustles into his overall
again.*] Now to business. What'll we do first ? The
rugs ?

Souhaun. There's no use of trying the rugs till you get

your quattrocento bureau in position. Then we'll be able to see if the colour of the rugs suits the bureau.

[*Avril has put on her mackintosh and sidled over to the entrance on right, leading to the hall, and is about to slip out when Basil darts to her side and catches her arm.*

Basil. Where are you slipping off to ?

Avril. I'm going for a brisk walk along the bank of the brimming river. I'm fed-up carrying things about to get this foolish old house in order.

Poges. In this weather ? Nonsense !

Basil. A good idea ; I'll go with you, darling.

Avril [*with a malevolent look at him*]. Wouldn't you like to, eh ? Take my advice and don't ! [*To Poges*] Ay, in this weather.

[*She goes quickly, leaving Basil, undecided, looking after her.*

Basil [*bitterly*]. She's going to go with O'Killigain !

Souhaun. Nonsense. She can't be out of your sight for a minute but you imagine the girl's with O'Killigain. The rain'll soon send her back. [*To Poges*] You see about locking the bureau, while I get the men to carry it in for you.

[*Poges goes by one of the entrances at the back.*

Basil [*going towards entrance at back*]. I tell you the jade's gone after O'Killigain.

Souhaun [*warningly*]. If I were you, Basil, I shouldn't press hard after little Avril ; you are a little too consequential to please her always.

Basil [*maliciously — as he goes out*]. And you, me lady, are a lot too old to please O'Killigain at any time !

[*Souhaun stands stiff for a few moments; then she goes quickly to the entrance to the hall and is seen beckoning for one of the workmen.*

Souhaun [*calling*]. One of you, come here, please.
[*The 2nd Workman comes into the room and stands near the entrance, looking quietly at Souhaun.*

Souhaun. Send Mr. O'Killigain in to me, please.

2nd Workman. He's gone to the station to see afther a wagon-load o' bricks.

Souhaun [*slowly, after a pause*]. By himself?

2nd Workman [*after a pause*]. With th' handsome young woman. [*A pause.*] You're a handsome woman yourself; you're Irish too; an' y'ought to be sensible.

Souhaun [*slowly — a little surprised*]. Am I not sensible, good man?

2nd Workman [*earnestly*]. Your shinin' eyes can always say you are; an' soon you'll tire o' nestin' in a dusty nook with the hills outside an' th' roads for walkin'.

Souhaun. I will, will I?

2nd Workman [*with his eyes looking steadily in hers*]. Ay will you, an' dance away from a smoky bragger who thinks th' world spins round on th' rim of a coin; you'll hurry away from him, I'm sayin', an' it's a glad heart'll lighten th' journey to a one'll find a place for your little hand in th' white clouds, an' a place for your saucy head in th' blue o' th' sky.

Souhaun [*with a touch of mockery*]. Yourself, for instance?

2nd Workman. It's waitin' warm, he'll be, to please you, highly, an' show you wondhers of a manly manner.

Souhaun [*laughing, with a little catch in the laugh*]. A
daughter of the Ormond with a workman !

2nd Workman [*raising his head proudly and looking steadily at
her*]. An oldher name is an O'Dempsey, an' an oldher
glory's in the name than the honour thrown to th'
Earl o' Ormond when he crouched for favour at the
English feet !

> [*The 2nd Workman looks at Souhaun and Souhaun looks
> at the 2nd Workman for a moment, then she turns and
> goes slowly out by right entrance at back.*

3rd Workman [*appearing at the back left entrance*]. Here,
Philib, what'r you doin' ?   You're to give us a hand to
get in the oul' codger's bureau.

> [*The two of them go out by the entrance to the left at back.
> After a second or two, the sound of scuffling and of voices
> are heard just outside the narrow entrance through which
> the two men have gone out, then Poges comes in with an
> anxious look on his face, turns and concentrates his gaze
> on the entrance. Presently the end of a big gilded desk-
> bureau comes in sight round the corner, with the three
> workmen puffing, pulling, pushing, and scuffling it
> along, each giving orders to the other two, to the concern of
> poor old Poges. When the bureau comes to the entrance,
> it can be seen to be a very tight fit.*

1st Workman. A little to the ayste, there, a little more
to the ayste, can't yous !

2nd Workman. No, west, west ; can't yous see it'll jam if
yous cant it to the ayste ? To th' west, I'm tellin'
yous !

Poges [*anxiously*]. Easy, boys, easy, now ; take care, take
great care ; that's a thing you won't meet every day,
you know.   I had an anxious time while it was coming
over.

3rd Workman [*taking no notice of Poges*]. Where th' hell are yous shovin' ? Are yous blind, or wha' ? No squirmin'll get it in that way. [*Recklessly*] Here, throw th' thing up on its hind legs an' let her go !

Poges [*loudly and anxiously*]. Eh, there, eh ; steady, steady. Careful how you handle that. It's not a thing to throw up on its hind legs. I can't have a precious thing like that scratched and mangled. That's a quattrocento piece of furniture, and there isn't another piece like it in the world.

1st Workman [*to the others*]. Hear what the gentleman's sayin' to yous ! Amn't I tired tellin' yous yous ud look long before yous ud find such a piece o' furniture in th' whole o' Clune na Geera ? Yous can't fling a thing like this about the way you'd fling about an oul' kitchen chair. [*To Poges*] Amn't I right, sir ?

Poges. Yes, yes ; quite right, my man. Thousands of people would give a fortune to possess a thing like that bureau. So gently, boys, gently. The slightest scratch will do irreparable damage.

1st Workman. See, boys, it's a quattrocento lump o' furniture, an' so needs gentle handlin'. [*To 2nd Workman*] You, Philib, there, give it a sudden swing to the ayste, an' while she's swingin' we'll shoot her ahead.

2nd Workman [*angrily*]. How am I goin' to give her a sudden swing to the ayste when there's no purchase to get a grip of her ? Squattrocento or nottrocento, I'm not goin' to let it whip a slice outa my hand !

3rd Workman [*thoughtfully*]. Th' only way to get it in proper is to get a sledge-hammer an' knock down some o' th' archway.

Poges [*indignantly*]. Knock down some of the archway ! You'll do no such thing ! You'll be suggesting that the house should be knocked down next. There's no sledge-hammer to be brought within sight of this precious bureau. [*Leaning over towards the men*] Listen : this is a piece of quattrocento — understand that, the whole of you, please !

1st Workman [*to the others*]. There, now, what did I tell yous ? Yous hear what the gentleman says.

Poges. It ought to go in easily, if you knew your job. The driver of the furniture van looked at this entrance and told me not to worry, that the bureau would slide in without the slightest trouble.

1st Workman [*scornfully*]. Is it Larry Lunigan said that, now, did he ? Don't mind anything Larry Lunigan says, sir. If your head was split he'd say it was only a scratch, to keep your heart up.

3rd Workman. Even if you were dead he'd tell your wife to wait, an' say you never could be sure of anything. An' we're not furniture shifters, sir.

Poges. Well, I'm sure of one thing : that bureau is coming into this room, and coming in without a scratch.

3rd Workman. 'Course it is.

1st Workman. Time an' patience'll do it.

Poges [*looking closely at the bureau — in anguish*]. Oh, my God, there's the stone wall eating into its edge ! Get it away, pull it out, shove it in, you fools ! [*As they shove*] Wait, wait !

1st Workman [*soothingly*]. I shouldn't worry, sir ; a shavin' or two off is th' worst that can happen to it.

Poges. Wait, wait a second. I'll go and get some cushions and pillows to guard the sides from the wall.
    [*He runs out by the adjoining entrance for the cushions.*

1st Workman. J'ever see such an oul' fustherer in your life ? You'd think the thing was on its way to the kingdom of heaven th' way he's cryin' over it.

3rd Workman. With a look on his ugly oul' gob like the tune th' oul' cow died of.

1st Workman. A quattrocento, mind you, says he.

3rd Workman. Seven hundred years an' more old, says he. Well, it's near time it met its death anyhow.

1st Workman. Here, let's get it in before he comes back billowin' with cushions. It's well able to take a knock or two.

2nd Workman. Here's th' crowbar he wouldn't let us use. [*He lifts up a big crowbar.*] We'll inch it in be main strength. Now, boys, get your shoulders to the quattrocento while I heave with th' bar ! [*To the 1st Workman*] Start a shanty, Bill, to give us encouragement.

1st Workman [*chanting quickly, while they all brace themselves*] :
    What shall we do with th' dhrunken sailor,
    What shall we do with th' dhrunken sailor,
    What shall we do with th' dhrunken sailor,
    Early in th' mornin' ?

All [*together — shoving and tugging vehemently*] :
    Pull away, an' up she rises,
    Pull away, an' up she rises,

Pull away, an' up she rises,
Early in th' mornin' !

[*Poges rushes in with some cushions in his arms. He is
frantic when he sees what the men are doing. As he rushes
in he is accompanied by a peal of thunder, louder than the
last, but still fairly faint. As he comes to a halt near the
bureau the peal ends.*

Poges [*enraged*]. What, in the devil's name, are you trying
to do ? Do you want to burst it to bits ? Oh, why
did I ever bring my poor quattrocento to a country like
this ! Shove it from the wall, shove it from the wall
till I put a cushion in !

1st Workman. Sure, it won't go far enough away from
the wall to fit a cushion, man.

Poges [*frantically*]. Do what you're told, do what you're
told. [*He drops the cushions, seizes the edge of the bureau and
tries to pull it from the wall.*] Here, somebody, help
me !

[*Before he is aware of it, the 1st Workman leaps on to the
top of the bureau to cross over to him, his heavy hobnailed
boots scraping the top of it.*

Poges [*shouting at him*]. Get down, get down, man !

1st Workman [*astonished*]. Amn't I only comin' across to
help you.

Poges [*yelling at him*]. That's a quattrocento, that's a
quattrocento, man !

1st Workman. Sure, I know it is.

Poges. Then get off it, get off it — sticking your hobnailed boots through and through it !

1st Workman [*lifting up a foot so that the sole of the boot can be seen*]. Is it that, sir ? Sure, th' nails are worn so soft an' smooth they wouldn't mark th' wing of a butther-fly.

Poges [*roaring*]. Get down, get down at once !
[*The 1st Workman jumps off the bureau back among his mates.*

2nd Workman [*muttering loudly*]. It ud be a godsend to some I know if they opened their eyes to th' signs an' wondhers showin'.

Poges. Now, no talk ; and don't do anything till I give the order.

Men. All right, sir ; go ahead ; we're waitin'.

Poges. When I say go, you swing it to the right, while I swing it to the left. Are you all ready ?

1st Workman. Ready an' waitin' an' willin'.

Poges. Go !
[*They all swing to the left, and Poges's foot is caught between the bureau and the archway. He lets a squeal out of him.*

Poges [*in anguish*]. Release my foot, my foot's caught ! Why did you all swing left ? Don't you know right from left ?

3rd Workman. You should have said ayste, sir.

Poges. Shove it off, shove it from my foot !

1st Workman [*placing the crowbar between archway, against the column, and the bureau*]. Now, boys, all together — heave yo-ho ! [*There is a mighty heave from them, one with*

the bar, the others with their shoulders. The bureau moves
slowly; a crack is heard; the column snaps with the push of
the bar against it and falls over the bureau, which suddenly
shoots forward right into the middle of the room, the men
stumbling after it. The men look triumphantly at the bureau,
the 1st Workman leaning on the crowbar like a warrior leaning
on his spear. Poges rubs his foot and contemplates the damage
to the bureau and the entrance.] There she is for you now,
sir ; right where you want her to be.

3rd Workman. I knew well patience ud do it in the end.

Poges. Oh, look at the bureau and look at the entrance !

1st Workman [*confidently*]. Oh, a spot o' cement an' a lick
o' white paint'll make th' entrance look as young as
ever again.
   [*Souhaun comes in, followed by Cloyne and Barney, who*
   are carrying a rug between them. They leave it on the
   floor. Basil is wearing very wide plus-fours.

Souhaun. We're getting the house into some kind of
order at last. [*She sees the damage.*] Oh, who's caused
all the wreckage ?

Poges [*sarcastically*]. Your very clever countrymen, dear.

Basil [*mockingly*]. And the high opinion they have of
themselves.

2nd Workman. There is sweet music in the land, but not
for th' deaf ; there is wisdom too, but it is not in a
desk it is, but out in th' hills, an' in the life of all
things rovin' round, undher th' blue sky.

Poges [*angrily and despairingly*]. Take this broken column

away and be off to your work again. Leave us, leave
us, before the house falls !
  [*The workmen take away the column and go out by entrance
  leading to the hall.*

Souhaun. Let us try the rugs, for God's sake ! I can't go
out o' th' room but there's damage done. [*Cloyne and
Barney spread on the floor a rug scattered over with brightly-
coloured geometrical patterns. Cloyne and Barney then go
out; the rest stare at the rug.*] Rather gay-looking for the
floor of a Tudor house, dear.

Basil [*decidedly*]. Too bright and too modern.

Poges. Where ? how ? why ?

Basil. The Tudors, my dear sir, were a sensible and
sober people, and wouldn't tolerate anything that was
vulgar or, shall I say, conspicuous.

Souhaun [*with some mockery*]. You see, darling, it was taste,
and not steam, that was everything in those days.

Basil. Quite, Souhaun ; taste was the Tudor — er — er
— *monumentum aere perennius.*

Poges. I don't know everything, my dear sir ; but I do
know something about the period that this house — er
— exemplifies ; in fact, the period was so riotous in
colour that the men's breeches had one leg blue, the
other leg red, or vice versa.

Basil [*with a patronising laugh*]. Ah, old boy, that wasn't the
Tudor period.

Poges. What period was it, then ?

Souhaun. The Hiawatha period.

Poges [*indignantly — to Souhaun*]. This is no joke, please.
[*To Basil*] What period was it, then?

Basil [*airily*]. Not the Tudor period, certainly; no,
certainly not, old boy.

Poges [*contemptuously*]. Pshaw! You don't know it yourself.
> [*From the entrance at back the 2nd Workman appears
> wheeling a barrow filled with bricks. Passing by the
> disputants, on his way to the hall entrance, he wheels the
> barrow over a rug.*

Poges [*shouting at him*]. Where the hell are you going with
your dirty barrow?

2nd Workman [*dropping the shafts of the barrow and turning
to answer Poges*]. I'm bringin' a barrow o' bricks to
O'Killigain, sir.

Basil. Oh, he's back, is he?

Poges. What the hell do you think you're doing, man?

2nd Workman. Amn't I after tellin' you, I'm bringin' a
barrow o' bricks to O'Killigain?

Poges. What d'ye mean, trundling your dirty barrow over
a handsome rug laid out for inspection?

2nd Workman. What d'ye want me to do? Take th'
barrow o' bricks up in me arms an' fly over it?

Basil [*with great dignity*]. Take it away at once, sir, and
don't show impertinence to your betters.

2nd Workman [*eyeing Basil with scorn*]. Jasus, looka what
calls itself a betther man than me!
> [*O'Killigain appears at the entrance leading to the hall.*

Poges [*earnestly — to the 2nd Workman*]. My man, you're cheeking a cousin of a K.G. whose family goes back to — to — [*turning to Basil*] — William the Conqueror, isn't it ?

Basil [*stiffening — with proud complacency*]. Further back, old boy — Alfred ; the last man of the last family fell at the battle of Hastings.

Poges [*impressively*]. There, you see.

Souhaun [*with a sign of mockery in her voice*]. And the ancient gentleman passed through Oxford, too.

O'Killigain [*from the archway*]. The city of dissolute might !

2nd Workman [*with mock deference*]. D'ye tell me that, now ? Why didn't you make me aware of all that glory before I began to speak ? Isn't it an alarmin' thing to hear of the ancientology of a being that I took to be an ordinary man ! An' what might be the ancient gentleman's ancient name ?

Poges. Basil Horatio Nelson Kaiser Stoke.

2nd Workman. A right worthy name. It mayn't have a musical sound, but it has a steady one. There's no flightiness in that name. An' now, would you like to know mine ?

Poges [*amusedly*]. Here, be off with you to your work ; as if your name mattered much.

2nd Workman. Me name's O'Dempsey, of the clan that were lords of Offaly ere his ancient highness here was a thousand years from bein' born ; a clan that sthretches back as far as the time before an Englishman thought of buildin' a weedy shelther ; an' further back to a day or two afther th' one when the sun herself was called upon to shine.

[*He takes hold of the shafts of the barrow preparatory to starting off.*

Poges [*contemptuously*]. You don't look it, my poor man !

2nd Workman [*as he wheels the barrow out*]. I feel it ; an' th' river's risin'.

Poges [*severely — to O'Killigain*]. You really oughtn't to allow, much more encourage, this silly, ignorant, and superstitious conceit among your men ; it is something close to scandalous !

O'Killigain [*quoting*]. They go their own gait : looking carelessly in the faces of presidents and governors, as to say, *Who are you?*

Poges [*imperatively*]. Well, it's not going to be heard in this house ! The bobtag and ragtail must be made to keep their free-and-easy manners at a distance. Dignity reigns here.

[*A louder peal of thunder is heard in the distance, and the room darkens a little.*

O'Killigain. It's raining.

Poges. Eh ?

O'Killigan. It's raining hard.

Souhaun [*shivering*]. And growing cold.

O'Killigain. And old things are perishing.

2nd Workman [*appearing at entrance*]. We're knocking off, O'Killigain, for the rain is heavier an' the winds are keen.

O'Killigain. You do well to knock off, for it is waste of time to try to butthress up a tumbling house.

Souhaun [*over to the 2nd Workman*]. The house'll be lone-some without you.

2nd Workman. Come, then, an' abide with the men o' th' wide wathers, who can go off in a tiny curragh o' thought to the New Island with th' outgoin' tide, an' come back be th' same tide sweepin' in again !

Poges [*mockingly — to Souhaun, clapping her on the back*]. There's a high and hearty invitation to you, me lady !
[*Avril comes in and dances over to Basil.*

Souhaun [*gleefully poking Poges in the ribs — to 2nd Workman*]. A long sail on the widening waters, no less ; what gift is offered when the tide returns, good man ?

2nd Workman. With firm-fed men an' comely, cordial women there'll be laughter round a red fire when the mists are risin', when th' roads an' fields are frosty, an' when th' nights is still.

Souhaun [*in a mocking voice — to Poges*]. There now, dear, is there anything more in the world than these that you can give ?

Poges [*with pretended dismay*]. He has me beaten ; what am I going to do at all, at all ?

2nd Workman. A portion, too, with them who, ruddy-faced, were first in battle, with crimson cloak, white coat, an' silver belt studded with splendour by a cunning hand ; a portion, too, with them of paler faces an' dhressed in dimmer clothes, who, fearless, stepped a straight way to th' gallows, silent an' darin' in th' midst of a yelled-out Sassenach song !

Souhaun [*trying to speak mockingly, but developing a slight catch in her voice; for she has been moved by the 2nd Workman's words*]. Where is the lady who would be slow to give a man with such a coaxing way an invitation to her pillow ?

Avril [*who sees her friend is affected. She comes closer to her, and touches her on the arm*]. Souhaun, Souhaun, come an' show me your newest dhresses, an' don't stay listenin' to his thrancin' talk. Don't leave me alone with them.

Souhaun [*shaking off Avril's hand. Falling into the Irish idiom*]. Let me be, girl, for it's right an' lovely listenin' to a voice that's makin' gold embroidery out o' dancin' words.

Poges [*angry and a little nervous*]. It's time to put an end to all this nonsense !

O'Killigain [*ignoring Poges's angry exclamation — to Avril*]. An' you, young girl, sweet bud of an out-spreading three, graft yourself on to the living, and don't stay hidden any longer here. Come where the rain is heavy ,where the frost frets, and where the sun is warm. Avril, pulse of me heart, listen to me, an' let longin' flood into your heart for the call of life. The young thorn-three withered away now, can awaken again, an' spread its fragrance around us. Spit out what's here, an' come where love is fierce an' fond an' fruitful. Come, lass, where there's things to say an' things to do an' love at the endings !

2nd Workman. Jack has spoken fair, an' there's no handsome hindrance near to stop yous. What's here but a creakin' grandeur an' poor witherin' talk ; salt food without a dhrink to go with it ; an' a purple dhryness turnin' timidly to dust !

O'Killigain [*coming close to Avril*]. Aren't my words a star
in your ear, lass ? Haven't you heard them ? They've
hit your young breast, lass. Come with me, I say ;
come away from where rich ignorance is a blessing,
an' foolishness a gift from God ! Come to th' house
on th' hill : the door is open, the fire's alight on the
hearth, and the table's laid with a clean white cloth.

Avril. Let another go in by the door ; let another eat
at the table ; let another sit by the fire. Why didn't
you come for me, O'Killigain, before the young thorn-
tree had shed its blossom, and before the stems began
to die ?

O'Killigain. I'd other things to do. While you were
livin' your lesser life, an' singin' your dowdy songs,
I was fightin' in Spain that you might go on singin' in
safety an' peace. [*He grips her arm*] I've come for you,
now, me love.

Avril [*emotionally and anxious*]. I cannot go where things
are said and things are done, for love has had no voice
in the beginning of them ! [*She tries to free her arm*] Oh,
Jack, let me go — you're hurting me !

O'Killigain. It's O'Killigain gives the pressure of comfort
and of care. D'ye mind th' hurt when th' hurt's th'
hurt of love ?

Avril [*passionately*]. Yes, I do ! Oh, no, no ; I don't,
O'Killigain ! I don't, I don't ! Your pressure on my
arm presses on my heart, too. Oh, go away an' leave
me lonely !
    [*She breaks away and runs to Souhaun, who puts an arm
    around her.*

O'Killigain. Avril, come out of th' guttherin' candlelight

C.P.—III   H

here to where th' wind puts a flush on the face, ruffles th' hair, and brings a catch to the breath ; come to th' one you want ; come to th' man who needs you !

2nd Workman [to Souhaun]. An' you, Souhaun, sturdy lily o' Clune na Geera, come into the love that can fix or flutther th' stars o' th' sky an' change th' shinin' moon into a lamp for two. Come to th' one you need ; come to th' man who wants you !

Souhaun [half joking, all in earnest]. If you only had a horse handy, I'd ride away with you !

2nd Workman [quietly]. He's outside waitin'. A loan from Mr. O'Killigain. An animal can gallop glorious the livelong day undher th' sound of a steady voice an' th' touch of a steady hand.

Souhaun [greatly moved]. N-no !

2nd Workman [firmly]. Yes.

Basil [rising out of astonishment — to Poges, angrily]. How long are you ready to stick this, man ? Send these impudent fellows away !

Poges [as if awaking from a stupor — furiously to the two men]. Get out, the two of you ! We haven't lived long enough here to be touched with your insanity ! Get out !

Souhaun [to 2nd Workman — gently]. I'll see ; I'll do whatever Avril advises. [To Avril] Come, dear, till we think out a wonderful answer.

O'Killigain [to Avril as she is going out]. Be ready : I'll call, and come to take you when the river rises !

[He goes out.

2nd Workman [*to Souhaun as she is going out after Avril*]. I'll wait outside be th' good gallopin' horse till th' snowy-breasted pearl comes to shimmer on me shouldher.

[*He goes out after O'Killigain.*

Poges [*furious and mocking*]. When the river rises! Come with me and be my love! Come into the garden, Maud. Were ever fools so foolish!

Basil [*in angry glee*]. And the fellow with the galloping horse outside! Boot, saddle, and away! I never expected to see and hear the like, even in this odd country. [*Slapping Poges on the back — jokingly*] You'd better watch out for the sound of the galloping horse!

Poges [*slapping Basil on the back*]. And you keep an ear open for O'Killigain's call when the river rises!

Basil [*in a mock tragical voice*]. Beware the sound of a galloping horse!

Poges [*in the same manner*]. Beware of O'Killigain's call!
[*Poges goes over to the bureau, opens a drawer, takes some papers out of it, and looks at them; then he sits down at the bureau, and arranges things in order to write a letter.*

Basil. And, for God's sake, did you hear that vulgar fellow chatting about making the moon do something or other?

Poges [*arranging things on the bureau*]. Poor crazy fool. They're all a bit demented. Must be the climate. Most amusing.

Basil [*gloomily*]. Yes, amusing up to a point, but hardly reassuring; no. [*He comes nearer to Poges.*] I don't like it, Poges.

Poges [*a little startled*]. Eh?

Basil. Well, it isn't exactly comfortable to be living in a community of crazy people, is it ? It may even become dangerous.

Poges [*sitting up straight*]. That's a serious thought, Stoke. Now that you mention it, I do feel the insidious influence of the place. We might become demented too.

Basil. If they allowed us to live long enough.

Poges. Good God, what a thought ! I must have a talk with you about this when I finish this letter.

Basil. You saw for yourself how this influence is even affecting the girls.

Poges [*emphatically*]. The girls ? There you are wrong, Stoke. No, no, not the girls, man. They were just humbugging the poor fools. Nonsense ; not the girls.

Basil [*about to go out*]. You watch. Come up to our room when you've finished the letter, will you ?

Poges. At once. [*Basil goes out. Poges takes some paper, and writes the date on the top right corner. Then he pauses, and evidently begins to think of what has happened. Shaking his head slowly from side to side — musingly*]. Erin, the tear and the smile in thine eye.

[*He clears his throat with a cough, and settles down to write. The room becomes darker. He has hardly been writing a minute when a curious face appears round the corner of the entrance leading to the hall. It is the stout little face of a little man dressed in neat black clothes covered with a saturated fawn-coloured mackintosh. Big spectacles cover his eyes. A huge fiery-red beard spreads over his chest like a breastplate, reaching to his belly, and*

extending out from his body like a fan turned downwards.
He wears a black jerry hat. When he speaks he is found
to have a little voice. He carries a blackthorn stick in his
hand. As he peeps round he sees Poges at the bureau, and
pulls in his head again. He thrusts it forward again,
steps out, and comes into full view. He pulls his coat
straight with a jerk and smoothes his trousers, and then
comes with a trot into the room, right over to Poges, bends
over towards him, and greets him in a hearty manner. He
is the Postmaster of the village.

Postmaster. An honour it is, sir, to meet the owner of such
a fine house. A house with a histhory. A house
where the genthry joined themselves to merriment and
danced th' stars to sleep ! [*He dances clumsily round the
room, singing*] See me dance the polka, see me dance the
polka, see me dance the polka, as I have done before.
[*He suddenly stops and comes close to Poges.*] I hope I see
you well, sir ? I bear a message from the Postmaster.

Poges [*amazed*]. I am well, thank you ; and what is your
message from the Postmaster ?

Postmaster. When I was outside, an' heard you coughin',
it's well I knew be th' sound of th' cough that the
cough was th' cough of a gentleman.

Poges [*impatiently*]. Yes, yes ; but what is your message ?

Postmaster. Well, as genuine gentleman, you'll be th'
first to agree that a Postmaster with a small wife an'
a large family, an' hardly any salary — I near forgot to
mention that — hardly any salary at all, if the thruth
was told, as a thrue gentleman, you'll agree that a man
like that is handicapped, an' has a claim on a gentleman's sympathy.

Poges. But I can't make his wife bigger or his family smaller, can I ?

Postmaster. Sure, I know you can't, an' that's not what the Postmaster's complainin' about. [*He leans over Poges.*] But th' poor man needs sleep, he needs his share o' sleep.

Poges [*humouring him — thinking his visitor is out of his mind*]. Yes, yes ; of course, the poor man needs sleep. We all need sleep. That's a fine stick you have in your hand, sir ; can I see it ?

Postmaster [*holding up the stick and stretching it away from Poges*]. Ay, ay, a fine blackthorn. There y'are ; look at it as long as you like — [*warningly*] — but don't lay a finger on it. There's a stick could give a man a crack a man ud remember !

Poges [*nervous*]. Oh ? I can't see it well from here ; let me take it in my hand for a moment.

Postmaster. Sorra a second you're goin' to have it in your hand. That stick has never been outa me father's hand an' it has never been outa mine. D'ye know why ?

Poges. No, friend, I don't.

Postmaster. Guess, now, guess.

Poges [*smiling sweetly*]. I haven't the slightest idea, friend ; I couldn't guess.

Postmaster. This's th' very stick that me oul' fellow made a swipe at Parnell with — th' scandaliser of Ireland's holy name, a swipe that, had it got home, ud a laid Parnell up for a month o' Sundays ! Now, as a thrue gentleman, wouldn't you say I was right ?

Poges. Yes, yes ; quite right.

Postmaster. Well, havin' settled that, let's settle th' other : amn't I right in sayin' that every man should have his share o' sleep ?

Poges. Yes, yes ; of course.

Postmaster. Well, then, amn't I right in sayin' that th' poor Postmaster should have his share o' sleep too ?

Poges. To be sure. [*Rising from his seat*] Now, I must be going. [*A fairly loud clap of thunder is heard, followed by the sound, first of a trotting horse, then of one going off at a gallop. They listen till the sounds die in the distance.*] A horse going off at a gallop. [*He makes a move away*] I must go to see what's wrong.

Postmaster [*waving him back with the stick*]. Wait a minute — I'm not done yet. You've just said the poor Postmaster should have his share o' sleep — didn't you?

Poges [*impatiently*]. Yes, yes, friend.

Postmaster. I knew you'd say that. [*He stretches out his hand to Poges.*] Lave it there. [*He shakes hands with Poges.*] Now I won't have to be keepin' one eye open an' me ear glued to the bell, for fear of a toll call or a thrunk call, afther ten o'clock at night, an' I settlin' down for a cosy sleep.

Poges [*the truth dawning on him*]. Oh, so you're the Postmaster, are you ? So it was you who delayed me when I wanted St. Paul ?

Postmaster. Didn't you know that ?

Poges. The telephonic system here is an all-night one, isn't it ?

Postmaster. 'Course it is, but that says nothin'.

Poges [*decidedly*]. Look here, my man ; I'm a business man, and have to make calls at all hours of the night ; I can't be thinking of every man having an honest night's sleep.

Postmaster. 'Course you can't ; it's only the poor Postmaster that you've got to keep in mind.

Poges [*severely*]. Look here, my man, as long as I pay for the service, the service will have to be supplied. Good day.

Postmaster. There isn't a gentleman in th' whole disthrict ud think, except in th' case o' sudden death or disasther, of givin' a tinkle afther th' hand o' th' clock had passed the figure of half-past nine o' night.

Poges. Take yourself and your stick away out of the house, man !

Postmaster [*mimicking him*]. Take yourself and your stick away outa the house, man. Is it comin' down here to teach us good manners an' feelin' y'are, an' you puttin' a surly gob on you when you're asked to fall in with the sensible an' thried institutions of the neighbourhood ?
    [*While they have been talking together, the room has darkened still more, and Poges sharply tugs the string that puts on the light; the wind has risen and can be heard occasionally blowing through the trees outside, and even shaking the old house.*

Poges [*in a rage*]. Go on, get out !
    [*As he says this, a long, loud peal of thunder is heard.*

Postmaster. D'ye hear that ? There won't be many thrunk

calls goin' for a while, an' th' poor Postmaster'll have
a sweeter night's sleep than some I know. [*He bends
towards Poges.*] When — the river — rises !

[*The room has darkened; the wind rises; the one light in the
room flickers. The Postmaster and Poges watch it. Then
the Postmaster turns to go, but halts when a Figure of a
man is seen standing at the entrance leading to the hall.
He is dressed from head to foot in gleaming black oilskins,
hooded over his head, just giving a glimpse of a blue mask,
all illumined by the rays of flickering lightning, so that
The Figure seems to look like the spirit of the turbulent
waters of the rising river. The Postmaster goes back,
startled, till he is beside Poges, and the two men stand
and stare at the ominous Figure. Basil, Barney, and
Cloyne appear at the entrances at back, each holding a lighted
lantern in his and her hand. They are very frightened.
They too hold up their lanterns and stare at The Figure.*]

Basil. The river is rising !

Barney. Risin' high !

Cloyne. An' will overwhelm us all !

The Figure [*in a deep voice*]. The river has broken her banks
and is rising high ; high enough to come tumbling in
on top of you. Cattle, sheep, and swine are moaning in
the whirling flood. Trees of an ancient heritage, that
looked down on all below them, are torn from the
power of the place they were born in, and are tossing
about in the foaming energy of the waters. Those
who have lifted their eyes unto the hills are firm of
foot, for in the hills is safety ; but a trembling perch
in the highest place on the highest house shall be the
portion of those who dwell in the valleys below !

[*The lightning ceases for a moment; the entrance becomes dark, and The Figure disappears.*

Poges [*frantic*]. What shall we do? what must we do? what can we do?

Basil [*in anguish*]. We're lost!

Cloyne [*sinking down on her knees*]. King o' th' Angels, save us!

Barney [*clasping his hands*]. Amen! A nice pass we've come to when we have to call for help in a Tudor house! [*To Basil and Poges*] It's the evil livin' of you two buckos that has brought this disaster upon us!

Poges [*bawling*]. Souhaun, Souhaun! O'Killigain, help!

Basil [*roaring at Poges*]. You made us come down here!

Poges [*roaring at Basil*]. You're a liar, it was you!

Postmaster [*bringing down the blackthorn stick with a bang on the quattrocento bureau*]. Eh, order, order, law an' order there; steady! Measures o' safety to be taken. [*Thrusting his stick towards Poges — sharply*] Has the highest room in the house a way to the roof — quick!

Poges [*answering at once*]. Yes.

Cloyne [*in anguish*]. Th' roof — oh, my God!

Postmaster [*rapidly*]. Up with us all with bread and wine, with firewood and coal, and an axe. Up!

Poges. An axe?

Postmaster. To hack whatever suitable furniture we can get into a raft if we're swirled off th' roof. [*Driving Cloyne and Barney before him*] Up!

Poges [*loudly*]. Souhaun, Souhaun, where's Souhaun?

Basil [*impatiently*]. Come on, and come up.
  [*Avril comes in from one of the back entrances. She is
  covered with a green mackintosh, and a coloured scarf,
  peasant-wise, is over her head. She carries a small case.
  She passes between the two men without a word, and
  stands still near the entrance leading to the hall, looking
  out before her.*

Poges [*staring at her*]. What are you doing here? What
  are you watching? [*Avril stands still and silent.*]
  Where's Souhaun, where's Souhaun?

Avril [*quietly — without looking round*]. She's gone.

Poges. Gone? How? Where?

Avril [*quietly — still not moving*]. Gone with the wind;
  gone with the waters; gone with the one man who
  alone saw something in her!

Poges [*raging*]. What, with that loud-mouthed, ignorant,
  superstitious, low-born, half-mad Irishman! Oh,
  she's nicely rooked me! She was with him on the
  galloping horse that galloped away, was she? Oh,
  she's nicely rooked a simple, honest, loving-hearted,
  foolish man! She's gone, is she?

Avril. An' well it would be if I was with her.

Poges. You damned slut, are you in your mind as bad
  as she is?

Avril [*indicating Basil*]. The mind that went with him is as
  bad as the mind that went with you.

Basil [*sneeringly*]. You lost the chance you had to get away
  from it.

Avril. He said he'd come when the river rises.

O'Killigain [*outside — loudly*]. Avril !

Avril [*with a start of joy*]. O'Killigain !   O'Killigain !
  [*O'Killigain appears, his trench coat drenched and his hair
  soaking, at the entrance.*

O'Killigain. My barque is waiting, love ; come !
                  [*Avril picks up the case and runs to O'Killigain.*

Basil. Honest, decent woman, she carries the booty of
her friends in her pack !

Avril [*quietly*]. I gave more than I got, you gilded monkey.
It's winnowed of every touch of life I'd be if I stayed
with th' waste of your mind much longer. [*She taps
the case.*] Th' thrinkets I wormed out of you are all
here, an' here they stay, for th' wages were low for
what was done for you.

Poges [*sneering*]. And gentleman O'Killigain will happier
be with a harlot's fortune !

O'Killigain [*good-humouredly*]. Of course he will. Th'
good things of this life are good for all, an' a pretty girl
looks handsomer in arms that are fit and fond to hold
her. You have had your day, like every dog. Your
Tudors have had their day, and they are gone ; and th'
little heap o' purple dust they left behind them will
vanish away in th' flow of the river. [*To Avril*] Come,
love, to my little house up on th' hill.
  [*He goes out with Avril.   After a moment the sound of oars
  are heard splashing the waters, and O'Killigain is heard
  singing.*

O'Killigain [*singing : other voices, outside, join in the chorus*] :

Come from the dyin' an' fly from th' dead,
Far away O !
An' now, with th' quick, make your home an' your bed,
With a will an' a way, away O !

Then away, love, away,
Far away O !
To live any life that is looming ahead,
With a will an' a way, away O !

Away from all mouldherin' ashes we row,
Far away O !
Takin' th' splendour of livin' in tow,
With a will an' a way, away O !

Then away, love, away,
Far away O !
Where th' lightning of life flashes vivid we go,
With a will an' a way, away O !

> [*Poges stands still, listening till the song fades away in the
> distance. Suddenly Basil clutches his arm.*

Basil [*frantically*]. Look, the waters are tumbling towards
us ! Run, man !
> [*He tears up the passage while Poges follows more slowly.*

Poges [*going out*]. My poor little quattrocento, the waters
are about to cover thee ! My comfort's gone, and my
house of pride is straining towards a fall. Would to
God I were in England, now that winter's here !
> [*He disappears down the passage as the green waters tumble
> into the room through the entrance from the hall.*

CURTAIN

COME FROM THE DYIN'

Come from the dy-in' an'   fly from the dead

Far— a-way O!— An' now, with the quick, make your

home an' your bed, With a   will and a way a-way

O! Then a-way, love—, a-way,

Far— a-way O!— To live an-y life that is

looming a-head, With a   will an' a way a-way   O!

THE MAID OF BUNCLODY

Oh— were I   at the   moss house, Where the

birds do   in-crease,   At the   foot   of   Mount

Lein-ster Or— some si-lent— place,   By the

streams of Bun - clo - dy Where all

plea - sures do— meet, And— all I would

ask is One kiss from you, sweet.

O'KILLIGAIN'S LILT

They may rail at this life, from the hour I be-gan it, I

found it a life full of kind-ness and bliss; And un-

-til they can show me some hap-pi-er pla-net, More

so-cial and bright, I'll con - tent me with this.

THERE ARE MANY FAIR THINGS IN THIS WORLD

There are ma-ny fair things in this world as it goes, The

blue skies of— sum-mer, the flush-ing red rose, But of

all the fair blossom-ing things that men see, A-come-ly-built lass is the near-est to me, A

come-ly-built lass is the dear-est to me.

HEY, HEY, THE COUNTRY'S HERE

Ru-ral scenes are now our joy, Farm-er's boy,

Milk-maid coy, Each like a new-ly paint-ed toy

CHORUS

In the bosk-y coun-try. Hey, hey, the country's here, The

country's there, It's ev-'ry where, We'll have it, now, last

thing at night, And the ve-ry first thing in the morn-ing!

THERE'S LIFE WITH TH' LASSES

Come in or go out or just stay at the door, With a

girl on each arm an' one stand-ing be-fore, Sure, the

more that I have, the more I a-dore, For there's
much slower

life with the lass-es, says Ro-ry O' More!

RED ROSES FOR ME

A Play in Four Acts

TO

D<small>R</small>. J. D. CUMMINS

IN MEMORY OF THE GRAND CHATS
AROUND HIS SURGERY FIRE

*My thanks to Bridgid Edwards
for setting down the airs to
the songs*

CHARACTERS IN THE PLAY

MRS. BREYDON

AYAMONN BREYDON, *her son*

EEADA
DYMPNA } *Mrs. Breydon's neighbours in the house*
FINNOOLA

SHEILA MOORNEEN, *Ayamonn's sweetheart*

BRENNAN O' THE MOOR, *owner of a few oul' houses*

A SINGER, *a young man with a good voice*

ROORY O'BALACAUN, *a zealous Irish Irelander*

MULLCANNY, *a mocker of sacred things*

REV. E. CLINTON, *Rector of St. Burnupus*

SAMUEL, *verger to the church*

INSPECTOR FINGLAS, *of the Mounted Police, and the Rector's churchwarden*

1ST MAN
2ND MAN } *neighbours in the next house to Breydons'*
3RD MAN

DOWZARD
FOSTER } *members of St. Burnupus' Select Vestry*

A LAMPLIGHTER

1ST RAILWAYMAN

2ND RAILWAYMAN

SCENES

ACT I.—Two-roomed home of the Breydons.

ACT II.—The same.

ACT III.—A Dublin street, beside a bridge over the river Liffey.

ACT IV.—Part of the grounds round the Protestant Church of St. Burnupus. In this Act the curtain is lowered for a few minutes to denote the passing of a few hours.

TIME.—A little while ago.

ACT I

The front one of two rather dilapidated rooms in a poor working-class locality. The walls, whitewashed, are dwindling into a rusty yellowish tinge. The main door, leading to the hall, is at the back, a little towards the right. The fireplace is in the right-hand wall, and a brilliant fire is burning in the large, old-fashioned grate. In the centre of the room is an old ebony-hued table on which stands a one-wick oil-lamp, its chimney a little smoky from the bad oil in the reservoir. Some books lie on the table, some paper, coloured chalks, a pen, and a small bottle of ink. In the left wall, up towards the back, is the door leading to the second room. Below this door is a horsehair sofa showing signs of old age. On it, to the head, is a neatly folded bundle of sheets and blankets, showing that it is used as a bed during the night. To the left of the main door at back is a large basket used by actors when on tour. On the other side of this door is an ordinary kitchen dresser on which some of the crockery is on the ledge, for the upper shelf is filled with a row of books, by the look of them second-hand. Over the basket, on the wall, is tacked a childlike brightly-coloured pastel of what is meant to be a copy of one of Fra Angelico's angels blowing a curved and golden trumpet; and beside it is a small coloured reproduction of Constable's " Cornfield ". In the same wall, towards the back, is a large, tall window, nearly reaching the ceiling, and, when one is in front of it, the top of a railway signal, with transverse arms, showing green and red lights, can be seen. Under this window, on a roughly made bench, stand three biscuit tins. In the first grows a geranium, in the second, musk, and in the third, a fuchsia. The disks of the geranium are extremely large and glowing; the tubular blooms of the golden musk, broad, gay, and rich; and the purple bells of the fuchsia, surrounded by their long white waxy sepals, seem to be as big as arum lilies. These crimson, gold, and purple flowers give a regal tint to the poor room. Occasionally in the distance can be heard the whistle of an engine, followed by its strenuous puffing as it pulls at a heavy rake of goods wagons. A chair or two stand about the room.

It is towards the evening of a mid-spring day, and the hour would make it dusk, but it is darker than that, for the sky is cloudy and rain is falling heavily over the city.

Ayamonn and his mother are in the room when the scene shows itself. He is tall, well built, twenty-two or so, with deep brown eyes, fair hair, rather bushy, but tidily kept, and his face would remind an interested observer of a rather handsome, firm-minded, thoughtful, and good-humoured bulldog. His mother is coming up to fifty, her face brownish, dark eyes with a fine glint in them, and she bears on her cheeks and brow the marks of struggle and hard work. She is dressed in a black jacket, fitting close, marred by several patches, done very neatly, dark-blue skirt, a little faded, and rather heavily-soled boots. At the moment this is all covered with a rich blue velvet cloak, broidered with silver lace, and she is sitting on a kitchen chair covered with a dark-red, rather ragged cloth.

Ayamonn wears a bright-green silk doublet over which is a crimson velvet armless cloak bordered with white fur. The back part of the cloak is padded so as to form a big hump between his shoulders. Across his chest is a dark-green baldric from which hangs a scabbard. A cross-hilted sword is in his hand. On his head he has a black felt hat with narrow turned-up rims. A black band goes round the hat, and a crimson feather sticks up from it. His legs are in heavy, black, working corduroy trousers, and he wears heavy hobnailed boots. She and he are in an intensely listening attitude.

Mrs. Breydon [*whispering over to Ayamonn*]. She's gone ;

wanted to borra something else, I suppose. They're feverish with borrowing in this blessed house !

Ayamonn. Damn her for a troublesome fool ! Where's this I was when the knock came ?

Mrs. Breydon. I was just goin' to say
    Ay, an' for much more slaughter after this,
    O God ! forgive my sins, and pardon thee !

Ayamonn [*looking at the floor*]. Oh yes ! [*He recites*] —
    What, will th' aspiring blood of Lancaster
    Sink to the ground ? I thought it would have
        mounted. [*He holds the sword aloft, and stares at it*]
    See how my sword weeps for the poor king's
        death !
    O, may such purple tears be always shed
    For those that wish the downfall of our house !
    If any spark of life be yet remaining,
    [*He stabs at the floor*] Down, down to hell ; and say
        I sent thee hither !

    [*A knuckle-knock is heard at the door. Ayamonn and Mrs. Breydon stiffen into a silent listening attitude. A fine baritone voice, husky with age, is heard speaking outside.*

Voice. Is anyone in or out or what ? [*Louder raps are given as Ayamonn steals over, and places his back to the door.*] Eh, in there — is there anyone movin', or is the oul' shack empty ?

Mrs. Breydon [*in a whisper*]. Oul' Brennan on the Moor. He was here before, today. He's got his rent for his oul' houses, an' he wants to be told again that the Bank of Ireland's a safe place to put it.

Ayamonn [*warningly*]. Ssshush !

Voice. No answer, eh? An' me afther seein' a light in
th' window. Maybe they are out. For their own
sakes, I hope they are ; for it's hardly an honourable
thing to gainsay a neighbour's knock.
  [*The sound of feet shuffling away is heard outside, and then
  there is silence for a few moments.*

Mrs. Breydon. He's gone. He's always a bit lively the
day he gets his rents. How a man, with his money,
can go on livin' in two rooms in a house an' sthreet
only a narrow way betther than this, I don't know.
What was he but an oul' painter an' paperhanger,
starvin' to save, an' usin' his cunnin' to buy up a few
oul' houses, give them a lick o' paint, and charge the
highest rent for th' inconvenience of livin' in them !

Ayamonn. I wish he'd keep himself and his throubles far
away from me now. I've higher things to think of
and greater things to do than to be attached to the
agony of an old fool for ever afraid a fistful of money'll
be snatched away from him. Still, he isn't a miser,
for he gives kids toys at Christmas, and never puts less
than half a crown on the plate in church on Sundays.

Mrs. Breydon. So well he may !

Ayamonn. What was he sayin' when he was here before ?

Mrs. Breydon. Oh, th' usual question of askin' me what I
thought about the Bank of Ireland ; mutterin' about
somebody not payin' the rent ; and that his birthday's
due tomorrow.

Ayamonn [*looking at the chair*]. I'll have to get a loan of a
chair with arms on, and someway make them golden to
do the thing proper in the Temperance Hall ; and
I'll paint for the back of it, on thin cardboard, a

cunning design of the House of Lancaster, the red rose, so that it'll look like a kingly seat.

Mrs. Breydon. Th' killin' o' th' king be th' Duke o' Gloster should go down well, an' th' whole thing should look sumptuous.

Ayamonn. So it will. It's only that they're afraid of Shakespeare out of all that's been said of him. They think he's beyond them, while all the time he's part of the kingdom of heaven in the nature of everyman. Before I'm done, I'll have him drinking in th' pubs with them !

Mrs. Breydon. I don't know that he'll go well with a Minstrel Show.

Ayamonn. He'll have to go well. If only King Henry doesn't rant too much, saw the air with his hands, and tear his passion to tatthers. The old fool saw someone do it that way, and thinks it must be right. [*With a sigh.*] I daren't attempt to recite my part now, for Oul' Brennan on the Moor's waitin' and listenin' somewhere down below ; so I'll just get it off by heart. How old does he say he'll be tomorrow ?

Mrs. Breydon. Only seventy-six, he says, an' feelin' as if he was lookin' forward to his twenty-first birthday.

Ayamonn. Well, he won't have long to wait.

Mrs. Breydon [*slyly*]. He was muttherin', too, about some air or other on the oul' piano he has at home.

Ayamonn [*springing up from where he has been sitting*]. It's one o' mine he's put an air to ! [*He rushes from the room and returns in a few moments.*] He's not there ; gone home, I suppose. [*Irritably*] I wish you'd told me that at first.

Mrs. Breydon. I'd thry to rest a little, Ayamonn, before you go to work. You're overdoing it. Less than two hours' sleep today, and a long night's work before you. Sketchin', readin', makin' songs, an' learnin' Shakespeare : if you had a piano, you'd be thryin' to learn music. Why don't you stick at one thing, an' leave the others alone ?

Ayamonn. They are all lovely, and my life needs them all.

Mrs. Breydon. I managed to get on well enough without them. [*A pause. She goes over to the window and tenderly touches the fuchsia.*] There's this sorryful sthrike, too, about to come down on top of us.

Ayamonn [*sitting in the red-covered chair and reading Shakespeare — quietly and confidently*]. There'll be no strike. The bosses won't fight. They'll grant the extra shilling a week demanded.

Mrs. Breydon [*now fingering the musk*]. I thought this Minstrel Show was being run to gather funds together ?

Ayamonn [*impatiently*]. So it is, so it is ; but only in case the strike may have to take place. I haven't much to do with it, anyway. I'm with the men, spoke at a meeting in favour of the demand, and that's all.

Mrs. Breydon. You'll undhermine your health with all you're doin', tearin' away what's left of your time be runnin' afther—— [*She checks herself, and becomes silent.*

Ayamonn [*lowering his book to his lap — angrily*]. Go on — finish what you started to say : runnin' afther who ?

Mrs. Breydon. Nobody, nobody.

Ayamonn. Runnin' afther Sheila Moorneen — that's what was in your mind to say, wasn't it ?

Mrs. Breydon. If it was aself; is there a new law out that a body's not to think of her own thoughts.

Ayamonn [*sharply*]. What have you got against the girl?

Mrs. Breydon. Nothing. As a girl, I'd say she's a fine coloured silken shawl among a crowd of cotton ones. A girl I'd say could step away from the shadowy hedges where others slink along, tiltin' her head as she takes the centre of the road for the entherprisin' light o' day to show her off to everyone. Still——

[*She stops speaking again.*

Ayamonn. Ay, but still what? You've a maddenin' way of never finishing some of your sentences.

Mrs. Breydon [*braving it out*]. She's a Roman Catholic; steeped in it, too, the way she'd never forgive a one for venturin' to test the Pope's pronouncement.

Ayamonn. And who wants to test the Pope's pronouncement? Life and all her vital changes'll go on testing everything, even to the Pope's pronouncement. D'ye think I've laboured as I have, and am labourin' now, to furnish myself with some of the greatness of the mighty minds of the past, just to sink down into passive acceptance of the Pope's pronouncement? Let the girl believe what she may, reverence what she can: it's her own use of her own mind. That she is fair to look upon, charming to talk with, and a dear companion, is well and away enough for me, were she even a believer in Mumbo Jumbo, and had a totem pole in her front garden.

Mrs. Breydon. There's worse still than that in it.

Ayamonn. Worse, is there? An' what may that be?

Mrs. Breydon. She's th' child of a sergeant in the Royal Irish Constabulary, isn't she?

Ayamonn. Well, she can't help it, can she?

Mrs. Breydon. I know that ; but many have murmured again' a son of mine goin' with the child of a man crouchin' close to their enemy.

Ayamonn. Everything, it seems, is against her, save herself. I like herself, and not her faith ; I want herself, and not her father.

Mrs. Breydon. The bigger half of Ireland would say that a man's way with a maid must be regulated by his faith an' hers, an' the other half by the way her father makes his livin'.

Ayamonn. And let the whole world join them ! Fair she is, and her little ear's open to hear all that I thry to say, so, were she the child of darkness aself, I'd catch her hand and lead her out and show her off to all men.

Mrs. Breydon. She wouldn't be a lot to look at afther she'd wended her way through poverty with you for a year an' a day.

Ayamonn. She gives no honour to gold ; neither does her warm heart pine for silks and satins from China and Japan, or the spicy isles of Easthern Asia. A sober black shawl on her shoulders, a simple petticoat, and naked feet would fail to find her craving finer things that envious women love.

Mrs. Breydon. Ah, go on with you, Ayamonn, for a kingly fool. I'm tellin' you th' hearts of all proper girls glow with the dhream of fine things ; an' I'm tellin' you, too, that the sword jinglin' on th' hip of Inspector Finglas, the red plume hangin' from his menacin' helmet, an' th' frosty silver sparklin' on his uniform, are a dazzle o' light between her tantalised eyes an' whatever she may happen to see in you.

Ayamonn. Tell me something else to add to my hope.

Mrs. Breydon. Go on readin', an' don't bother to listen to your mother.

Ayamonn [*going over and gently putting his hands on her shoulders*]. I do listen, but I am drifting away from you, Mother, a dim shape now, in a gold canoe, dipping over a far horizon.

Mrs. Breydon [*with a catch in her voice*]. I did an' dared a lot for you, Ayamonn, my son, in my time, when jeerin' death hurried your father off to Heaven.

Ayamonn. It's I who know that well : when it was dark, you always carried the sun in your hand for me ; when you suffered me to starve rather than thrive towards death in an Institution, you gave me life to play with as a richer child is given a coloured ball. [*He gently lifts up her face by putting a hand under her chin.*] The face, the dear face that once was smooth is wrinkled now ; the eyes, brown still, that once were bright, have now been dimmed by a sthrained stare into the future ; the sturdy back that stood so straight, is bending. A well-tried leaf, bronzed with beauty, waiting for a far-off winter wind to shake it from the tree.

Mrs. Breydon [*gently removing his hand from her chin*]. I have a tight hold still. My back can still bear many a heavy burden; and my eyes, dimmer now than once they were, can still see far enough. Well, I betther take this fancy robe from off me, lest it give me gorgeous notions.

[*She takes off her robe, and leaves it carefully folded on the basket, then goes over and arranges the fire. Ayamonn looks thoughtfully out of the window, then takes off cloak, sword, and hat, leaving them carefully on the basket.*]

Ayamonn [*musingly*]. He'll hardly come tonight in this

rain. If he does, I'll get him to read the King's part, and do mine over again.

Mrs. Breydon. Who's to come tonight?

Ayamonn. Mullcanny : he's searching Dublin for a book he wants to give me ; and, if he got it, he was to bring it tonight — *The Riddle of the Universe.*

Mrs. Breydon. That's another one I wouldn't see too much of, for he has the whole neighbourhood up in arms against his reckless disregard of God, an' his mockery of everything solemn, set down as sacred.

Ayamonn. Oh, Tim is all right. The people are sensible enough to take all he says in good part ; and a black flame stands out in a brightly-coloured world.

Mrs. Breydon. You don't know them, if you say that ; he'll meet with a mishap, some day, if he doesn't keep his mouth shut.

Ayamonn. Nonsense.

[*She has quietly slipped a shawl around her, and is moving to the door so silently as to seem to want to prevent Ayamonn from noticing her movements, when the door opens and Eeada, Dympna, Finnoola, and several men, appear there. The three women come a little way into the room; the men stay around the door. All their faces are stiff and mask-like, holding tight an expression of dumb resignation; and are traversed with seams of poverty and a hard life. The face of Eeada is that of an old woman; that of Dympna, one coming up to middle age ; and that of Finnoola, one of a young girl. Each shows the difference of age by more or less furrows, but each has the same expressionless stare out on life.*

[*Dympna is carrying a statue of the Blessed Virgin, more than two feet high, in her arms. The figure was once a*

*glory of purest white, sparkling blue, and luscious gilding;
but the colours have faded, the gilt is gone, save for a spot
or two of dull gold still lingering on the crown. She is
wearing a crown that, instead of being domed, is castellated
like a city's tower, resembling those of Dublin ; and the
pale face of the Virgin is sadly soiled by the grime of the
house. The men are dressed in drab brown, the women in
a chill grey, each suit or dress having a patch of faded
blue, red, green, or purple somewhere about them.*

Eeada [*to Mrs. Breydon*]. Could you spare a pinch or two of
your Hudson's soap, Mrs. Breydon, dear, to give the
Blessed Virgin a bit of a wash? [*To all in general*]
Though I've often said it's th' washin' that's done
away with the bonnie blue of th' robe an' th' braver
gold of its bordhers an' th' most o' th' royalty outa th'
crown. Little Ursula below's savin' up her odd
pennies to bring Her where She'll find a new blue
robe, an' where they'll make the royalty of th' gilt
glow again ; though whenever she's a shillin' up, it's
needed for food an' firin' ; but we never yet found
Our Lady of Eblana averse to sellin' Her crown an'
Her blue robe to provide for Her people's need. [*Mrs.
Breydon gives half a packet of soap powder. Gratefully*]
Thank you, ma'am, an' though y'are of a different
persuasion, Our Blessed Lady of Eblana's poor'll bless
you an' your fine son for this little tribute to Her
honour and circumspect appearance before the world.

The Rest [*murmuring*]. Ay will She, an' that's a sure thing.
      [*They open a way for Eeada to pass out, with Dympna
      carrying the statue, following in a kind of simple pro-
      cession. Mrs. Breydon is moving slowly after them.*

Ayamonn [*who has noticed her under his eyes*]. You're not
going out again, surely — on a night like this, too ?

Mrs. Breydon. Not really ; only down the road to Mrs. Cashmore's. She's not too well ; I promised I'd dhrop in, and see to a hot dhrink or something for her before she wandhered off to sleep.

Ayamonn [*irritably*]. You think more of other homes than you do of your own ! Every night for the past week you've been going out on one silly mission or another like an imitation sisther of charity.

Mrs. Breydon. I couldn't sit quiet knowin' the poor woman needed me. I'd hear her voice all through the night complainin' I never came to give her a hot dhrink, settle her bed soft, an' make her safe for th' lonely hours of th' slow-movin' night.

Ayamonn. A lot they'd do for you if you happened to need help from them.

Mrs. Breydon. Ah, we don't know. A body shouldn't think of that, for such a belief would dismay an' dismantle everything done outside of our own advantage. No harm to use an idle hour to help another in need.

Ayamonn. An' wear yourself out in the process ?

Mrs. Breydon [*with a sigh*]. I'll wear out, anyway, sometime, an' a tired ould body can, at least, go to its long rest without any excuse.

    [*As she opens the door to go out, Sheila appears on the threshold. She is a girl of about twenty-three, fairly tall, a fine figure, carrying herself with a sturdiness never ceasing to be graceful. She has large, sympathetic brown eyes that dim, now and again, with a cloud of timidity. Her mouth is rather large but sweetly made; her hair is brown and long, though now it is gathered up into a*

*thick coil that rests on the nape of her neck. She is
dressed in a tailor-made suit of rich brown tweed, golden-
brown blouse, and a bright-blue hat. These are now
covered with a fawn-coloured mackintosh, darkened with
heavy rain, and a hastily folded umbrella is dripping on
to the floor. She comes in shyly, evidently conscious of
Mrs. Breydon's presence; but fighting her timidity with a
breezy and jovial demeanour. Mrs. Breydon tries, but
can't keep a little stiffness out of her greeting.*

Sheila. Oh! good evening, Mrs. Breydon. What a
night! I'm nearly blown to bits; and the rain — oh,
the wind and the weather!

Mrs. Breydon. You must be perished. Take off your
mac, and come over to the fire. Get Ayamonn to make
you a cup o' tea, and bring you back to life again.

Sheila. No, really; I'm burning — the battle with the
wind and the rain has made me warm and lively.

Ayamonn. Hey ho, the wind and the rain, for the rain it
raineth every day. Sit down and take the weight off
your legs.

Sheila. Not worth while, for I can't stop long. [*To Mrs.
Breydon*] Going out on a night like this, Mrs. Breydon?

Ayamonn [*hastily*]. She has to go: got an urgent call from
a poor sick neighbour.

Sheila [*hesitatingly*]. What is it? Could . . . could I do
it for you?

Ayamonn [*decidedly*]. No, no, you couldn't. The woman
knows my mother. It's only to see her safe and warm
in bed for the night; Mother won't be long.

C.P.—III   K

Mrs. Breydon. Good night, Miss Sheila ; perhaps you'll be here when I come back.

Sheila. I don't think so.   I must go almost at once.

Mrs. Breydon. Well, good night, then.
   [*She goes out, and Ayamonn goes over to Sheila, kisses her, and helps her off with the mac.*

Sheila. You shouldn't let your mother go out on a night like this — she's no longer a young woman.

Ayamonn. I don't like to interfere with her need to give help to a neighbour.   She likes it, and it does her good.

Sheila. But the rain's coming down in sheets, and she's got but a thin shawl round her shoulders.

Ayamonn [*impatiently*]. Oh, she hasn't very far to go. Let's think of greater things than the pouring rain and an old woman on her way to smooth pillows on a sick bed.   Look ! — [*he feels her skirt*] — the hem's wringing. Better dry it at the fire.   Turn round and I'll unfasten it for you.

Sheila [*forcing his hand away*]. It's nothing — you are thinking now of your own pleasure.   You weren't so eager to see me when I was knocking at the door a while ago.

Ayamonn. You !   But it was Old Brennan o' the Moor that was there.

Sheila. Before him, I was there.   He hammered at the door too.

Ayamonn [*angry with himself*]. And I thinking the rapping was that of a pestering neighbour !   I might have guessed it wasn't, it was so gentle.

Sheila. After trying to slip in unnoticed, there I was left
with the whole house knowing I was at the door, and
when I ran down, I heard them yelling that the
stylish-dressed pusher was trying to get into Breydon's
again ! A nice time I'll have with my people when
they hear it.

Ayamonn. I was doing my Shakespeare part, and didn't
want disturbance, so there I was, standing stiff and
breathless like a heron in a pond, keeping my dear one
away from me ! [*Going over and taking her in his arms*]
Well, it's all over now, and here you are in my arms,
safe and sure and lovely.

Sheila [*struggling away from him*]. No, it's not all over ;
and don't press me so hard ; don't ruffle me tonight,
for I feel a little tired.

Ayamonn [*peevishly*]. Tired again ? Well, so am I, more
than a little tired ; but never too tired to put a
sparkle into a welcome for a loved one.

Sheila. Oh, Ayamonn, I do want you to be serious for one
night.

Ayamonn. Very well, very well, Sheila. [*He moves away
from her, and stands at the other side of the fire.*] Let us
plan, then, of how we can spin joy into every moment
of tomorrow's day.

Sheila. That's why I hurried here to see you — I can't be
with you tomorrow.   [*There is a long pause.*

Ayamonn. Why can't you be with me tomorrow ?

Sheila. The Daughters of St. Frigid begin a retreat
tomorrow, to give the Saint a warm devotion, and
Mother insists I go.

Ayamonn. And I insist that you go with me. Is the Saint Frigid more to you than the sinner Ayamonn? Would you rather go to the meeting than come to see me? [*A pause.*] Would you, would you, Sheila?

Sheila [*in a hesitant whisper*]. God forgive me, I'd rather come to see you.

Ayamonn. Come then ; God will be sure to forgive you.

Sheila. I daren't. My mother would be at me for ever if I failed to go. I've told you how she hates me to be near you. She chatters red-lined warnings and black-bordered appeals into my ears night and day, and when they dwindle for lack of breath, my father shakes them out of their drowsiness and sends them dancing round more lively still, dressed richly up in deadly black and gleaming scarlet.

Ayamonn. Sheila, Sheila, on the one day of the month when I'm free, you must be with me. I wouldn't go to a workers' meeting so that I might be with you.

Sheila. There's another thing, Ayamonn — the threatened strike. Oh, why do you meddle with those sort of things !

Ayamonn. Oh, never mind that, now. Don't be like a timid little girl ensconced in a clear space in a thicket of thorns — safe from a scratch if she doesn't stir, but unable to get to the green grass or the open road unless she risks the tears the thorns can give.

Sheila. Oh, Ayamonn, for my sake, if you love me, do try to be serious.

Ayamonn [*a little wildly*]. Oh, Sheila, our time is not yet come to be serious in the way of our elders. Soon enough to browse with wisdom when Time's grey finger puts a warning speck on the crimson rose of youth. Let no damned frosty prayer chill the sunny sighs that dread the joy of love.

Sheila [*wildly*]. I won't listen, Ayamonn, I won't listen ! We must look well ahead on the road to the future. You lead your life through too many paths instead of treading the one way of making it possible for us to live together.

Ayamonn. We live together now ; live in the light of the burning bush. I tell you life is not one thing, but many things, a wide branching flame, grand and good to see and feel, dazzling to the eye of no-one loving it. I am not one to carry fear about with me as a priest carries the Host. Let the timid tiptoe through the way where the paler blossoms grow ; my feet shall be where the redder roses grow, though they bear long thorns, sharp and piercing, thick among them !

Sheila [*rising from the chair — vehemently*]. I'll listen no more ; I'll go. You want to make me a spark in a mere illusion. I'll go !

Ayamonn. Rather a spark from the althar of God, me girl ; a spark that flames on a new path for a bubbling moment of life, or burns a song into the heart of a poet.

Sheila. I came here as a last chance to talk things quiet with you, but you won't let me ; so I'll go. [*As he seizes her in his arms*] Let me go ! [*Pleadingly*] Please, Ayamonn, let me go !

Ayamonn. I tell you it is a gay sight for God to see joy shine for a moment on the faces of His much-troubled children.

Sheila [*fearfully*]. Oh, don't bring God's name into this, for it will mean trouble to the pair of us. And your love for me lasts only while I'm here. When I'm gone, you think more of your poor painting, your poor oul' Ireland, your songs, and your workers' union than you think of Sheila.

Ayamonn. You're part of them all, in them all, and through them all ; joyous, graceful, and a dearer vision ; a bonnie rose, delectable and red. [*He draws her to him, presses her hard, lifts her on to his lap, and kisses her.*] Sheila, darling, you couldn't set aside the joy that makes the moon a golden berry in a hidden tree. You cannot close your ear to the sweet sound of the silver bell that strikes but once and never strikes again !

> [*The door opens, and the head of Brennan o' the Moor looks into the room. It is a bald one, the dome highly polished ; the face is wrinkled a lot, but the eyes are bright and peering. A long white beard gives him a far-away likeness to St. Jerome. He is dressed in a shabby-genteel way, and wears a long rain-soaked mackintosh. A faded bowler hat is on his head.*

Brennan. Oh, dear, dear, dear me !

> [*He comes into the room showing that his back is well bent, though he still has a sturdy look about him. A strap around his body holds a melodeon on his back. Sheila and Ayamonn separate ; he rises to meet the old man, while she stares, embarrassed, into the fire.*

Ayamonn. Now what th' hell do you want ?

Brennan [*taking no notice of Ayamonn's remark — taking off his hat in a sweeping bow*]. Ah, me two sweet, snowy-breasted Dublin doves ! Me woe it is to come ramblin' in through marjoram moments scentin' the serious hilarity of a genuine courtin' couple. I'm askin' now what's the dear one's name, if that isn't thresspassin' on others who are in a firmer condition of friendship? Though, be rights, it's a fair an' showy nosegay I should be throwin' through a shyly opened window into the adorable lady's lap.

Sheila [*shyly*]. Me name is Sheila.

Brennan. Sheila is it? Ay, an' a Sheila are you. Ay, an' a suitable one too, for there's a gentle nature in the two soft sounds, an' a silver note in the echo, describin' grandly the pretty slendher lass me two ould eyes are now beholdin'.

Ayamonn [*going over and catching him by an arm to guide him out*]. I can't see you now, old friend, for the pair of us are heavily harnessed to a question that must be answered before either of us is a day older.

Brennan. Sure I know. An' isn't it only natural, too, that young people should have questions to ask and answers to give to the dewy problems that get in th' way of their dancin' feet?

Ayamonn [*impatiently*]. Come again, old friend, when time has halted us for an hour of rest.

Brennan. It isn't me, I'm sayin', that would be dense enough to circumvent your longin' to be deep down in the silent consequence of regardin' each other without let or hindrance. [*He goes towards Sheila, eagerly, pulling Ayamonn after him.*] It's easy seen, sweet lady, that you're well within the compass of your young man's knowledge, an' unaware of nothin', so I may speak as man to lady, so with cunnin' confidence, tell me what you think of the Bank of Ireland?

Ayamonn. Oh, for goodness' sake, old man.   Sheila's no intherest in the Bank of Ireland.   She cares nothing for money, or for anything money can buy.

Brennan [*staring at Ayamonn for a moment as if he had received a shock*].   Eh ?   Arra, don't be talkin' nonsense, man !   Who is it daren't think of what money can buy ?   [*He crosses to the door in a trot on his toes, opens it, looks out, and closes it softly again.   Then he tiptoes back to Sheila, bends down towards her, hands on knees, and whispers hoarsely*] I've just a little consideration of stocks and bonds nestin' in the Bank of Ireland, at four per cent — just enough to guard a poor man from ill, eh ?   Safe an' sound there, isn't it, eh ?   [*To Ayamonn*]   Now, let the fair one speak out on her own.   [*Twisting his head back to Sheila.*]   Safe there as if St. Pether himself had the key of where the bonds are stationed, eh ?

Sheila.   I'm sure they must be, sir.

Brennan [*with chuckling emphasis*].   Yehess !   Aren't you the sensible young lady ;   sure I knew you'd say that, without fear or favour.   [*Turning towards Ayamonn.*] What do you say ?   You're a man, now, of tellin' judgement.

Ayamonn.   Oh, the State would have to totther before you'd lose a coin.

Brennan [*gleefully*].   Go bang, absolutely bang !   Eh ?

Ayamonn.   Go bang !

Brennan.   Bang !   [*To Sheila*]   Hear that, now, from a man climbin' up to scholarship ?   Yehess !   Stony walls, steely doors, locks an' keys, bolts an' bars, an' all th' bonds warm an' dhry, an' shinin' safe behind them.

Sheila. Safe behind them.

Brennan [*gleefully*]. Ay, so. An' none of it sthrollin' into Peter's Pence. [*Chuckling.*] Wouldn't the Pope be mad if he knew what he was missin' ! Safe an' sound. [*To Ayamonn*] You think so, too, eh ?

Ayamonn. Yes, yes.

Brennan [*soberly*]. Ay, of course you do. [*To Sheila — indicating Ayamonn*] A good breed, me sweet an' fair one, brought up proper to see things in their right light.

Ayamonn [*catching him impatiently by the arm*]. And now, old friend, we have to get you to go.

Brennan. Eh ?

Ayamonn. To go ; Sheila and I have things to talk about.

Brennan [*suddenly*]. An' what about the song, then ?

Ayamonn. Song ?

Brennan. Th' one for the Show. Isn't that what brought me up ? At long last, afther hard sthrainin', me an' Sammy have got the tune down in tested clefs, crotchets, an' quavers, fair set down to be sung be anyone in thrue time. An' Sammy's below, in his gay suit for the Show, waitin' to be called up to let yous hear th' song sung as only Sammy can sing it.

Ayamonn. Bring him up, bring him up — why in hell didn't you tell me all this before ?

Brennan [*stormily*]. Wasn't I thryin' all the time an' you wouldn't let a man get a word in edgeways. [*Gesturing towards Sheila.*] He'll jib at singin' in front of her. [*He whispers hoarsely towards Sheila.*] He's as shy as a kid in his first pair o' pants, dear lady.

Ayamonn [*impatiently pushing him out of the room*]. Oh, go on, go on, man, and bring him up.   [*Brennan goes out.*

Sheila [*earnestly*]. Wait till I'm gone, Ayamonn; I can't stop long, and I want to talk to you so much.

Ayamonn [*a little excited*]. Oh, you must hear the song, Sheila; they've been working to get the air down for a week, and it won't take a minute.

Sheila [*angrily*]. I've waited too long already! Aren't you more interested in what I want to say than to be listening to some vain fool singing a song?

Ayamonn [*a little taken aback*]. Oh, Sheila, what's wrong with you tonight? The young carpenter who'll sing it, so far from being vain, is as shy as a field-mouse, and you'll see, when he starts to sing, he'll edge his face away from us. You do want to hear it, Sheila, don't you?

Sheila [*appealingly*]. Let it wait over, Ayamonn; I can come to hear it some other time. I do want to say something, very serious, to you about our future meetings.

Ayamonn [*hastily*]. All right then; I'll hurry them off the minute the song's sung. Here they are, so sit down, do, just for one minute more.

[*But she goes towards the door, and reaches it just as Old Brennan returns shoving in before him a young man of twenty-three, shy, and loth to come in. He is tall, but his face is pale and mask-like in its expression of resignation to the world and all around him. Even when he shows he's shy, the mask-like features do not alter. He is dressed in a white cut-away coat, shaped like a tailed evening dress, black waistcoat over a rather soiled shirt-*

front, frilled, and green trousers. He carries a sheet of manuscript music in his hand. Brennan unslings his melodeon from his back, fusses the young Singer forward; bumping against Sheila, who has moved towards the door, he pushes her back with a shove of his backside; and puts Ayamonn to the other end of the room with a push on the shoulder.

Brennan [*as he pushes Sheila*]. Outa th' way, there! Stem your eagerness for a second, will yous? All in good time. Give the man a chance to get himself easy. [*As he pushes Ayamonn*] Farther back, there, farther back! Give the performer a chance to dispose himself. Isn't he a swell, wha'? The centre group's to be dhressed the same way, while th' corner men'll be in reverse colours — green coats, black trousers, an' white vest, see? Th' whole assembly'll look famous. Benjamin's lendin' all the set o' twelve suits for five bob, 'cause o' th' reason we're runnin' th' Show for. [*To Sheila — in a hoarse whisper*] You stare at the fire as if he wasn't here. He's extravagant in shyness, an' sinks away into confusion at the stare of an eye — understand?

[*She slowly, and a little sullenly, sits down to stare into the fire. The door is opened, and in comes Roory O'Balacaun with a small roll of Irish magazines under an arm. He is a stout middle-aged man, dressed in rough homespun coat, cap, and knee-breeches, wearing over all a trench coat.*

Roory. Here y'are, Ayamonn, me son, avic's th' Irish magazines I got me friend to pinch for you. [*He looks at the Singer.*] Hello, what kind of a circus is it's goin' on here?

Ayamonn. Mr. Brennan Moore here's organising the singers for the Minsthrel Show to help get funds in case we have to go on sthrike, Roory.

Roory. I'm one o' th' men meself, but I don't stand for a foreign Minsthrel Show bein' held, an' the Sword of Light gettin' lifted up in th' land. We want no coon or Kaffir industry in our country.

Brennan [indignantly]. Doesn't matter what you stand for before you came here, you'll sit down now. Thry to regard yourself as a civilised member of the community, man, an' hold your peace for th' present. [*To the Singer*] Now, Sam, me son o' gold, excavate the shyness out of your system an' sing as if you were performin' before a Royal Command !

Roory [with a growl]. There's no royal commands wanted here.

Brennan [with a gesture of disgusted annoyance]. Will you for goodness' sake not be puttin' th' singer out ? I used the term only as an allegory, man.

Roory. Allegory man, or allegory woman, there's goin' to be no royal inthrusions where the Sword o' Light is shinin'.

Ayamonn. Aw, for Christ's sake, Roory, let's hear the song !

Brennan [to the Singer, who has been coughing shyly and turning sideways from his audience]. Now, Sam, remember you're not in your working clothes, an' are a different man, entirely. Chin up and chest out. [*He gives a note or two on the melodeon.*] Now !

Singer [singing] :
    A sober black shawl hides her body entirely,
    Touch'd by th' sun and th' salt spray of the sea ;
    But down in th' darkness a slim hand, so lovely,
    Carries a rich bunch of red roses for me.

[*He turns away a little more from his audience, and coughs shyly.*

Brennan [*enthusiastically*]. Sam, you're excellin' yourself ! On again, me oul' son !

Singer [*singing*] :
    Her petticoat's simple, her feet are but bare,
    An' all that she has is but neat an' scantie ;
    But stars in th' deeps of her eyes are exclaiming
    I carry a rich bunch of red roses for thee !

Brennan [*after giving a few curling notes on the melodeon*]. A second Count McCormack in th' makin' ! An' whenever he sung *Mother Mo Chree*, wasn't there a fewroory in Heaven with the rush that was made to lean over an hear him singin' it !
    [*While Brennan has been speaking, the door has opened, and Mullcanny now stands there gaping into the room. He is young, lusty, and restless. He is wearing fine tweeds that don't fit too well ; and his tweed cap is set rakishly on his head. He, too, wears a mackintosh.*

Mullcanny. Is this a home-sweet-away-from-home hippodhrome, or what ?

Brennan [*clicking his tongue in annoyance*]. Dtchdtchdtch !

Mullcanny. An' did I hear someone pratin' about Heaven, an' I coming in ? [*To Brennan — tapping him on the shoulder*] Haven't you heard, old man, that God is dead ?

Brennan. Well, keep your grand discovery to yourself for a minute or two more, please. [*To the Singer*] Now, Sam, apologisin' for th' other's rudeness, the last verse, please.

Singer [*singing*] :

No arrogant gem sits enthron'd on her forehead,
Or swings from a white ear for all men to see ;
But jewel'd desire in a bosom, most pearly,
Carries a rich bunch of red roses for me !

Brennan [*after another curl of notes on the melodeon*]. Well, fair damsel and gentlemen all, what do you think of the song and the singer ?

Ayamonn. The song was good, and the singer was splendid.

Mullcanny. What I heard of it wasn't bad.

Singer [*shyly*]. I'm glad I pleased yous all.

Roory [*dubiously*]. D'ye not think th' song is a trifle indecent ?

Mullcanny [*mockingly*]. Indecent ! And what may your eminence's specification of indecency be ? [*Angrily*] Are you catalogued, too, with the Catholic Young Men going about with noses long as a snipe's bill, sthripping the gayest rose of its petals in search of a beetle, and sniffing a taint in the freshest breeze blowing in from the sea ?

Brennan [*warningly*]. Lady present, lady present, boys !

Roory. It ill becomes a thrue Gael to stand unruffled when either song or story thries to introduce colour to the sabler nature of yearnin's in untuthored minds.

Brennan [*more loudly*]. Lady present, boys !

Sheila [*rising out of the chair and going towards the door*]. The lady's going now, thank you all for the entertainment.

[*To Ayamonn*] I won't stay any longer to disturb the important dispute of your friends.

Ayamonn [*going over to her*]. Don't be foolish, Sheila, dear ; but if you must go, you must. We'll see each other again tomorrow evening.

Sheila [*firmly*]. No, not tomorrow, nor the next night either.

Ayamonn [*while Brennan plays softly on the melodeon to hide embarrassment*]. When then ?

Sheila. I can't tell. I'll write. Never maybe. [*Bitterly*] I warned you this night might be the last chance of a talk for some time, and you didn't try to make use of it !

Ayamonn [*catching her arm*]. I made as much use of it as you'd let me. Tomorrow night, in the old place, near the bridge, the bridge of vision where we first saw Aengus and his coloured birds of passion passing.

Sheila [*wildly*]. I can't ; I won't, so there—oh, let me go ! [*She breaks away from him, runs out, and a silence falls on the room for a few moments.*

Roory [*breaking the silence*]. Women is strange things ! Elegant animals, not knowin' their own minds a minute.

Brennan [*consolingly*]. She'll come back, she'll come back.

Ayamonn [*trying to appear unconcerned*]. Aw, to hell with her !

Singer [*faintly*]. Can I go now ?

Brennan. Wait, an' I'll be with you in a second.

Mullcanny [*to Ayamonn*]. I just dropped in to say, Ayamonn, that I'll be getting Haeckel's *Riddle of the Universe* to-morrow, afther long searching, and I'll let you have it the minute it comes into my hand.

[*The door is suddenly flung open, and Eeada, followed by Dympna and Finnoola, with others, mingled with men behind them, rushes into the room in a very excited state. She comes forward, with her two companions a little behind, while the rest group themselves by the door.*

Eeada [*distractedly*]. It's gone She is, an' left us lonesome; vanished She is like a fairy mist of an early summer mornin'; stolen She is be some pagan Protestan' hand, envious of the love we had for our sweet Lady of Eblana's poor !

Chorus. Our Lady of Eblana's gone !

Ayamonn. Nonsense; no Protestant hand touched Her. Where was She?

Dympna. Safe in Her niche in th' hall She was, afther Her washin', lookin' down on the comin's an' goin's of Her strugglin' children: an' then we missed Her, an' th' niche was empty !

Chorus. Our Lady of Eblana's gone !

Single Voice. An' dear knows what woe'll fall on our poor house now.

Brennan. An' a good job, too. [*Passionately*] Inflamin' yourselves with idols that have eyes an' see not; ears, an' hear not; an' have hands that handle not; like th' chosen people settin' moon-images an' sun-images, cuttin' away the thrue and homely connection between the Christian an' his God ! Here, let me and me singer out of this unholy place !

[*He pushes his way through the people, followed by the Singer, and goes out.*

Eeada [*nodding her head, to Ayamonn*]. All bark, but no
bite ! We know him of old : a decent oul' blatherer.
Sure, doesn't he often buy violets and snowdhrops,
even, for little Ursula, below, tellin' her she mustn't put
them before a graven image, knowin' full well that
that was th' first thing she'd hurry home to do. An'
she's breakin' her young heart below, now, because her
dear Lady has left her. [*Suspiciously*] If oul' Brennan
had a hand in Her removal, woe betide him.

Mullcanny [*mocking*]. Couldn't you all do betther than
wasting your time making gods afther your own
ignorant images ?

Ayamonn [*silencing him with a gesture*]. That's enough,
Paudhrig. [*To Eeada*] Tell little Ursula not to worry.
Her Lady'll come back. If your Lady of Eblana hasn't
returned by tonight, I'll surrender my sleep afther my
night's work to search for Her, and bring Her back safe
to Her niche in the hall. No one in this house touched
Her.

Eeada. An' you'll see She'll pay you back for your kind-
ness, Ayamonn — [*looking at Mullcanny*] — though it's
little surprised I'd be if, of Her own accord, She came
down indignant, an' slipped off from us, hearin' the
horrid talk that's allowed to float around this house
lately.

Mullcanny [*mocking*]. Afraid of me, She was. Well,
Ayamonn, I've some lessons to get ready, so I'll be off.
I'll bring you the book tomorrow. [*To the crowd —
mocking*] I hope the poor Lady of Eblana's poor'll find
Her way home again.

[*He goes out through a surly-faced crowd.*

Ayamonn [*to Eeada*]. Don't mind Mullcanny. Good

night, now ; and don't worry about your dear statue.
If She doesn't come back, we'll find another as bright
and good to take Her place.

Eeada [*growling*]. The fella that's gone'll have a rough end,
jeerin' things sacred to our feelin'.
  [*They all go out, and Ayamonn is left alone with Roory.
  Ayamonn takes off his doublet, folds it up, and puts it
  back in the basket. He goes into the other room and comes
  back with oilskin coat and thigh-high leggings. He puts
  the leggings on over his trousers.*

Ayamonn [*putting on the leggings*]. Th' shunting-yard'll be a
nice place to be tonight. D'ye hear it ?
  [*He listens to the falling rain, now heavier than ever.*

Roory. Fallin' fast. That Mullcanny'll get into throuble
yet.

Ayamonn. Not he. He's really a good fellow. Gave up
his job rather than his beliefs — more'n many would do.

Roory. An' how does he manage now ?

Ayamonn. Hammering knowledge into deluded minds
wishing to be civil servants, bank clerks, an' constables
who hope to take the last sacraments as sergeants in the
Royal Irish Constabulary or the Metropolitan Police.

Roory. By God, he's his work cut out for him with the
last lot !
  [*The door is again opened and Eeada sticks her head into the
  room.*

Eeada. Your mother's just sent word that the woman
she's mindin's bad, an' she'll have to stay th' night.
I'm just runnin' round meself to make your mother a
cup o' tea.

Ayamonn [*irritably*]. Dtch dtch — she'll knock herself up before she's done ! When I lock up, I'll leave the key with you for her, Eeada.

    [*He lights a shunter's lantern and puts out the lamp.*

Eeada. Right y'are.   [*She goes.*

Roory. What kid was it sketched th' angel on th' wall ?

Ayamonn. Oh, I did that. I'd give anything to be a painter.

Roory. What, like Oul' Brennan o' th' Moor ?

Ayamonn. No, no ; like Angelico or Constable.

Roory [*indifferently*]. Never heard of them.

Ayamonn [*musingly*]. To throw a whole world in colour on a canvas though it be but a man's fine face, a woman's shape asthride of a cushioned couch, or a three-bordered house on a hill, done with a glory ; even delaying God, busy forgin' a new world, to stay awhile an' look upon their loveliness.

Roory. Aw, Ayamonn, Ayamonn, man, put out your hand an' see if you're awake ! [*He fiddles with the books on the table.*] What oul' book are you readin' now ?

Ayamonn [*dressed now in oilskin leggings and coat, with an oilskin sou'wester on his head, comes over to look at the book in Roory's hand, and shines the lantern on it*]. Oh, that's Ruskin's *Crown of Wild Olive* — a grand book — I'll lend it to you.

Roory. What for ? What would I be doin' with it ? I've no time to waste on books. Ruskin. Curious name ; not Irish, is it ?

Ayamonn. No, a Scotsman who wrote splendidly about a

lot of things. Listen to this, spoken before a gathering of business men about to build an Exchange in their town.

Roory. Aw, Ayamonn — an Exchange ! What have we got to do with an Exchange ?

Ayamonn [*impatiently*]. Listen a second, man ! Ruskin, speakin' to the business men, says : " Your ideal of life is a pleasant and undulating world, with iron and coal everywhere beneath it. On each pleasant bank of this world is to be a beautiful mansion ; stables, and coach-houses ; a park and hot-houses ; carriage-drives and shrubberies ; and here are to live the votaries of the Goddess of Getting-on — the English gentle-man——"

Roory [*interrupting*]. There you are, you see, Ayamonn — th' *English* gentleman !

Ayamonn. Wait a second — Irish or English — a gentle-man's th' same.

Roory. 'Tisn't. I'm tellin' you it's different. What's in this Ruskin of yours but another oul' cod with a gift of the gab ? Right enough for th' English, pinin' afther little things, ever rakin' cindhers for th' glint of gold. We're different — we have th' light.

Ayamonn. You mean th' Catholic Faith ?

Roory [*impatiently*]. No, no ; that's there, too ; I mean th' light of freedom ; th' tall white candle tipped with its golden spear of flame. The light we thought we'd lost ; but it burns again, sthrengthenin' into a sword of light. Like in th' song we sung together th' other night. [*He sings softly :*]

Our courage so many have thought to be agein',
Now flames like a brilliant new star in th' sky ;
And Danger is proud to be call'd a good brother,
For Freedom has buckled her sword on her thigh.

Ayamonn [*joining in*] :
Then out to th' place where th' battle is bravest,
Where th' noblest an' meanest fight fierce in th' fray,
Republican banners shall mock at th' foemen,
An' Fenians shall turn a dark night into day !
[*A pause as the two of them stand silent, each clasping the
other's hand. Ayamonn opens the door to pass out.*

Roory [*in a tense whisper*]. Th' Fenians are in force again,
Ayamonn ; th' Sword o' Light is shinin' !
[*They go out, and Ayamonn closes the door as the Curtain
falls.*

ACT II

The same as in Act I.

It is about ten o'clock at night. The rain has stopped, and there is a fine moon sailing through the sky. Some of its rays come in through the window at the side.

Ayamonn, in his shirt-sleeves, is sitting at the table. He has an ordinary tin money-box in his hand, and a small pile of coppers, mixed with a few sixpences, are on the table beside him. He is just taking the last coin from the slit in the box with the aid of a knife-blade. His mother is by the dresser piling up the few pieces of crockery used for a recent meal. The old one-wick lamp is alight, and stands on the table near to Ayamonn. Several books lie open there, too.

Ayamonn. There's th' last one out, now. It's quite a job getting them out with a knife.

Mrs. Breydon. Why don't you put them in a box with a simple lid on ?

Ayamonn. The harder it is to get at, the less chance of me spending it on something more necessary than what I seek. [*He counts the money on the table.*] One bob — two — three — an' sixpence — an' nine — three an' nine-pence ; one an' threepence to get yet — a long way to go.

Mrs. Breydon. Maybe, now, th' bookseller would give you it for what you have till you can give him th' rest.

Ayamonn [*in agony*]. Aw, woman, if you can't say sense, say nothing ! Constable's reproductions are five shillings second-hand, an' he that's selling is the bastard that nearly got me jailed for running off with his Shakespeare. It's touch an' go if he'll let me have it for the five bob.

Mrs. Breydon [*philosophically*]. Well, seein' you done without it so long, you can go without it longer.

Ayamonn [*with firm conviction*]. I'll have it the first week we get the extra shilling the men are demandin'.

Mrs. Breydon. I shouldn't count your chickens before they're hatched.

Ayamonn [*joking a little bitterly*]. Perhaps our blessed Lady of Eblana's poor will work a miracle for me.

Mrs. Breydon [*a little anxiously*]. Hush, don't say that ! Jokin' or serious, Ayamonn, I wouldn't say that. We don't believe in any of their Blessed Ladies, but as it's somethin' sacred, it's best not mentioned. [*She shuffles into her shawl.*] Though it's a queer thing, Her goin' off out of Her niche without a one in th' house knowin' why. They're all out huntin' for Her still.

[*The door opens, and Brennan comes in slowly, with a cute grin on his face. He has a large package, covered with paper, under his arm.*

Brennan. Out huntin' still for Her they are, are they ? Well, let them hunt ; She's here ! A prisoner under me arm !

Mrs. Breydon [*indignantly*]. Well, Mr. Brennan Moore, it's ashamed of yourself you should be yokin' th' poor people to throubled anxiety over their treasure ; and little Ursula breakin' her heart into th' bargain.

Ayamonn. It's god-damned mean of you, Brennan ! What good d'ye think you'll do by this rowdy love of your

own opinions — forcing tumult into the minds of
ignorant, anxious people ?

Brennan [*calmly*]. Wait till yous see, wait till yous see,
before yous are sorry for sayin' more. [*He removes the
paper and shows the lost image transfigured into a figure looking
as if it had come straight from the shop : the white dress is
spotless, the blue robe radiant, and the gold along its border
and on the crown is gleaming. He holds it up for admiration.
Triumphantly*] There, what d'ye think of Her now ?
Fair as th' first grand tinge of th' dawn, She is, an'
bright as th' star of the evenin'.

Mrs. Breydon. Glory be to God, isn't She lovely ! But
hurry Her off, Brennan, for She's not a thing for
Protestant eyes to favour.

Ayamonn [*a little testily*]. Put it back, Brennan, put it back,
and don't touch it again.

Brennan. Isn't that what I'm going to do ? Oh, boy
alive, won't they get th' shock o' their lives when they
see Her shinin' in th' oul' spot. [*He becomes serious.*]
Though, mind you, me thrue mind misgives me for
decoratin' what's a charm to the people of Judah in th'
worship of idols ; but th' two of you is witness I did it
for the sake of the little one, and not in any tilt towards
honour to a graven image.

Mrs. Breydon [*resignedly*]. It's done now, God forgive us
both, an' me for sayin' She's lovely. Touchin' a thing
forbidden with a startled stir of praise !

Ayamonn. Put it back, put it back, man, and leave it
quiet where you got it first.
    [*Brennan goes out, looking intently out, and listening,
    before he does so.*

Mrs. Breydon. He meant well, poor man, but he's done a dangerous thing. I'll be back before you start for work. [*With a heavy sigh.*] It won't take us long to tend her for the last time. The white sheets have come, th' tall candles wait to be lit, an' th' coffin's ordhered, an' th' room'll look sacred with the bunch of violets near her head. [*She goes out slowly — as she goes*] Dear knows what'll happen to th' three children.

[*Ayamonn sits silent for a few moments, reading a book, his elbows resting on the table.*]

Ayamonn [*with a deep sigh — murmuringly*]. Sheila, Sheila, my heart cries out for you ! [*After a moment's pause, he reads :*]

But I am pigeon-livered, an' lack gall
To make oppression bitther ; or, ere this,
I should have fatted all th' region kites
With this slave's offal : Bloody, bawdy villain !

Oh, Will, you were a boyo ; a brave boyo, though, and a beautiful one !

[*The door opens and Old Brennan comes in, showing by his half-suppressed chuckles that he is enjoying himself. He wanders over the room to stand by the fire.*]

Brennan [*chuckling*]. In Her old place she is, now, in Her new coronation robe ; and funny it is to think it's the last place they'll look for Her.

Ayamonn. I'm busy, now.

Brennan [*sitting down by the fire*]. Ay, so you are ; so I see ; busy readin'. Read away, for I won't disturb you ; only have a few quiet puffs at th' oul' pipe. [*A pause.*] Ah, then, don't I wish I was young enough to bury meself in th' joy of readin' all th' great books of th'

world. Ah ! but when I was young, I had to work
hard.

Ayamonn. I work hard, too.

Brennan. 'Course you do ! Isn't that what I'm sayin' ?
An' all th' more credit, too, though it must be thryin'
to have thoughtless people comin' in an' intherferin'
with the golden movements of your thoughts.

Ayamonn. It's often a damned nuisance !

Brennan. 'Course it is. Isn't that what I'm sayin' ? [*As
the door opens*] An' here's another o' th' boobies
entherin' now. [*Roory comes in, and shuts the door rather
noisily.*] Eh, go easy, there — can't you see Ayamonn's
busy studyin' ?

Roory [*coming and bending over Ayamonn*]. Are you still
lettin' oul' Ruskin tease you ?

Ayamonn [*angrily*]. No, no ; Shakespeare, Shakespeare,
this time ! [*Springing from his chair*] Damn it, can't
you let a man alone a minute ? What th' hell d'ye
want now ?

Brennan [*warningly*]. I told you he was busy.

Roory [*apologetically*]. Aw, I only came with the tickets
you asked me to bring you for the comin' National
Anniversary of Terence Bellew MacManus.

Ayamonn. All right, all right ; let's have them.

Roory. How many d'ye want ? How many can you sell ?

Ayamonn. Give me twelve sixpennies ; if the sthrike
doesn't come off I'll easily sell that number.

Roory [*counting out the tickets which Ayamonn gathers up and*

puts into his pocket]. I met that Mullcanny on the way
with a book for you ; but he stopped to tell a couple of
railwaymen that the Story of Adam an' Eve was all a
cod.

Brennan [*indignantly*]. He has a lot o' the people here in a
state o' steamin' anger, goin' about with his bitther
belief that the patthern of a man's hand is nearly at
one with a monkey's paw, a horse's foot, th' flipper of
a seal, or th' wing of a bat !

Ayamonn. Well, each of them is as wonderful as the hand
of a man.

Roory. No, Ayamonn, not from the Christian point of
view. D'ye know what they're callin' him round
here ? Th' New Broom, because he's always sayin'
he'll sweep th' idea of God clean outa th' mind o' man.

Brennan [*excited*]. There'll be dire damage done to him
yet ! He was goin' to be flattened out be a docker th'
other day for tellin' him that a man first formin'
showed an undoubted sign of a tail.

Ayamonn. Ay, and when he's fully formed, if he doesn't
show the tail, he shows most signs of all that goes
along with it.

Roory. But isn't that a nice dignity to put on th' sacred-
ness of a man's conception !

Brennan [*whisperingly*]. An' a lot o' them are sayin', Ayamonn, that your encouragement of him should come
to an end.

Ayamonn. Indeed ? Well, let them. I'll stand by any
honest man seekin' th' truth, though his way isn't
my way. [*To Brennan*] You, yourself, go about deriding
many things beloved by your Catholic neighbours.

Brennan. I contest only dangerous deceits specified be the Council o' Thrent, that are nowhere scheduled in th' pages of the Holy Scriptures.

Roory. Yes, Ayamonn, it's altogether different ; he just goes about blatherin' in his ignorant Protestant way.

Brennan [*highly indignant*]. Ignorant, am I ? An' where would a body find an ignorance lustier than your own, eh ? If your Council o' Thrent's ordher for prayers for the dead who are past help, your dismal veneration of Saints an' Angels, your images of wood an' stone, carved an' coloured, have given you the image an' superscription of a tail, th' pure milk of the gospel has made a man of me, God-fearin', but stately, with a mind garlanded to th' steady an' eternal thruth !

> [*While they have been arguing, Mullcanny has peeped round the door, and now comes into the room, eyeing the two disputants with a lot of amusement and a little scorn. They take no notice of him.*

Roory. Sure, man, you have the neighbourhood hectored with your animosity against Catholic custom an' Catholic thought, never hesitatin' to give th' Pope even a deleterious name.

Brennan [*lapsing, in his excitement, into a semi-Ulster dialect*]. We dud ut tae yeh in Durry, on' sent your bravest floatin' down dud in th' wathers of th' Boyne, like th' hosts of Pharaoh tumblin' in the rush of th' Rud Sea ! Thut was a slup in th' puss tae your Pope !

Mullcanny. You pair of damned fools, don't you know that the Pope wanted King Billy to win, and that the Vatican was ablaze with lights of joy afther King James's defeat over the wathers of the Boyne ?

Roory. You're a liar, he didn't !

Brennan. You're a liar, it wasn't !
  [*They turn from Mullcanny to continue the row with themselves.*

Brennan. Looksee, if I believed in the ministhration of Saints on' Angels, I'd say thut th' good Protestant St. Puthrick was at the hud of what fell out at Durry, Aughrim, on' th' Boyne.

Roory [*stunned with the thought of St. Patrick as a Protestant*]. Protestant St. Patrick ? Is me hearin' sound, or what ? What name did you mention ?

Brennan. I said St. Puthrick — th' evangelical founder of our thrue Church.

Roory. Is it dhreamin' I am ? Is somethin' happenin' to me, or is it happenin' to you ? Oh, man, it's mixin' mirth with madness you are at thinkin' St. Pathrick ever looped his neck in an orange sash, or tapped out a tune on a Protestant dhrum !

Brennan [*contemptuously*]. I refuse to argue with a one who's no' a broad-minded mon. Abuse is no equivalent for lugic — so I say God save th' King, an' tae hull with th' Pope !

Roory [*indignantly*]. You damned bigot — to hell with th' King, an' God save th' Pope !

Mullcanny [*to Ayamonn*]. You see how they live in bittherness, the one with the other. Envy, strife, and malice crawl from the coloured slime of the fairy-tales that go to make what is called religion. [*Taking a book from his pocket*] Here's something can bear a thousand tests, showing neatly how the world and all it bears upon it came into slow existence over millions of years, doing away for ever with the funny wonders of the seven days' creation set out in the fairy book of the Bible.

Ayamonn [*taking the book from Mullcanny*]. Thanks, Pether, oul' son ; I'm bound to have a good time reading it.

Mullcanny. It'll give you the true and scientific history of man as he was before Adam.

Brennan [*in a woeful voice*]. It's a darkened mind that thries tae lower us to what we were before th' great an' good God fashioned us. What does ony sensible person want to know what we were like before the creation of th' first man ?

Ayamonn [*murmuringly*]. To know the truth, to seek the truth, is good, though it lead to th' danger of eternal death.

Roory [*horror-stricken — crossing himself*]. Th' Lord between us an' all harm !

Brennan [*whispering prayerfully*]. Lord, I believe, help Thou mine unbelief.

Mullcanny [*pointing out a picture in the book*]. See ? The human form unborn. The tail — look ; the os coccyx sticking a mile out ; there's no getting away from it !

Brennan [*shaking his head woefully*]. An' this is holy Ireland !

Roory [*lifting his eyes to the ceiling — woefully*]. Poor St. Pathrick !

Mullcanny [*mockingly*]. He's going to be a lonely man soon, eh ? [*To Ayamonn*] Keep it safe for me, Ayamonn. When you've read it, you'll be a different man. [*He goes to the door*] Well, health with the whole o' you, and goodbye for the present.   [*He goes out.*

Roory. Have nothin' to do with that book, Ayamonn, for that fellow gone out would rip up the floor of Heaven to see what was beneath it. It's clapped in jail he ought to be !

Brennan. An' th' book banned !

Ayamonn. Roory, Roory, is that th' sort o' freedom you'd bring to Ireland with a crowd of green branches an' th' joy of shouting ? If we give no room to men of our time to question many things, all things, ay, life itself, then freedom's but a paper flower, a star of tinsel, a dead lass with gay ribbons at her breast an' a gold comb in her hair. Let us bring freedom here, not with sounding brass an' tinkling cymbal, but with silver trumpets blowing, with a song all men can sing, with a palm branch in our hand, rather than with a whip at our belt, and a headsman's axe on our shoulders.

[*There is a gentle knock at the door, and the voice of Sheila is heard speaking.*

Sheila [*outside*]. Ayamonn, are you there ?   Are you in ?

Brennan [*whispering*]. The little lass ; I knew she'd come back.

Ayamonn. I don't want her to see you here.   Go into the other room — quick. [*He pushes them towards it.*] An' keep still.

Roory [*to Brennan*]. An' don't you go mockin' our Pope, see ?

Brennan [*to Roory*]. Nor you go singlin' out King Billy for a jeer.

Ayamonn. In with yous, quick !

Brennan. I prophesied she'd come back, didn't I, Aya-monn ? that she'd come back, didn't I ?

Ayamonn. Yes, yes ; in you go.
[*He puts them in the other room and shuts the door. Then he crosses the room and opens the door to admit Sheila. She comes in, and he and Sheila stand silently for some moments, she trying to look at him, and finding it hard.*

Sheila [*at last*]. Well, haven't you anything to say to me ?

Ayamonn [*slowly and coldly*]. I waited for you at the bridge today ; but you didn't come.

Sheila. I couldn't come ; I told you why.

Ayamonn. I was very lonely.

Sheila [*softly*]. So was I, Ayamonn, lonely even in front of God's holy face.

Ayamonn. Sheila, we've gone a long way in a gold canoe over many waters, bright and surly, sometimes send-ing bitter spray asplash on our faces. But you were ever listening for the beat from the wings of the angel of fear. So you got out to walk safe on a crowded road.

Sheila. This is a cold and cheerless welcome, Ayamonn.

Ayamonn. Change, if you want to, the burning kiss falling on the upturned, begging mouth for the chill caress of a bony, bearded Saint. [*Loudly*] Go with th' yelling crowd, and keep them brave, and yell along with them !

Sheila. Won't you listen, then, to the few words I have to say ?

Ayamonn [*sitting down near the fire, and looking into it, though he leaves her standing*]. Go ahead ; I won't fail to hear you.

Sheila. God knows I don't mean to hurt you, but you must know that we couldn't begin to live on what you're earning now — could we ? [*He keeps silent.*] Oh, Ayamonn, why do you waste your time on doing foolish things ?

Ayamonn. What foolish things ?
[*A hubbub is heard in the street outside ; voices saying loudly " Give him one in the bake " or " Down him with a one in th' belly "; then the sound of running foot- steps, and silence.*

Sheila [*when she hears the voices — nervously*]. What's that ?

Ayamonn [*without taking his gaze from the fire*]. Some drunken row or other.   [*They listen silently for a few moments.*

Ayamonn. Well, what foolish things ?

Sheila [*timid and hesitating*]. You know yourself, Ayamonn : trying to paint, going mad about Shakespeare, and con- sorting with a kind of people that can only do you harm.

Ayamonn [*mockingly prayerful — raising his eyes to the ceiling*]. O Lord, let me forsake the foolish, and live ; and go in the way of Sheila's understanding !

Sheila [*going over nearer to him*]. Listen, Ayamonn, my love ; you know what I say is only for our own good, that we may come together all the sooner. [*Trying to speak jokingly*] Now, really, isn't it comical I'd look if I were to go about in a scanty petticoat, covered in a sober black shawl, and my poor feet bare ! [*Mocking*] Wouldn't I look well that way !

C.P.—III   M

Ayamonn [*quietly*]. With red roses in your hand, you'd look beautiful.

Sheila [*desperately*]. Oh, for goodness' sake, Ayamonn, be sensible ! I'm getting a little tired of all this. I can't bear the strain the way we're going on much longer. [*A short pause.*] You will either have to make good, or—— [*She pauses.*

Ayamonn [*quietly*]. Or what ?

Sheila [*with a little catch in her voice*]. Or lose me ; and you wouldn't like that to happen.

Ayamonn. I shouldn't like that to happen ; but I could bear the sthrain.

Sheila. I risked a big row tonight to come to tell you good news : I've been told that the strike is bound to take place ; there is bound to be trouble ; and, if you divide yourself from the foolish men, and stick to your job, you'll soon be a foreman of some kind or other.

Ayamonn [*rising from his seat and facing her for the first time*]. Who told you all this ? The Inspector ?

Sheila. Never mind who ; if he did, wasn't it decent of him ?

Ayamonn. D'ye know what you're asking me to do, woman ? To be a blackleg ; to blast with th' black frost of desertion the gay hopes of my comrades. Whatever you may think them to be, they are my comrades. Whatever they may say or do, they remain my brothers and sisters. Go to hell, girl, I have a soul to save as well as you. [*With a catch in his voice*] Oh, Sheila, you shouldn't have asked me to do this thing !

Sheila [*trying to come close, but he pushes her back*]. Oh,
Ayamonn, it is a chance ; take it, do, for my sake !
　　[*Rapid footsteps are heard outside. The door flies open and
　　Mullcanny comes in, pale, frightened, his clothes dis-
　　hevelled, and a slight smear of blood on his forehead. His
　　bowler hat is crushed down on his head, his coat is torn,
　　and his waistcoat unbuttoned, showing his tie pulled out of
　　its place. He sinks into a chair.*

Ayamonn. What's happened ? Who did that to you ?

Mullcanny. Give's a drink, someone, will you ?
　　[*Ayamonn gets him a drink from a jug on the dresser.*

Mullcanny. A gang of bowseys made for me, and I talking
to a man. Barely escaped with my life. Only for
some brave oul' one, they'd have laid me out completely. She saved me from worse.

Ayamonn. How th' hell did you bring all that on you ?

Mullcanny [*plaintively*]. Just trying to show a fellow the
foolishness of faith in a hereafter, when something
struck me on the head, and I was surrounded by feet
making kicks at me !
　　[*A crash of breaking glass is heard from the other room, and
　　Brennan and Roory come running out of it.*

Roory. A stone has done for th' window ! [*He sees
Mullcanny.*] Oh, that's how th' land lies, is it ?
Haven't I often said that if you go round leerin' at
God an' His holy assistants, one day He's bound to
have a rap at you !

Brennan. Keep away from that window, there, in case
another one comes sailin' in.
　　[*Immediately he has spoken, a stone smashes in through the
　　window. Brennan lies down flat on the floor ; Mull-*

canny slides from the chair and crouches on the ground;
Roory gets down on his hands and knees, keeping his head
as low as possible, so that he resembles a Mohammedan
at his devotions; Sheila stands stiff in a corner, near the
door; and Ayamonn, seizing up a hurley lying against
the dresser, makes for the door to go out.

Brennan. I guessed this was comin'.

Ayamonn [*angrily*]. I'll show them !

Sheila [*to Ayamonn*]. Stop where you are, you fool !
  [*But Ayamonn pays no attention to the advice and hurries out*
  of the door.

Roory [*plaintively and with dignity — to Mullcanny*]. This
is what you bring down on innocent people with your
obstinate association of man with th' lower animals.

Mullcanny [*truculently*]. Only created impudence it is that
strives to set yourselves above the ape's formation,
genetically present in every person's body.

Brennan [*indignantly*]. String out life to where it started,
an' you'll find no sign, let alone a proof, of the dignity,
wisdom, an' civility of man ever having been associated
with th' manners of a monkey.

Mullcanny. And why do children like to climb trees, eh ?
Answer me that ?

Roory [*fiercely*]. They love it more where you come from
than they do here.

Sheila [*from her corner*]. It's surely to be pitied you are,
young man, lettin' yourself be bullied by ignorant
books into believing that things are naught but what
poor men are inclined to call them, blind to the glorious
and eternal facts that shine behind them.

Mullcanny [*pityingly*]. Bullied be books — eternal facts — aw ! Yous are all scared stiff at the manifestation of a truth or two. D'ye know that the contraction of catharrah, apoplexy, consumption, and cataract of the eye is common to the monkeys ? Knowledge you have now that you hadn't before ; and a lot of them even like beer.

Roory. Well, that's something sensible, at last.

Brennan [*fiercely*]. Did they get their likin' for beer from us, or did we get our likin' of beer from them ? Answer me that, you, now ; answer me that !

Roory. Answer him that. We're not Terra Del Fooay-geeans, but sensible, sane, an' civilised souls.

Mullcanny [*gleefully*]. Time's promoted reptiles — that's all ; yous can't do away with the os coccyges !

Brennan. Ladies present, ladies present.

Roory [*creeping over rapidly till his face is close to that of Mull-canny's — fiercely*]. We stand on the earth, firm, upright, heads cocked, lookin' all men in th' face, afraid o' nothin' ; men o' goodwill we are, abloom with th' blessin' o' charity, showin' in th' dust we're made of, th' diamond-core of an everlastin' divinity !

Sheila [*excitedly*]. Hung as high as Gilderoy he ought to be, an' he deep in the evil of his rich illusions, spouting insults at war with th' mysteries an' facts of our holy faith !

Brennan [*to Sheila*]. Hush, pretty lady, hush. [*To the others*] Boys, boys, take example from a poor oul' Pro-testant here, never lettin' himself be offended be a quiver of anger in any peaceable or terrified discussion.

Now, let that last word finish it ; finis — the end, see ?

Roory [*angrily — to Brennan*]. Finis yousself, you blurry-eyed, wither-skinned oul' greybeard, singin' songs in th' public streets for odd coppers, with all th' boys in th' Bank of Ireland workin' overtime countin' all you've got in their front room ! Finis you !

Brennan [*indignantly*]. An office-boy, in a hurry, wouldn't stop to pick up from th' path before him the few coins I have. An' as for being withered, soople as you I am, hands that can tinkle a thremblin' tune out of an oul' melodeon, legs that can carry me ten miles an' more, an' eyes that can still see without hardship a red berry shinin' from a distant bush !

> [*The door opens and Ayamonn and his mother come in. She runs over to the blossoms at the window, tenderly examining the plants growing there — the musk, the geranium, and the fuchsia.*

Mrs. Breydon [*joyfully*]. Unharmed, th' whole of them. Th' stone passed them by, touchin' none o' them — thank God for that mercy !

Ayamonn. What th' hell are you doin' on your knees ? Get up, get up. [*They rise from the floor shamefacedly.*] Th' rioters all dispersed. [*To Mullcanny*] Mother was th' oul' one who saved you from a sudden an' unprovided death. An' th' Blessed Image has come back again, all aglow in garments new. Listen !

> [*A murmur of song has been heard while Ayamonn was speaking, and now Eeada, Dympna, Finnoola, and the Men appear at the door — now wide open — half backing into the room singing part of a hymn softly, their pale faces still wearing the frozen look of resignation; staring at the Image shining bright and gorgeous as Brennan has*

made it for them, standing in a niche in the wall,
directly opposite the door. Eeada, Dympna, Finnoola,
and the Men singing softly —

Oh ! Queen of Eblana's poor children,
Bear swiftly our woe away;
An' give us a chance to live lightly
An hour of our life's dark day !
Lift up th' poor heads ever bending,
An' light a lone star in th' sky,
To show thro' th' darkness, descending,
A cheerier way to die.

Eeada [*coming forward a little*]. She came back to Her poor
again, in raiment rich. She came back ; of Her own
accord. She came to abide with Her people.

Dympna. From her window, little Ursula looked, and
saw Her come in ; in th' moonlight, along the street
She came, stately. Blinded be the coloured light that
shone around about Her, the child fell back, in a
swoon she fell full on the floor beneath her.

1st Man. My eyes caught a glimpse of Her too, glidin'
back to where She came from. Regal an' proud She
was, an' wondrous, so that me eyes failed ; me knees
thrembled an' bent low, an' me heart whispered a
silent prayer to itself as th' vision passed me by, an' I
fancied I saw a smile on Her holy face.

Eeada. Many have lived to see a strange thing this
favoured night, an' blessin' will flow from it to all
tempered into a lively belief ; and maybe, too, to
some who happen to be out of step with the many
marchin' in the mode o' thruth. [*She comes a little
closer to Mrs. Breydon. The others, backs turned towards the
room, stand, most of them outside the door, a few just across*

the threshold, in a semicircle, heads bent as if praying, facing towards the Image.] Th' hand of a black stranger it was who sent the stones flyin' through your windows ; but ere tomorrow's sun is seen, they will be back again as shelther from th' elements. A blessin' generous on yous all — [*pause*] — except th' evil thing that stands, all stiff-necked, underneath th' roof !

Mullcanny [*mockingly*]. Me !

Sheila [*fiercely*]. Ay, you, that shouldn't find a smile or an unclenched hand in a decent man's house !

Mullcanny. I'll go ; there's too many here to deal with — I'll leave you with your miracle.

Ayamonn. You can stay if you wish, for whatever surety of shelther's here, it's open to th' spirit seeking to add another colour to whatever thruth we know already. Thought that has run from a blow will find a roof under its courage here, an' a fire to sit by, as long as I live an' th' oul' rooms last !

Sheila [*with quiet bitterness*]. Well, shelter him, then, that by right should be lost in the night, a black night, an' bitterly lonely, without a dim ray from a half-hidden star to give him a far-away companionship ; ay, an' a desolate rest under a thorny and dripping thicket of lean and twisted whins, too tired to thry to live longer against th' hate of the black wind and th' grey rain. Let him lie there, let him live there, forsaken, forgotten by all who live under a kindly roof and close to a cosy fire !

Mullcanny [*with pretended alarm*]. Good God, I'm done, now ! I'm off before worse befall me. Good night, Ayamonn.

Ayamonn. Good night, my friend.   [*Mullcanny goes out.*

Brennan. We're keepin' decent people out of their beds — so long, all.

Roory. I'll be with you some o' th' way, an' we can finish that argument we had. Good night all.
   [*He and Brennan go out together, closing the door after them. Sheila stands where she was, sullen and silent.*

Mrs. Breydon. Shame on you, Sheila, for such a smoky flame to come from such a golden lamp ! [*Sheila stays silent.*] Tired out I am, an' frightened be th' scene o' death I saw today. Dodge about how we may, we come to th' same end.

Ayamonn [*gently leading her towards the other room*]. Go an' lie down, lady ; you're worn out. Time's a perjured jade, an' ever he moans a man must die. Who through every inch of life weaves a patthern of vigour an' elation can never taste death, but goes to sleep among th' stars, his withered arms outstretched to greet th' echo of his own shout. It will be for them left behind to sigh for an hour, an' then to sing their own odd songs, an' do their own odd dances, to give a lonely God a little company, till they, too, pass by on their bare way out. When a true man dies, he is buried in th' birth of a thousand worlds.
   [*Mrs. Breydon goes into the other room, and Ayamonn closes the door softly behind her. He comes back and stands pensive near the fire.*

Ayamonn [*after a pause*]. Don't you think you should go too ?

Sheila [*a little brokenly*]. Let me have a few more words with you, Ayamonn, before we hurry to our separation.

Ayamonn [*quietly*]. There is nothing more to be said.

Sheila. There's a lot to be said, but hasty time won't stretch an hour a little out to let the words be spoken. Goodbye.

Ayamonn [*without turning his head*]. Goodbye.

[*Sheila is going slowly to the door when it partly opens, and half the head of Eeada peeps around it, amid an indistinct murmur as of praying outside.*

Eeada [*in half a whisper*]. Th' Protestan' Rector to see Mr. Breydon. [*The half of her head disappears, but her voice is heard saying a little more loudly*] This way, sir ; shure you know th' way well, anyhow.

[*The door opening a little more, the Rector comes in. He is a handsome man of forty. His rather pale face wears a grave scholarly look, but there is kindness in his grey eyes, and humorous lines round his mouth, though these are almost hidden by a short, brown, pointed beard, here and there about to turn grey. His black clothes are covered by a warm black topcoat, the blackness brightened a little by a vivid green scarf he is wearing round his neck, the fringed ends falling over his shoulders. He carries a black, broad-brimmed, soft clerical hat and a walking-stick in his left hand. He hastens towards Ayamonn, smiling genially, hand outstretched in greeting.*

Rector. My dear Ayamonn.   [*They shake hands.*

Ayamonn [*indicating Sheila*]. A friend of mine, sir — Sheila Moorneen. [*Moving a chair.*] Sit down, sir.

[*The Rector bows to Sheila ; she returns it quietly, and the Rector sits down.*

Rector. I've hurried from home in a cab, Ayamonn, to see you before the night was spent. [*His face forming grave lines*] I've a message for you — and a warning.

[*The door again is partly opened, and again the half head of Eeada appears, mid the murmurs outside, unheard the moment the door closes.*

Eeada. Two railwaymen to see you, Ayamonn ; full house tonight you're havin', eh ?

[*The half head goes, the door opens wider, and the two railwaymen come into the room. They are dressed drably as the other men are, but their peaked railway uniform caps (which they keep on their heads) have vivid scarlet bands around them. Their faces, too, are like the others, and stonily stare in front of them. They stand stock still when they see the Rector.*

1st Railwayman [*after a pause*]. 'Scuse us. Didn' know th' Protestan' Minister was here. We'll wait outside till he goes, Ayamonn.

Ayamonn. Th' Rector's a dear friend of mine, Bill ; say what you want, without fear — he's a friend.

1st Railwayman [*a little dubiously*]. Glad to hear it. You know th' sthrike starts tomorrow ?

Ayamonn. I know it now.

2nd Railwayman. Wouldn' give's th' extra shillin'. Offered us thruppence instead — th' lowsers ! [*Hastily — to Rector*] 'Scuse me, sir.

1st Railwayman [*taking a document from his breast pocket*]. An' th' meetin's proclaimed.

Rector [*to Ayamonn*]. That's part of what I came to tell you.

1st Railwayman [*handing document to Ayamonn*]. They handed that to our Committee this evening, a warrant of warning.

Rector [*earnestly — to Ayamonn*]. I was advised to warn you, Ayamonn, that the Authorities are prepared to use all the force they have to prevent the meeting.

Ayamonn. Who advised you, sir — th' Inspector ?

Rector. My churchwarden, Ayamonn. Come, even he has good in him.

Ayamonn. I daresay he has, sir ; I've no grudge against him.

Rector [*convinced*]. I know that, Ayamonn.

Ayamonn [*indicating document — to 1st Railwayman*]. What are th' Committee going to do with this ?

1st Railwayman. What would you do with it, Ayamonn ?

Ayamonn [*setting it alight at the fire and waiting till it falls to ashes*]. That !

2nd Railwayman [*gleefully*]. Exactly what we said you'd do !

Sheila [*haughtily*]. It's not what any sensible body would think he'd do.

1st Railwayman [*ignoring her*]. Further still, Ayamonn, me son, we want you to be one of the speakers on the platform at the meeting.

Sheila [*bursting forward and confronting the railwaymen*]. He'll do nothing of the kind — hear me ? Nothing of the kind. Cinder-tongued moaners, who's to make any bones about what you suffer, or how you die ? Ayamonn's his reading and his painting to do, and his mother to mind, more than lipping your complaints in front of gun muzzles, ready to sing a short and sudden death-song !

1st Railwayman [*a little awed*]. To see Ayamonn we came, an' not you, Miss.

2nd Railwayman [*roughly*]. Let th' man speak for himself.

Ayamonn [*catching Sheila's arm and drawing her back*]. It's my answer they're seeking. [*To railwaymen*] Tell the Committee, Bill, I'll be there ; and that they honour me when they set me in front of my brothers. The Minstrel Show must be forgotten.

Sheila [*vehemently — to the Rector*]. You talk to him ; you're his friend. You can influence him. Get him to stay away, man !

Rector. It's right for me to warn you, Ayamonn, and you, men, that the Authorities are determined to prevent the meeting ; and that you run a grave risk in defying them.

2nd Railwayman [*growling*]. We'll chance it. We've barked long enough, sir ; it's time to bite a bit now.

Sheila [*to Rector*]. Warning's no good ; that's not enough — forbid him to go. Show him God's against it !

Rector [*standing up*]. Who am I to say that God's against it ? You are too young by a thousand years to know the mind of God. If they be his brothers, he does well among them.

Sheila [*wildly*]. I'll get his mother to bar his way. She'll do more than murmur grand excuses.
　　[*She runs to the door of the other room, opens it, and goes in. After a few moments, she comes out slowly, goes to the*

*chair left idle by the Rector, sits down on it, leans her
arms on the table, and lets her head rest on them.*

Ayamonn. Well ?

Sheila [*brokenly*]. She's stretched out, worn and wan, fast
asleep, and I hadn't the heart to awaken her.

Rector [*holding out a hand to Ayamonn*]. Come to see me
before you go, Ayamonn. Be sure, wherever you may
be, whatever you may do, a blessing deep from my
breast is all around you. Goodbye. [*To the railwaymen*] Goodbye, my friends.

Railwaymen. Goodbye, sir.

[*The Rector glances at Sheila, decides to say nothing, and
goes towards the door; Ayamonn opens it for him, and he
goes out through the semicircle of men and women, still
softly singing before the Statue of the Queen of Eblana's
poor. Sheila's quiet crying heard as a minor note through
the singing.*

Oh, Queen of Eblana's poor children,
Bear swiftly our woe away,
An' give us a chance to live lightly
An hour of our life's dark day !

CURTAIN

*A part of Dublin City flowering into a street and a bridge across
the river Liffey. The parapets are seen to the right and left so
that the bridge fills most of the scene before the onlooker. The
distant end of the bridge leads to a street flowing on to a point
in the far distance; and to the right and left of this street are
tall gaunt houses, mottled with dubious activities, with
crowds of all sorts of men and women burrowing in them in a
pathetic search for a home. These houses stand along another
street running parallel with the river. In the distance, where
the street, leading from the bridge, ends in a point of space, to the
right, soars the tapering silver spire of a church; and to the left,
Nelson's Pillar, a deep red, pierces the sky, with Nelson, a deep
black, on its top, looking over everything that goes on around
him. A gloomy grey sky is over all, so that the colours of the
scene are made up of the dark houses, the brown parapets of the
bridge, the grey sky, the silver spire, the red pillar, and Nelson's
black figure.*

*On one of the bridge parapets a number of the men seen in
the previous scenes are gathered together, their expressionless
faces hidden by being bent down towards their breasts. Some
sit on the parapets, some lounge against the gaunt houses at the
corner of the street leading from the bridge, and, in one corner, a
man stands wearily against the parapet, head bent, an unlit pipe
dropping from his mouth, apparently forgotten. The sun shines
on pillar and church spire, but there is no sign of sun where
these people are.*

*On the pavement, opposite to where the men sit, nearer to this
end of the bridge, sit Eeada, Dympna, and Finnoola, dressed so
in black that they appear to be enveloped in the blackness of a dark*

night. In front of Eeada is a drab-coloured basket in which cakes and apples are spending an idle and uneasy time. Dympna has a shallower basket holding decadent blossoms, and a drooping bunch of violets hangs from a listless hand.

Eeada [*drowsily*]. This spongy leaden sky's Dublin ; those tomby houses is Dublin too — Dublin's scurvy body ; an' we're Dublin's silver soul. [*She spits vigorously into the street.*] An' that's what Eeada thinks of th' city's soul an' body !

Dympna. You're more than right, Eeada, but I wouldn't be too harsh. [*Calling out in a sing-song way*] Violets, here, on'y tuppence a bunch ; tuppence a bunch, th' fresh violets !

Eeada [*calling out in a sing-song voice*]. Apples an' cakes, on'y tuppence a head here for th' cakes ; ripe apples a penny apiece !

Dympna. Th' sun is always at a distance, an' th' chill grey is always here.

Finnoola. Half-mournin' skies for ever over us, frownin' out any chance of merriment that came staggerin' to us for a little support.

Eeada. That's Dublin, Finnoola, an' th' sky over it. Sorrow's a slush under our feet, up to our ankles, an' th' deep drip of it constant overhead.

Dympna. A graveyard where th' dead are all above th' ground.

Eeada. Without a blessed blink of rest to give them hope. An' she cockin' herself up that she stands among other cities as a queen o' counsel, laden with

knowledge, afire with th' song of great men, enough
to overawe all livin' beyond th' salty sea, undher
another sun be day, an' undher a different moon be
night.   [*They drowse, with heads bent lower.*

1st Man [*leaning wearily against the parapet*]. Golden
Gander'll do it, if I'm e'er a thrue prophet. [*Raising
his voice a little*] He'll flash past th' winnin' post like an
arra from th' bow, in the five hundhred guinea West's
Awake Steeplechase Championship.

2nd Man [*drowsily contradicting*]. In me neck he will!
He'd have a chance if it was a ramble. Copper
Goose'll leave him standin', if I'm e'er a thrue prophet.

Eeada [*waking up slightly*]. Prophets? Do me ears deceive
me, or am I afther hearin' somebody say prophets?

Dympna. You heard a murmur of it, Eeada, an' it's a bad
word to hear, remindin' us of our low estate at th'
present juncture. Th' prophets we once had are well
hidden behind God be now, an' no wondher, for we
put small pass on them, an' God in His generous
anger's showin' us what it is to be saddled with
Johnnies-come-marchin'-home, all song an' shirt an'
no surety.

Finnoola [*shaking her head sadly*]. A gold-speckled candle,
white as snow, was Dublin once; yellowish now,
leanin' sideways, an' guttherin' down to a last shaky
glimmer in th' wind o' life.

Eeada. Well, we've got Guinness's Brewery still, givin'
us a needy glimpse of a betther life an hour or so on a
Saturday night, though I hold me hand at praisin' th'
puttin' of Brian Boru's golden harp on every black
porther bottle, destined to give outsiders a false im-
C.P.—III   N

pression of our pride in th' tendher an' dauntless
memories of th' past.

[*The Rector and the Inspector appear at the farther end of the
bridge, and come over it towards where the men and
women are. The Rector is dressed in immaculate black,
wears a glossy tall hat, and carries a walking-stick. He
has shed his topcoat, but wears his green scarf round his
neck. The Inspector is clad in a blue uniform, slashed
with silver epaulettes on the shoulders, and silver braid
on collar and cuffs. He wears a big blue helmet, back
and front peaks silver-bordered, and from a long silver
spike on the top flows a graceful plume of crimson hair.
On the front is a great silver crown throned on a circle of
red velvet. A sword, in a silver scabbard, hangs by his
side. He is wearing highly-polished top-boots. They
both pause on the bridge, the Rector looking pensively down
over the parapet at the flowing river.*

Inspector. It was a great wedding, sir. A beautiful bride
and an elegant bridegroom ; a distinguished congregation, and the Primate in his fine sermon did justice to
the grand occasion, sir. Fittingly ended, too, by the
organ with *The Voice that Breathed o'er Eden.*

Rector [*apparently not very interested*]. Oh yes, yes ; quite.

Inspector. Historic disthrict, this, round here : head-
quarters of a Volunteer Corp in Grattan's time — not,
of course, that I agree with Grattan. A great-great-
grandfather of mine was one of the officers.

Rector. Oh yes ; was he ?

Inspector. Yes. Strange uniform he wore : richly black,
with sky-blue facings, a yellow breast-piece, ribbed with
red braid, and, capping all, a huge silver helmet having
a yellow plume soaring over it from the right-hand side.

Rector [*smiling*]. Your own's not too bad, Mr. Church-warden.

Inspector. Smart ; but a bit too sombre, I think, sir.

Eeada [*whining towards them*]. On'y a penny each, th' rosy apples, lovely for th' chiselurs — Jasus ! what am I sayin' ? Lovely for th' little masters an' little misthresses, stately, in their chandeliered an' carpeted dwellin'-houses ; or a cake — on'y tuppence a piece — daintily spiced, an' tastin' splendid.

Dympna [*whining towards them*]. Tuppence, here, th' bunch o' violets, fit for to go with th' white an' spotless cashmere gown of our radiant Lady o' Fair Dealin'.

Eeada [*deprecatingly*]. What are you sayin', woman ? That's a Protestan' ministher, indeed, gentleman, Dympna !

Dympna. Me mind slipped for a poor minute ; but it's pity he'll have on us, an' regulate our lives with what'll bring a sudden cup o' tea within fair reach of our hands.

Eeada. Apples, here, penny each, rosy apples, picked hardly an hour ago from a laden three ; cakes tuppence on'y, baked over scented turf as th' dawn stepped over th' blue-gowned backs o' th' Dublin Mountains.

Dympna. Tuppence a bunch, th' violets, shy an' dhrunk with th' dew o' th' mornin' ; fain to lie in the white bosom of a high-born lady, or fit into th' lapel of a genuine gentleman's Sunday courtin' coat.

[*The Rector takes a few coins from his pocket and throws them to the women, who pick them up and sink into silence again.*

Inspector. Swift, too, must have walked about here with the thorny crown of madness pressing ever deeper into his brain.

Rector [*indicating the men and women*]. Who are these?

Inspector [*indifferent*]. Those? Oh, flotsam and jetsam. A few of them dangerous at night, maybe; but harmless during the day.

Rector. I've read that tens of thousands of such as those followed Swift to the grave.

Inspector. Indeed, sir? A queer man, the poor demented Dean; a right queer man.

> [*A sleepy lounger suddenly gives a cough, gives his throat a hawk, and sends a big spit on to one of the Inspector's polished boots, then sinks back into sleep again.*

Inspector [*springing back with an angry exclamation*]. What th' hell are you after doing, you rotten lizard! Looka what you've done, you mangy rat!

> [*He takes hold of the lounger and shakes him sharply.*

2nd Man [*sleepily resentful*]. Eh, there! Wha' th' hell?

Inspector [*furiously*]. You spat on my boots, you tousled toad — my boots, boots, boots!

2nd Man [*frightened and bewildered*]. Boots, sir? Is it me, sir? Not me, sir. Musta been someone else, sir.

Inspector [*shaking him furiously*]. You, you, you!

2nd Man. Me, sir? Never spit in public in me life, sir. Makin' a mistake, sir. Musta been someone else.

Rector. Inspector Finglas! Remember you wear the King's uniform! Quiet, quiet, man!

Inspector [*subsiding*]. Pardon me. I lost my temper. I'm more used to a blow from a stone than a dirty spit on my boot.

Rector [*shuddering a little*]. Let us go from here. Things here frighten me, for they seem to look with wonder on our ease and comfort.

Inspector. Frighten you ? Nonsense — and with me !

Rector. Things here are of a substance I dare not think about, much less see and handle. Here, I can hardly bear to look upon the same thing twice.

Inspector. There you are, and as I've said so often, Breydon's but a neat slab of a similar slime.

Rector. You wrong yourself to say so : Ayamonn Breydon has within him the Kingdom of Heaven. [*He pauses.*] And so, indeed, may these sad things we turn away from.   [*They pass out.*

Eeada [*thinking of the coins given*]. Two tiny sixpences — fourpence a head. Oh, well, beggars can't be choosers. But isn't it a hard life to be grindin' our poor bums to powder, for ever squattin' on the heartless pavements of th' Dublin streets !

Dympna. Ah, what is it all to us but a deep-written testament o' gloom : grey sky over our heads, brown an' dusty streets undher our feet, with th' black an' bitther Liffey flowin' through it all.

Eeada [*mournfully*]. We've dhrifted down to where there's nothin'. Younger I was when every quiet-clad evenin' carried a jaunty jewel in her bosom. Tormented with joy I was then as to whether I'd parade th' thronged sthreets on th' arm of a 16th Lancer, his black-breasted crimson coat a sight to see, an' a black plume droopin' from his haughty helmet ; or lay claim to a red-breasted Prince o' Wales's Own, th' red plume in his hat a flame over his head.

Dympna. It was a 15th King's Own Hussar for me, Eeada, with his rich blue coat an' its fairyland o' yellow braid, two yellow sthripes down his trousers, an' a red bag an' plume dancin' on his busby.

Eeada. Lancers for me, Dympna.

Dympna. Hussars for me, Eeada.

Eeada. An' what for you, Finnoola ?

Finnoola. What would a girl, born in a wild Cork valley, among the mountains, brought up to sing the songs of her fathers, what would she choose but the patched coat, shaky shoes, an' white hungry face of th' Irish rebel ? But their shabbiness was threaded with th' colours from the garments of Finn Mac Cool of th' golden hair, Goll Mac Morna of th' big blows, Caoilte of th' flyin' feet, an' Oscar of th' invincible spear.

Eeada [*nudging Dympna*]. That was some time ago, if y'ask me.

    [*Brennan comes slowly over the bridge from the far side. His melodeon is hanging on his back. He looks around for a likely place to play. He leans against a parapet, some distance off, and unslings his melodeon from his back.*

Eeada. Here's that oul' miser creepin' after coppers, an' some bank bulgin' with what he has in it already.

2nd Man [*waking suddenly, spitting out vigorously, and speaking venomously*]. Rowlin' in th' coin o' th' realm—bastard !
    [*He sinks into a coma again.*

Brennan [*giving himself confidence*]. Evenin', ladies an' gentlemen. Good thing to be alive when th' sun's kind. [*They take no heed of what he says. Brennan sighs ; then plays a few preliminary notes on the melodeon to make sure it is in tune. He begins to sing in a voice that was once a mellow baritone, but now is a little husky with age, now and again quavering a little on the higher notes in the song. Singing :]*

I stroll'd with a fine maid far out in th' counthry,
Th' blossoms around us all cryin' for dew ;
On a violet-clad bench, sure, I sat down beside her,
An' tuck'd up my sleeves for to tie up her shoe.
An' what's that to anyone whether or no
If I came to th' fore when she gave me th' cue ?
She clos'd her eyes tight as she murmur'd full low,
Be good enough, dear, for to tie up my shoe.

Eeada [with muttered indignation]. Isn't that outrageous, now ; on a day like this, too, an' in a sober mood !

Dympna. In front o' decent women as well !

1st Man [waking up suddenly]. Disturbin' me dhreams of Golden Gandher gallopin' home to win in a canther !

Brennan [singing] :

Th' hawthorn shook all her perfume upon us,
Red poppies saluted, wherever they grew,
Th' joyous exertion that flaunted before me,
When I tuck'd up my sleeves for to fasten her shoe.
An' what's it to anyone, whether or no
I learn'd in that moment far more than I knew,
As she lifted her petticoat, shyly an' slow,
An' I tuck'd up my sleeves for to fasten her shoe ?

The heathery hills were all dancin' around us,
False things in th' world turn'd out to be thrue,
When she put her arms round me, an' kiss'd me an'
    murmur'd,
You've neatly an' tenderly tied up my shoe.

An' what's that to anyone whether or no,
I ventur'd quite gamely to see th' thing through,
When she lifted her petticoat, silent an' slow,
An' I tuck'd up my sleeves for to tie up her shoe?

[*Some pennies have been thrown from the windows of the
houses. Brennan picks them up, and taking off a shabby,
wide-brimmed hat, bestows a sweeping bow on the houses.
During the singing of the last verse of the song, Ayamonn
and Roory have strolled in, and have listened to the old
man singing while they leant against the balustrade of
the bridge. The scene has grown darker as the old man
is singing his song, for the sun is setting.*

2nd Man [*waking up suddenly*]. Off with you, old man,
thinkin' to turn our thoughts aside from th' way we
are, an' th' worn-out hope in front of us.

1st Man [*waking up — wrathfully*]. Get to hell outa that,
with your sootherin' songs o' gaudy idleness!

Eeada. Makin' his soul, at his age, he ought to be,
instead o' chantin' ditties th' way you'd fear what
would come upon you in th' darkness o' th' night, an'
ne'er a sword be your side either.

3rd Man. Away with you an' your heathen songs to parts
renowned for ignorance an' shame!

Finnoola. Away to where light women are plenty, an' free
to open purple purses to throw you glitterin' coins!

[*Brennan slings his melodeon on to his back, puts his hat back
on his head, and wends his way across the bridge.*

Roory [*as he passes*]. Isn't it a wondher, now, you wouldn't
sing an Irish song, free o' blemish, instead o' one
thickly speckled with th' lure of foreign enthertain-
ment?

[*Brennan heeds him not, but crosses the bridge and goes out.
The men and women begin to sink into drowsiness again.*

Ayamonn. Let him be, man ; he sang a merry song well,
and should have got a fairer greeting.

Roory [*taking no notice of Ayamonn's remark — to the men and
women*]. Why didn't yous stop him before he began ?
Pearl of th' White Breasts, now, or *Battle Song o' Munster*
that would pour into yous Conn's battle-fire of th'
hundhred fights. Watchman o' Tara he was, his arm
reachin' over deep rivers an' high hills, to dhrag out a
host o' sthrong enemies shiverin' in shelthers. Leadher
of Magh Femon's Host he was, Guardian of Moinmoy,
an' Vetheran of our river Liffey, flowin' through a city
whose dhrinkin' goblets once were made of gold, ere
wise men carried it with frankincense an' myrrh to
star-lit Bethlehem.

Eeada [*full of sleep — murmuring low*]. Away you, too,
with your spangled memories of battle-mad warriors
buried too deep for words to find them. Penny, here,
each, th' ripe apples.

Dympna [*sleepily — in a low murmur*]. Away, an' leave us
to saunter in sleep, an' crave out a crust in the grey
kingdom of quietness. Tuppence a bunch the fresh
violets.

Finnoola [*sleepily*]. Run away, son, to where bright eyes
can see no fear, an' white hands, idle, are willin' to
buckle a sword on a young man's thigh.

1st Man [*with a sleepy growl*]. Get to hell where gay life
has room to move, an' hours to waste, an' white praise
is sung to coloured shadows. Time is precious here.

2nd and 3rd Men [*together—murmuringly*]. Time is precious here.

Ayamonn. Rouse yourselves ; we hold a city in our hands !

Eeada [*in a very low, but bitter voice*]. It's a bitther city.

Dympna [*murmuring the same way*]. It's a black an' bitther city.

Finnoola [*speaking the same way*]. It's a bleak, black, an' bitther city.

1st Man. Like a batthered, tatthered whore, bullied by too long a life.

2nd Man. An' her three gates are castles of poverty, penance, an' pain.

Ayamonn. She's what our hands have made her. We pray too much and work too little. Meanness, spite, and common pattherns are woven thick through all her glory ; but her glory's there for open eyes to see.

Eeada [*bitterly — in a low voice*]. Take your fill of her glory, then ; for it won't last long with your headin' against them who hold the kingdom an' who wield th' power.

Dympna [*reprovingly*]. He means well, Eeada, an' he knows things hid from us ; an' we know his poor oul' mother's poor feet has worn out a pathway to most of our tumbling doorways, seekin' out ways o' comfort for us she sadly needs herself.

Eeada [*in a slightly livelier manner*]. Don't I know that well ! A shabby sisther of ceaseless help she is, blind to herself for seein' so far into th' needs of others. May th' Lord be restless when He loses sight of her !

Finnoola. For all her tired look an' wrinkled face, a pure white candle she is, blessed this minute by St. Colmkille of th' gentle manner, or be Aidan, steeped in th' lore o' Heaven, or be Lausereena of th' silver voice an' snowy vestments — th' blue cloak o' Brigid be a banner over her head for ever !

The Other Two Women [together]. Amen.

Roory [impatiently]. We waste our time here — come on !

Ayamonn. Be still, man ; it was dark when th' spirit of God first moved on th' face of th' waters.

Roory. There's nothin' movin' here but misery. Gun peal an' slogan cry are th' only things to startle them. We're useless here. I'm off, if you're not.

Ayamonn. Wait a moment, Roory. No-one knows what a word may bring forth. Th' leaves an' blossoms have fallen, but th' three isn't dead.

Roory [hotly]. An' d'ye think talkin' to these tatthered second-hand ghosts'll bring back Heaven's grace an' Heaven's beauty to Kaithleen ni Houlihan ?

Ayamonn. Roory, Roory, your Kaithleen ni Houlihan has th' bent back of an oul' woman as well as th' walk of a queen. We love th' ideal Kaithleen ni Houlihan, not because she is false, but because she is beautiful ; we hate th' real Kaithleen ni Houlihan, not because she is true, but because she is ugly.

Roory [disgusted]. Aw, for God's sake, man !

[*He hurries off angrily.*

Eeada [calling scornfully after him]. God speed you, scut !

Ayamonn [placing a hand softly on Eeada's head]. Forget him, an' remember ourselves, and think of what we can do

to pull down th' banner from dusty bygones, an' fix it up
in th' needs an' desires of today.

[*The scene has now become so dark that things are but dimly
seen, save the silver spire and the crimson pillar in the
distance; and Ayamonn's head set in a streak of sunlight,
looking like the severed head of Dunn-Bo speaking out of
the darkness.*]

Finnoola. Songs of Osheen and Sword of Oscar could do
nothing to tire this city of its shame.

Ayamonn. Friend, we would that you should live a
greater life ; we will that all of us shall live a greater
life. Our sthrike is yours. A step ahead for us today ;
another one for you tomorrow. We who have known,
and know, the emptiness of life shall know its fullness.
All men and women quick with life are fain to venture
forward. [*To Eeada*] The apple grows for you to eat.
[*To Dympna*] The violet grows for you to wear. [*To
Finnoola*] Young maiden, another world is in your
womb.

Eeada [*still a little gloomily*]. Th' soldiers will be chasin'
us with gunfire ; th' polis hoppin' batons off our
heads ; our sons an' husbands hurried off to prison, to
sigh away th' time in gloomier places than those they
live in now.

Ayamonn. Don't flinch in th' first flare of a fight. [*He
looks away from them and gazes meditatively down the
river.*] Take heart of grace from your city's hidden
splendour. [*He points with an outstretched hand.*] Oh,
look ! Look there ! Th' sky has thrown a gleaming
green mantle over her bare shoulders, bordhered with
crimson, an' with a hood of gentle magenta over her
handsome head — look !

[*The scene has brightened, and bright and lovely colours are being brought to them by the caress of the setting sun. The houses on the far side of the river now bow to the visible world, decked in mauve and burnished bronze ; and the men that have been lounging against them now stand stalwart, looking like fine bronze statues, slashed with scarlet.*

Ayamonn. Look ! Th' vans an' lorries rattling down th' quays, turned to bronze an' purple by th' sun, look like chariots forging forward to th' battle-front.

[*Eeada, rising into the light, now shows a fresh and virile face, and she is garbed in a dark-green robe, with a silvery mantle over her shoulders.*

Eeada [*gazing intently before her*]. Shy an' lovely, as well as battle-minded !

[*Dympna rises now to look where Ayamonn is pointing. She is dressed like Eeada, and her face is aglow. The men have slid from the parapets of the bridge, turning, too, to look where Ayamonn is pointing. Their faces are aglow, like the women's, and they look like bronze statues, slashed with a vivid green. Finnoola rises, last, and stands a little behind the others, to look at the city showing her melody of colours. Finnoola is dressed in a skirt of a brighter green than the other two women, a white bodice slashed with black, and a flowing silvery scarf is round her waist.*

Finnoola. She's glowin' like a song sung be Osheen himself, with th' golden melody of his own harp helpin' !

1st Man [*puzzled*]. Something funny musta happened, for, 'clare to God, I never noticed her shinin' that way before.

2nd Man. Looka the loungers opposite have changed to

sturdy men of bronze, and th' houses themselves are
gay in purple an' silver !

3rd Man. Our tired heads have always haunted far too
low a level.

Ayamonn. There's th' great dome o' th' Four Courts
lookin' like a golden rose in a great bronze bowl ! An'
th' river flowin' below it, a purple flood, marbled with
ripples o' scarlet ; watch th' seagulls glidin' over it —
like restless white pearls astir on a royal breast. Our
city's in th' grip o' God !

1st Man [*emotionally*]. Oh, hell, it's grand !

Eeada. Blessed be our city for ever an' ever.

Ayamonn [*lifting his right hand high*]. Home of th' Ostmen,
of th' Norman, an' th' Gael, we greet you ! Greet
you as you catch a passing hour of loveliness, an' hold
it tightly to your panting breast ! [*He sings :*]
Fair city, I tell thee our souls shall not slumber
Within th' warm beds of ambition or gain ;
Our hands shall stretch out to th' fullness of labour,
Till wondher an' beauty within thee shall reign.

The Rest [*singing together*] :
We vow to release thee from anger an' envy,
To dhrive th' fierce wolf an' sly fox from thy gate,
Till wise men an' matrons an' virgins shall murmur
O city of splendour, right fair is thy fate !

Ayamonn [*singing*] :
Fair city, I tell thee that children's white laughter,
An' all th' red joy of grave youth goin' gay,
Shall make of thy streets a wild harp ever sounding,
Touch'd by th' swift fingers of young ones at play !

The Rest [*singing*] :
    We swear to release thee from hunger an' hardship,
    From things that are ugly an' common an' mean ;
    Thy people together shall build a brave city,
    Th' fairest an' finest that ever was seen !

> [*Finnoola has been swaying her body to the rhythm of the
> song, and now, just as the last part is ending, she swings
> out on to the centre of the bridge in a dance. The tune,
> played on a flute by someone, somewhere, is that of a
> Gavotte, or an air of some dignified and joyous dance,
> and, for a while, it is played in fairly slow time. After
> some time it gets quicker, and Ayamonn dances out to
> meet her. They dance opposite each other, the people
> around clapping their hands to the tap of the dancers'
> feet. The two move around in this spontaneous dance,
> she in a golden pool of light, he in a violet-coloured
> shadow, now and again changing their movements so that
> she is in the violet-coloured shadow, and he in the golden
> pool.*

Eeada [*loudly*]. The finest colours God has to give are all
    around us now.

Finnoola [*as she dances*]. The Sword of Light is shining !

1st Man [*exultantly*]. Sons an' daughters of princes are we
    all, an' one with th' race of Milesius !
    [*The dance comes to an end with Ayamonn and Finnoola
    having their arms round each other.*

Eeada. Praise God for th' urge of jubilation in th' heart
    of th' young.

1st Man. An' for th' swiftness of leg an' foot in th' heart
    of a dance.

2nd Man. An' for th' dhream that God's right hand still
holds all things firmly.

> [*The scene darkens slightly. Ayamonn loosens his hold on
> Finnoola and raises his head to listen to something. In the
> distance can be heard the sound of many feet marching in
> unison.*

Finnoola [*a little anxiously*]. What is it you're listenin'
to ?

Ayamonn. I must go ; goodbye, fair maid, goodbye.

Finnoola. Is it goin' to go you are, away from the fine
things shinin' around us ? Amn't I good enough for
you ?

Ayamonn [*earnestly*]. You're lovely stayin' still, an'
brimmin' over with a wilder beauty when you're
dancin' ; but I must go. May you marry well, an'
rear up children fair as Emer was, an' fine as Oscar's
son ; an' may they be young when Spanish ale foams
high on every hand, an' wine from th' royal Pope's a
common dhrink ! Goodbye.

> [*He kisses her, and goes across the bridge, passing out of sight
> on the farther bank of the river. The figures left behind
> have shrunk a little; the colours have faded a good deal,
> and all look a little puzzled and bewildered. The
> loungers have fallen back to the walls of the houses, and,
> though they do not lie against them, they stand close to
> them, as if seeking their shelter. There is a fairly long
> pause before anyone speaks. They stand apart, as if shy
> of each other's company.*

Eeada [*murmuringly*]. Penny each, th' ripe apples. Who
was it that spoke that time ? Jasus ! I musta been
dhreamin'.

Dympna [*in a bewildered voice*]. So must I, th' way I thought I was lost in a storm of joy, an' many colours, with gay clothes adornin' me.

Finnoola [*puzzled and dreamy*]. Dhreamin' I musta been when I heard strange words in a city nearly smothered be stars, with God guidin' us along th' banks of a purple river, all of us clad in fresh garments, fit to make Osheen mad to sing a song of the revelry dancin' in an' out of God's own vision.

Eeada [*murmuringly, but a little peevishly*]. For God's sake give over dwellin' on oul' songs sung by Osheen, th' way you'd be kindlin' a fire o' glory round some poor bog-warbler chantin' hoarse ditties in a sheltered corner of a windy street. [*Very sleepily*] Th' dewy violets, here, on'y tuppence a bunch — Jasus, apples I mean !
    [*Now the tramp-tramp of marching men is heard more plainly.*

Dympna [*a little more awake*]. Tuppence each, the bunch of vio—— What can that be, now ?

1st Man [*gloomily, but with a note of defiance in his voice*]. Th' thramp of marchin' soldiers out to prevent our meetin' an' to stop our sthrike.

2nd Man [*in a burst of resolution*]. We'll have both, in spite of them !
    [*The scene darkens deeply now. In the pause following the 2nd Man's remark, nothing is heard but the sound of the tramping feet ; then through this threatening sound comes the sound of voices singing quietly, voices that may be of those on and around the bridge, or of those singing some little distance away.*

C.P.—III   O

Voices [singing quietly] :
    We swear to release thee from hunger and hardship,
    From things that are ugly and common and mean ;
    Thy people together shall build a great city,
    The finest and fairest that ever was seen.

CURTAIN

*Part of the grounds surrounding the Protestant church of St.
Burnupus. The grounds aren't very beautiful, for they are in
the midst of a poor and smoky district; but they are trim, and,
considering the surroundings, they make a fair show. An iron
railing running along the back is almost hidden by a green and
golden hedge, except where, towards the centre, a fairly wide
wooden gate gives admittance to the grounds. Beyond this gateway, on the pathway outside, is a street lamp. Shrubs grow
here and there, and in the left corner, close to the hedge, are lilac
and laburnum trees in bloom. To the right is the porch of the
church, and part of the south wall, holding a long, rather narrow
window, showing, in coloured glass, the figures of SS. Peter and
Paul. Some distance away from the porch is a rowan tree, also
in blossom, its white flowers contrasting richly with the gay
yellow of the laburnum and the royal purple of the lilac. The
rest of the grounds are laid out in grass, except for the path leading
from the gateway to the entrance of the church. It is a warm,
sunny evening, the Vigil of Easter, and the Rector is sitting on
a deck-chair, before a table, on which are some books and papers.
He is evidently considering the services that are to be held in the
church on the following day.*

*The Rector is wearing a thick black cassock lined with red
cloth, and at the moment is humming a verse of a hymn softly to
himself, as he marks down notes on a slip of paper before him. A
square black skull-cap covers his head.*

Rector [*singing to himself, softly*]:
    As Thou didst rise from Thy grim grave,
    So may we rise and stand to brave

Th' power bestow'd on fool or knave ;
We beseech Thee !

[*The verger comes out from the porch and walks towards the
Rector.   He is bald as an egg, and his yellowish face is
parched and woebegone-looking.   He is a man of sixty,
and shows it.   His ordinary clothes are covered with a
long black mantle of thin stuff, with a small cape-like
addition or insertion of crimson velvet on the shoulders.*]

Rector [*noticing the verger beside him*]. Hymn 625 : we must
have that as our opening hymn, Samuel.

Samuel. It's got to go in, sir.

Rector. As you say — it's got to go in.   Did you want to
speak to me, Samuel ?

Samuel. Excuse me, sir, for what I'm agoin' to say.

Rector [*encouragingly*]. Yes, yes, Samuel, go on.

Samuel [*mysteriously*]. Somethin's afther happenin', sir,
that I don't like.

Rector [*turning a little in his chair.*]. Oh ! What's that,
Sam ?

Samuel. Mr. Fosther was here this mornin' runnin' a
hand through th' daffodils sent for Easther, an' found
somethin' he didn't like.

Rector. Yes ?

Samuel. It's not for me to remark on anything that
manœuvres out in front o' me, or to slip in a sly word
on things done, said, or thought on, be th' pastors,
masthers, or higher individuals of th' congregation ;
but, sometimes, sir, there comes a time when a true
man should, must speak out.

Rector [*with a sigh*]. And the time has come to say something now — what is it, Sam ?

Samuel [*in a part whisper*]. This mornin', sir, and th' dear
spring sun shinin' through th' yellow robes of Pether
an' th' purple robes o' Paul, an' me arrangin' th' books
in th' pews, who comes stealin' in, but lo and behold
you, Fosther an' Dowzard to have a squint round.
Seein' they're Select Vesthrymen, I couldn't ask them
why they were nosin' about in th' silence of th' church
on an ordinary week-day mornin'.

Rector [*patiently*]. Yes ; but a long time ago, you said
something about daffodils.

Samuel. I'm comin' at a gallop to them, sir.

Rector. Good ; well, let's hear about the daffodils.

Samuel. Aha, says I, when I seen th' two prowlers with
their heads close together, whisperin', aha, says I,
there's somethin' on th' carpet.

Rector. Is what you have to tell me something to do with
Dowzard and Foster, or the daffodils ?

Samuel. Wait till you hear ; sometimes Fosther an'
Dowzard'll be to th' fore, an' sometimes th' daffodils.
What can these two oul' codgers be up to? says I,
sidlin' up to where they were, hummin' a hymn.

Rector. Humming a hymn ? I'm glad to hear it ; for
I'd be surprised to hear either of them humming a
hymn.

Samuel. Me it was, sir, who was hummin' th' hymn ; for
in a church, I like me thoughts to go with th' work
I'm doin', if you know what I mean.

Rector [*impatiently*]. It'll be nightfall before you get to the daffodils, man.

Samuel. Wait till you hear, sir. There I was gettin' close to them be degrees, when, all of a sudden, didn't Fosther turn on me, shoutin' " Are you goin' to be a party to th' plastherin' of Popish emblems over a Protestan' church ? "

Rector. Popish emblems ?

Samuel. Th' daffodils, sir.

Rector. The daffodils ? But they simply signify the new life that Spring gives ; and we connect them in a symbolic way, quite innocently, with our Blessed Lord's Rising. And a beautiful symbol they are : daffodils that come before the swallow dares, and take the winds of March with beauty. Shakespeare, Sam.

Samuel [*lifting his eyes skywards and pointing upwards*]. Altogether too high up for poor me, sir. [*He bends down close to the Rector's ear.*] When he seen the cross o' daffodils made be Breydon, he near went daft. [*A pause, as if Samuel expected the Rector to speak, but he stays silent.*] God knows what'll be th' upshot if it's fixed to the Communion Table, sir. [*Another slight pause.*] Is it really to go there, sir ? Wouldn't it look a little more innocent on th' pulpit, sir ?

Rector [*in a final voice*]. I will place it myself in front of the Communion Table, and, if Mr. Foster or Mr. Dowzard ask anything more about it, say that it has been placed there by me. And, remember, when you say Mr. Foster and Mr. Dowzard, it's to be Mr. Breydon too. [*He hands some leaflets to Samuel.*] Distribute these through the pews, Sam, please. The arranging of the flowers is finished, is it ?

Samuel. Yessir ; all but the cross.

Rector. I will see to that myself. Thanks, Sam.
    [*Samuel goes off into the church, and the Rector, leaning back in his chair with a book in his hand, chants softly.*

Rector [*chanting*] :
        May wonders cease when we grow tame,
        Or worship greatness in a name ;
        May love for man be all our fame,
        We beseech Thee !
    [*As he pauses to meditate for a moment, Mrs. Breydon is seen coming along, outside the hedge. She enters by the gate, and comes over to the Rector. Sheila has come with her, but lags a little behind when they enter the grounds. The Rector rises quickly from his chair to greet Mrs. Breydon.*

Rector [*warmly*]. My dear Mrs. Breydon ! Hasn't it been a lovely day ? The weather promises well for Easter.

Mrs. Breydon. It would be good if other things promised as well as the weather, sir.

Rector. We must be patient, and more hopeful, my friend. From the clash of life new life is born.

Mrs. Breydon. An' often new life dies in th' clash too. Ah, when he comes, sir, speak th' word that will keep my boy safe at home, or here.

Rector [*laying a gentle hand on her arm*]. I wish I could, dear friend ; I wish I could.

Mrs. Breydon. His mind, like his poor father's, hates what he sees as a sham ; an' shams are powerful things,

mustherin' at their broad backs guns that shoot, big
jails that hide their foes, and high gallows to choke th'
young cryin' out against them when th' stones are
silent.

Rector. Let those safely sheltered under the lawn of the
bishop, the miniver of the noble, the scarlet and
ermine of the judge, say unto him, this thing you
must not do ; I won't, for sometimes out of the
mouths of even babes and sucklings cometh wisdom.

Sheila. If what's against him be so powerful, he is helpless ; so let this power go on its way of darkened
grandeur, and let Ayamonn sit safe by his own fireside.

[*To the left, on the path outside the hedge, the Inspector, in
full uniform, appears, evidently coming to see the Rector;
on the right, followed by the men and women of the
previous scenes, appears Ayamonn. He and the Inspector
meet at the gate. The Inspector and he halt. The
Inspector indicates he will wait for Ayamonn to pass, and
Ayamonn comes into the grounds towards the Rector.
The Inspector follows, but, in the grounds, stands a
little apart, nearer the hedge. The men and women
spread along the path outside, and stay still watching
those in the grounds from over the hedge. They hold
themselves erect, now ; their faces are still pale, but are
set with seams of resolution. Each is wearing in the
bosom a golden-rayed sun. Brennan comes in and, crossing
the grass, sidles over to sit down on the step of the porch.*

Rector [*shaking Ayamonn's hand*]. Ah, I'm so glad you've
come ; I hope you'll stay.

Ayamonn [*hastily.*] I come but to go. You got the cross of
daffodils ?

Rector. Your mother brought it to us ; it will hang in

front of our church's greatest promise. Come and place it there with your own loyal hands, Ayamonn.

Inspector. Loyal hands engaged in rough rending of the law and the rumpling-up of decency and order ; and all for what ? For what would but buy blacking for a pair of boots, or a sheet of glass to mend a broken window !

Brennan [*from his seat on the porch's step*]. He's right, Ayamonn, me son, he's right : money's the root of all evil.

Ayamonn [*to the Inspector*]. A shilling's little to you, and less to many ; to us it is our Shechinah, showing us God's light is near ; showing us the way in which our feet must go ; a sun-ray on our face ; the first step taken in the march of a thousand miles.

Inspector [*threateningly*]. I register a lonely warning here that the people of power today will teach a lesson many will remember for ever ; though some fools may not live long enough to learn it.

Mrs. Breydon. Stay here, my son, where safety is a green tree with a kindly growth.

Men and Women [*in chorus — above*]. He comes with us !

Sheila. Stay here where time goes by in sandals soft, where days fall gently as petals from a flower, where dark hair, growing grey, is never noticed.

Men and Women [*above*]. He comes with us !

Ayamonn [*turning towards them*]. I go with you !

Inspector [*vehemently*]. Before you go to carry out all your heated mind is set to do, I warn you for the last time that today swift horses will be galloping, and swords will be out of their scabbards !

Rector [*reprovingly — to Inspector*]. I hope you, at least, will find no reason to set your horses moving.

Inspector [*stiffly*]. I'll do my duty, sir ; and it would be a good thing if someone we all know did his in that state of life unto which it has pleased God to call him.

Rector [*losing his temper*]. Oh, damn it, man, when you repeat the Church's counsel, repeat it right ! Not *unto which it has pleased God to call him*, but *unto which it shall please God to call him.*

Inspector [*losing his temper too*]. Damn it, man, do you believe that what the fellow's doing now is the state of life unto which it has pleased God to call him ?

Rector [*hotly*]. I have neither the authority nor the know-ledge to deny it, though I have more of both than you, sir !
     [*The Inspector is about to answer angrily, but Sheila catches his arm.*

Sheila. Oh, cancel from your mind the harder things you want to say, an' do your best to save us from another sorrow !

Inspector [*shaking off Sheila's hand roughly, and going to the gateway, where he turns to speak again*]. Remember, all ! When swords are drawn and horses charge, the kindly Law, so fat with hesitation, swoons away, and sees not, hears not, cares not what may happen.

Mrs. Breydon [*angrily — up to the Inspector*]. Look at th' round world, man, an' all its wondhers, God made, flaming in it, an' what are you among them, standing here, or on a charging horse, but just a braided an' a tasselled dot !

[*The Inspector hurries off, to pause, and stands outside the hedge, to the right, the men and women shrinking back a little in awe to give him a passage.*

Mrs. Breydon [*to Ayamonn*]. Go on your way, my son, an' win. We'll welcome another inch of the world's welfare.

Rector [*shaking his hand*]. Go, and may the Lord direct you ! [*He smiles.*] The Inspector's bark is louder than his bite is deep.

Ayamonn. For the present — goodbye !

[*Ayamonn hurries away through the gate, pausing, outside the hedge to the left, turning to give a last look at the Inspector.*

Inspector. Bear back, my boy, when you see the horsemen charging !

[*He goes out by the right, and Ayamonn goes out left, followed by the men and the women. There is a slight pause.*

Rector [*briskly — to banish a gloomy feeling*]. Now, Mrs. Breydon, you run along to the vestry, and make us a good cup of tea — I'm dying for one. [*To Sheila*] You'll join us, Miss Moorneen, won't you?

Sheila [*immediately anxious*]. Oh no, thanks. I . . . I shouldn't even be here. I'm a Catholic, you know.

Rector. I know, and I'd be the last to ask you do anything you shouldn't ; but rest assured there's no canonical law against taking tea made by a Protestant. Off you go, and help Mrs. Breydon. I'll join you in a moment.

[*Sheila and Mrs. Breydon go off by the south wall of the church.*

Brennan [*as the Rector is gathering his books and papers from the table*]. Hey, sir ; hey there, sir ! It won't shatther th' community at large this disturbance, will it, eh ?

Rector. I hope not.

Brennan [*with a forced laugh*]. No, no, of course not. Bank of Ireland'll still stand, eh ? Ay. Ravenous to break in, some of them are, eh ? Ay, ay. Iron doors, iron doors are hard to open, eh ?

Rector [*going off to get his tea*]. I suppose so.

Brennan. Ay, are they. He supposes so ; only supposes — there's a responsible man for you !
[*The verger comes into the porch and bends over Brennan.*

Samuel [*in a hoarse whisper*]. Come in an' have a decko at our grand cross.

Brennan. Cross ? What cross ?

Samuel. One o' daffodils for Easther, to be put in front of th' Communion Table.

Brennan. Popery, be God !
[*Booing is heard a little distance away, followed by the rattling fall of a shower of stones.*

Brennan. What's that ; what's happenin' ?

Samuel [*going to back, and looking down the street*]. A crowd flingin' stones ; flingin' them at two men runnin' for their life.

Brennan [*nervously*]. Let's get into the church, quick. Throuble's beginnin' already.
[*They both go into the church, and Samuel closes the door. A crowd can be heard booing. Men and women, among them Eeada, Finnoola, Dympna, the Railwaymen, and the*

Lurchers who were on the bridge, pass across outside the hedge. The Leader carries a red flag, and all march with determination. They are all singing the following song:

Leaders [*singing*] :
  If we can't fire a gun, we can fire a hard stone,
  Till th' life of a scab shrivels into a moan ;

Crowd [*chorusing*] :
  Let it sink in what I say,
  Let me say it again —
  Though the Lord made an odd scab, sure, He also made men !

Leaders [*singing*] :
  Th' one honour he'll get is a dusty black plume,
  On th' head of th' nag taking him to the tomb ;

Crowd [*chorusing*] :
  Let it sink in what I say,
  Let me say it again :
  Th' scab's curs'd be th' workers, book, candle an' bell !

[They cross over and disappear. After a pause, Dowzard and Foster come running in ; they hurry through the gateway, and dash over to the church's porch.

[Dowzard is a big, beefy, red-faced man, rolls of flesh pouring out over the collar of his coat. His head is massive and bald, with jet-black tufts behind his ear, and a tiny fringe of it combed across high over his forehead. Foster is small and scraggy, with aggression for ever lurking in his cranky face, ready to leap into full view at the slightest opportunity. His cheeks and lips are shaven, but spikes of yellowish whiskers point defiantly out from under his chin. His voice is squeaky and, when it is strengthened in

*anger, it rises into a thin piping scream. Both are
dressed in the uniforms of railway foremen, blue cloth,
with silver buttons, and silver braid on Dowzard's
peaked hat and coat-sleeves, and gold braid on those of
Foster. Both have their coats tightly buttoned up on
them. They take off their peaked caps and wipe sweat
from their foreheads. Dowzard pushes the door.*

Dowzard. We're safe here in th' grounds ; Church
grounds sacred. Unguarded, verminous villains —
Papists, th' lot o' them !

Foster [*venomously*]. On' one o' their leaders a Select
Vestryman. On' thot domned Rector stondin' by
him. Steeped in Popery : sign o' th' cross ; turnin'
eastward sayin' th' Creed ; sung Communion — be
Gud, it's a public scondal !

Dowzard. Some o' them stones scorched me ear passin'
by. We shouldn't have worn our uniforms. Gave us
away. I knew we were in for it when they called us
scabs.

Foster. Scobs themselves ! Smoky, vonomous bastards !
I tull you I'd wear me uniform in th' Vutican. [*He
unbuttons his coat and shows that he is wearing a vivid orange
sash, bordered with blue.*] Thor's me sash for all tae see.
You should ha' stud with me, mon ; stud like th'
heroes o' Dully's Brae !

Dowzard [*shouting and knocking at door*]. Ey, there, in there,
come out, open th' blasted door an' help a half-dead
man !

[*The church door is opened, and the Rector, followed by the
verger and Brennan, comes out into the grounds.*

Rector. What's wrong ; what has happened ?

Dowzard. Th' Pope's bullies with hard stones have smitten us sore. Honest men, virtuous an' upright, loyal to th' law an' constitution, have this day been smitten sore with Popish stones — oh, me poor head !

Foster. St. Bartholomew's Day's dawnin' again, I'm tullin' yous, an' dismumbered Protestants'll lie on all th' sthreets !

Rector. You can't be badly hurt when you complain so grandly.

Foster. Stand up for th' ruffians be makin' luttle of our hurts, so do, ay, do. [*Noticing Brennan who has edged towards the gate and is about to go away.*] Eh, you, aren't you goin' to stay an' put tustimony to the fullness o' th' Protestan' feth ?

Brennan [*with slight mockery*]. Ay, I would, an' welcome, if I hodn't to go, forbye, at this hour of on uvery day, I mak' ut a rule tae be sturdy in th' readin' of a chapther o' God's word so's I won't hold on tae wordly things too strongly.   [*He goes out.*

Foster [*fiercely*]. A jully-fush Protestant ! [*To the Rector*] Look see, I tull you th' fires o' Smithfield 'ull be blazin' round Protestant bodies again, an' coloured lights 'ull be shown in th' Vatican windows soon !

Dowzard. An' we'll be th' first to go up in th' flames.

Rector [*laughing contemptuously*]. Nonsense, oh, nonsense.

Foster [*almost screaming*]. It's not nonsense, mon ! Every sable-robed Jesuit's goin' about chucklin', his honds twitchin' to pounce out on men like me here, an' Eddie Dowzard there, tae manacle us, head, hond, and fut, for th' wheel, th' thumbscrew, an' th' rack, an'

then finish us up at th' stake in a hoppy Romish auto-
dey-fey ! The Loyola boyos are out to fight another
buttle with th' men o' King Bully !

Rector [*amused*]. Well, let the Loyola boyos and King
Bully fight it out between them. I'm too busy to join
either side. Goodbye.

Foster [*catching his arm as he is going — viciously*]. You're
no' goin' tae be lut slide off like thot, now, with your
guilty conscience, mon. There's things to be done,
and things tae be ondone in yon church, there ; ay, ay.

Rector [*quietly*]. Indeed ?

Foster [*angrily — to Dowzard*]. Uh, speak, speak a word,
mon, on' don't leave ut all tae me.

Dowzard. First, sir, we want you to get rid o' Breydon
from the Vesthry an' from th' church.

Rector. Oh, indeed ?

Foster [*almost screaming*]. It's no' oh, indeed ; answer th'
question — plain yes or no !

Rector [*coldly*]. Gentlemen, Mr. Breydon stays in the
Vestry till the parishioners elect someone else ; as for
the church, God has seen fit to make him a member of
Christ, and it is not for me, or even for you, gentlemen,
to say that God did wrong.

Dowzard [*sneeringly*]. An' when did that wondherful thing
hoppen ?

Rector. At his baptism, as you yourself should know.

Foster [*with an agonised squeal*]. Popery, Popery, nothin' but
Popery ! Th' whole place's infusted with it !

[*The verger appears at the porch door with the cross of daffodils in his hand. It has a Keltic shape, the shafts made of the flowers, and the circle of vivid green moss. The verger shows it to Dowzard, behind the Rector's back, and Dowzard sidling over, takes it from him, the verger returning into the church again.*

Rector. And now be good enough, Mr. Foster, to let my arm go.

[*In the distance, a bugle-call sounding the charge is heard. Foster lets go of the Rector's arm; and they all listen.*

Foster [*gleefully*]. Aha, there's the bugle soundin' th' charge, an' soon the King's horses an' th' King's men'll be poundin' th' riothers undher their feet! Law an ordher in th' State an' law an' ordher in th' Church we must have. An' we're fightin' here as they're fightin' there — for th' Crown an' ceevil an' releegious liberty!

[*The sound of galloping horses is heard, followed by several volleys of rifle-fire. They all listen intently for a few moments.*

Foster [*gleefully*]. Hear that now? Your Breydon fullow'll soon be doshin' in here for th' church to hide him.

Rector. The cross of Christ be between him and all harm!

Dowzard [*dancing out in front of the Rector, holding out the cross — with exultant glee*]. The cross — a Popish symbol! There y'urre, see? A Popish symbol flourished in th' faces o' Protestant people! [*With a yell*] Ichabod!

Foster [*venomously*]. I'll no' stick it, no; I'll no' stick it. Look-see, th' rage kindlin' godly Luther is kindlin' me! Here, go, gimme a holt of thot. [*He snatches the cross of flowers from Dowzard, flings it on the ground, and dances on it.*] Th' bible on' th' crown! The twa on' a

C.P.—III   P

half, th' orange on' blue ; on' th' Dagon of Popery
undher our Protestant feet !

Dowzard [*wildly*]. Th' dhrum, th' dhrum, th' Protestant
dhrum !

> [*While Foster and Dowzard have been dancing about and
> shouting their last few words, the men and women have
> run frightened along the path, behind the hedge. Those
> running from the right, turn, and run back to the left;
> those running from the left, turn, and run back to the
> left again, passing each other as they run. They suddenly
> see the men and women running about behind the hedge,
> and at once plunge into the porch, almost knocking the
> Rector down.*

Foster [*as they fly — to the Rector*]. Out uh th' way, mon,
out uh th' way !

> [*After a pause Eeada comes running through the gate, into
> the garden, over to the Rector.*

Eeada [*beseechingly*]. Oh, sir, please let me into the church,
till all th' sthrife is over — no place's safe with the
soldiers firin' an' th' police runnin' mad in a flourish o'
batons !

Rector [*reassuringly*]. Be calm, be quiet, they won't touch
a woman.   They remain men, however furious they may
be for the moment.

Eeada. Arra, God help your innocence ! You should ha'
seen them sthrikin' at men, women, an' childher.
An' me own friend, Dympna, in hospital gettin' her
face laced with stitches, th' way you'd lace a shoe !
An' all along of followin' that mad fool, Breydon !

Rector. Go in, then. [*To the verger, who has come to the
entrance*] See her safe.

> [*Eeada and the verger go into the church.   Finnoola comes*

slowly along the path outside the hedge, holding on to the
railings as she moves, step by step. When she comes to the
gateway, she sinks down to the ground and turns a white
and distorted face towards those in the grounds.

Finnoola [*painfully*]. For th' love o' God, one of you tell
me if th' Reverend something Clinton's here, or have
I to crawl a long way further ?

Rector [*hurrying over to her*]. He's here ; I'm he, my good
woman. What is it you want of me ?

Finnoola. I've a message for you from Ayamonn Breydon.

Rector [*eagerly*]. Yes, yes ; where is he ?

Finnoola. He's gone.

Rector. Gone ? Gone where ?

Finnoola. Gone to God, I hope.   [*A rather long pause.*

Rector [*in a low voice*]. May he rest in peace ! And the
message ?

Finnoola. Yes. He whispered it in me ear as his life
fled through a bullet-hole in his chest — th' soldiers,
th' soldiers. He said this day's but a day's work done,
an' it'll be begun again tomorrow. You're to keep an
eye on th' oul' woman. He wants to lie in th' church
tonight, sir. Me hip's hurt ; th' fut of a plungin'
horse caught me, an' I flat on th' ground. He sent a
quick an' a long farewell to you. Oh, for Christ's
sake get's a dhrink o' wather ! [*The verger runs for a*
drink.] We stood our groun' well, though. [*The verger*
comes back with the water, and she drinks.] Now I can have
a thrickle of rest at last.

                    [*She stretches herself out on the ground.*

Rector. Where did you leave him ? Where is he lying

now? [*She lies there, and makes no answer. He picks up the broken cross of flowers and is silent for a few moments. With head bent low — sorrowfully*] Oh, Ayamonn, Ayamonn, my dear, dear friend. Oh Lord, open Thou mine eyes that I may see Thee, even as in a glass, darkly, in all this mischief and all this woe!

[*The curtain comes down to indicate the passing of some hours. When it rises again, it is evening. The lamp over the porch door is lighted, and so is the church, the light shining through the yellow robe of St. Peter and the purple robe of St. Paul from the window in the church's wall. The church organ is playing, very softly, a dead march. The lamp on the path, outside the hedge, isn't yet lighted. The dark figures of men and women can be faintly seen lining themselves along the hedge. Mrs. Breydon is standing in the grounds, near to the gateway. Foster and Dowzard stand on the steps of the porch. A little in front, with his back turned towards them, stands the Rector, now with white surplice over his cassock, his stole around his neck, and the crimson-lined hood of a Doctor of Divinity on his shoulders. Sheila, holding a bunch of crimson roses in her hand, stands under the rowan tree. Partly behind the tree, the Inspector is standing alone. A lamplighter comes along the path, carrying his pole with the little flower of light in the brass top. He lights the lamp on the path, then comes over to peer across the hedge.*]

Lamplighter. What's up? What's on? What's happenin' here? What's they all doin' now?

1st Man. Bringin' th' body o' Breydon to th' church.

Lamplighter. Aw, is that it? Guessed somethin' was goin' on.

1st Man. He died for us.

Lamplighter. Looka that, now ! An' they're all ac-couthered in their best to welcome him home, wha' ? Aw, well, th' world's got to keep movin', so I must be off ; so long !   [*He goes.*

Dowzard [*speaking to the Rector's back*]. For th' last time, sir, I tell you half of the Vestry's against him comin' here ; they don't want our church mixed up with this venomous disturbance.

Rector [*without moving, and keeping his eyes looking towards the gateway*]. All things in life, the evil and the good, the orderly and disorderly, are mixed with the life of the Church Militant here on earth. We honour our brother, not for what may have been an error in him, but for the truth for ever before his face. We dare not grudge him God's forgiveness and rest eternal because he held no banner above a man-made custom.

Foster [*savagely*]. Aw, looksee, I'm no' a mon to sut down on' listen to a tumblin' blether o' words — wull ye, or wull ye not, give intil us ?
          [*In the distance a bagpipe is heard playing* Flowers of the Forest. *Mrs. Breydon's body stiffens, and Sheila's head bends lower on her breast.*

Rector. It is a small thing that you weary me, but you weary my God also. Stand aside, and go your way of smoky ignorance, leaving me to welcome him whose turbulence has sunken into a deep sleep, and who cometh now as the waters of Shiloah that go softly, and sing sadly of peace.
          [*As he is speaking, the lament ceases, and a moment after, a stretcher bier, bearing the covered-up body of Ayamonn,*

*appears at the gateway. It is carried down towards the
church, and the Rector goes to meet it.*

Rector [*intoning*]. Lord, Thou hast been our refuge from
one generation to another. For a thousand years in
Thy sight are but as yesterday. [*He chants:*]
    All our brother's mordant strife
    Fought for more abundant life ;
    For this, and more — oh, hold him dear.
    Jesu, Son of Mary, hear !

    Gather to Thy loving breast
    Ev'ry laughing thoughtful jest,
    Gemm'd with many a thoughtful tear.
    Jesu, Son of Mary, hear !

    When Charon rows him nigh to shore,
    To see a land ne'er seen before,
    Him to rest eternal steer.
    Jesu, Son of Mary, hear !

[*The bier is carried into the church, and, as it passes, Sheila
lays the bunch of crimson roses on the body's breast.*

Sheila. Ayamonn, Ayamonn, my own poor Ayamonn !
[*The Rector precedes the bier, and Mrs. Breydon walks beside
it, into the church, the rest staying where they are.
There is a slight pause.*

Dowzard. We'd betther be goin'. Th' man's a malignant
Romaniser. Keep your eye on th' rabble goin' out.

Foster [*contemptuously*]. There's little fight left in thom,
th' now. I'll no' forgive thot Inspector fur refusin' to
back our demond.
[*They swagger out through the gateway and disappear along
the path outside the hedge, as those who carried the bier
come out of the church.*

2nd Man. That's the last, th' very last of him — a core o' darkness stretched out in a dim church.

3rd Man. It was a noble an' a mighty death.

Inspector [*from where he is near the tree*]. It wasn't a very noble thing to die for a single shilling.

Sheila. Maybe he saw the shilling in th' shape of a new world.

> [*The 2nd and 3rd Men go out by the gateway and mingle with the rest gathered there. The Inspector comes closer to Sheila.*

Inspector. Oughtn't you to go from this gloom, Sheila? Believe me, I did my best. I thought the charge would send them flying, but they wouldn't budge; wouldn't budge, till the soldiers fired, and he was hit. Believe me, I did my best. I tried to force my horse between them and him.

Sheila [*calmly*]. I believe you, Inspector Finglas.

Inspector [*gently catching her by the arm*]. Tom to you, dear. Come, Sheila, come, and let us put these things away from us as we saunter slowly home.

Sheila [*with a quiver in her voice*]. Oh, not now; oh, not tonight! Go your own way, and let me go mine, alone tonight.

Inspector [*taking her hand in his*]. Sheila, Sheila, be sparing in your thought for death, and let life smile before you. Be sparing in thought of death on one who spent his life too rashly and lost it all too soon. Ill-gotten wealth of life, ill-gone for ever!

Sheila [*withdrawing her hand from his gently*]. Oh, Tom, I hope you're right; you are right, you must be right.

[They have walked to the gateway, and now stand there together, the men and women along the hedge eyeing them, though pretending to take no notice.

Inspector. You'll see it clearer, dear, when busy Time in space has set another scene of summer's glory, and new-born spring's loud voice of hope hushes to silence th' intolerant dead.

Sheila [musingly]. He said that roses red were never meant for me ; before I left him last, that's what he said. Dear loneliness tonight must help me think it out, for that's just what he said. *[Suddenly — with violence]* Oh, you dusky-minded killer of more worthy men !
[She runs violently away from him, and goes out, leaving him with the men and women, who stand idly by as if noticing nothing.

Inspector [after a pause]. What are ye doing here ? Get home ! Home with you, you lean rats, to your holes and haunts ! D'ye think th' like o' you alone are decked with th' dark honour of trouble ? *[Men and women scatter, slowly and sullenly, till only Brennan, with his melodeon on his back, is left, leaning by the gate. To Brennan]* Heard what I said ? Are you deaf, or what ?

Brennan [calmly]. I'm a Protestant, an' a worshipper in this church.

Inspector. One of the elect ! So was Breydon. Well, keep clear of unruly crowds — my men don't wait to ask the way you worship when they raise their arms to strike.
[He goes slowly away down the path. A few moments pass, then the Rector and Mrs. Breydon come out of the church. He arranges a shawl round her shoulders.

Rector. There ; that's better ! My wife insists you stay the night with us, so there's no getting out of it.

Mrs. Breydon. She's kind. [*She pauses to look at the rowan tree.*] There's th' three he loved, bare, or dhrenched with blossom. Like himself, for fine things grew thick in his nature : an' lather come the berries, th' red berries, like the blood that flowed today out of his white body. [*Suddenly — turning to face the church.*] Is it puttin' out th' lights he is ?

Rector. Yes, before he goes home for the night.

Mrs. Breydon. Isn't it a sad thing for him to be lyin' lonesome in th' cheerless darkness of th' livelong night !

Rector [*going to the porch and calling out*]. Sam, leave the lights on tonight.
                    [*The church, which had dimmed, lights up again.*

Rector. He's not so lonesome as you think, dear friend, but alive and laughing in the midst of God's gay welcome. Come.
    [*They slowly go through the gate and pass out. The verger comes from the church and swings the outer door to, to lock up for the night. Brennan comes down into the grounds.*

Samuel [*grumbling*]. Light on all night — more of his Romanisin' manœuvres.

Brennan. Eh, eh, there ; houl' on a second !

Samuel. What th' hell do you want ?

Brennan. Just to sing a little song he liked as a sign of respect an' affection ; an' as a finisher-off to a last farewell.

Samuel [*locking the door*]. An what d'ye take me for ? You an' your song an' your last farewell !

Brennan [*giving him a coin*]. For a bare few minutes, an'
leave th' door open so's th' sound'll have a fair chance
to go in to him. [*The verger opens the door.*] That's it.
You're a kind man, really. [*Brennan stands facing into
the porch, the verger leaning against the side of it. Brennan
unslings his melodeon, plays a few preliminary notes on it, and
then sings softly:*]

A sober black shawl hides her body entirely,
Touch'd be th' sun an' th' salt spray of th' sea ;
But down in th' darkness a slim hand, so lovely,
Carries a rich bunch of red roses for me !

[*The rest of the song is cut off by the ending of the play.*

CURTAIN

RED ROSES FOR ME

A so-ber black shawl hides her bod-y en-ti-re-ly, Touch'd by th'
sun and th' salt spray of th' sea; But down in th' dark-ness a
slim hand, so love-ly, Car-ries a rich bunch of red ro-ses for me.—

TH' BOULD FENIAN MEN

Our cour-age so ma-ny have thought to be age-in', Now
flames like a bril-liant new star in th' sky; An' Dan-ger is proud to be
call'd a new bro-ther, Since Freedom has buckled her sword on her thigh. Then
out to th' place where th' bat-tle is brav-est, Where th'
noblest an' meanest fight fierce in th' fray, Re-pub-lic-an ban-ners shall
mock at th' foe-men, An' Fen-ians shall turn a dark night in-to day!

OH, QUEEN OF EBLANA'S POOR CHILDREN

Oh, Queen of Eb - la-na's poor child - ren, Bear swift - ly our woe a -
way; An' give us a chance to live light - ly An hour of our life's dark
day! Lift up th' poor heads ev - er bend - ing, An' light a lone star in th'
sky, To show thro' th' dark-ness, de-scend-ing, A cheer-i-er way to die.

I TUCK'D UP MY SLEEVES

I stroll'd with a fine maid far out in th' coun-try, Th'
blos - soms a - round us all cry - in' for dew; On a
dai-sy deckt bench, sure, I sat down be-side her, An' tuck'd up my sleeves for to
tie up her shoe. An' what's that to a - ny one wheth-er or no, If I
came to th' fore when she gave me th' cue? She clos'd her eyes tight as she
mur-mured full low, Be good e-nough, dear, for to tie up my shoe.

FAIR CITY

Fair ci - ty, I tell thee our souls shall not slum-ber With- in th' warm beds of am - bi - tion or gain; Our hands shall stretch out to th' full-ness of la-bour, Till won-dher an' beau-ty with - in thee shall reign!

WE BESEECH THEE

As Thou didst rise from Thy_ grim grave, So may we rise to stand and brave Th' pow'r be - stow'd on fool _ or knave. _ We be - seech Thee!

THE SCAB

If we can't fire a gun, we can fire a hard stone, Till th' life of th' scab shriv-els in-to a moan. Let it sink in what I say, Let me say it a - gain— Tho' th' Lord God made an odd scab He al - so made men!

BROTHERS

All our bro - ther's mord - ant strife

Fought for more a - bund - ant life; For

this, and more, oh, hold him dear.

Je - su, Son of Ma - ry, hear!

HALL OF HEALING

A Sincerious Farce in One Scene

CHARACTERS IN THE PLAY

ALLELUIA (ALOYSIUS), *the Caretaker of the Dispensary*
THE OLD WOMAN ⎫
THE YOUNG WOMAN ⎪
BLACK MUFFLER ⎬ *patients attending the Dispensary*
GREEN MUFFLER ⎪
JENTREE ⎭
A LAD
THE DOCTOR, *the Dispensary's Medical Officer*
THE APOTHECARY, *the Dispensary's Dispenser*
RED MUFFLER
GREY SHAWL, *Red Muffler's wife*

SCENE

The waiting-room of the Dublin Parish Dispensary for the Poor. It is a winter's day.

The waiting-room of the Parish Dispensary in Dublin, on a winter's day. It is a place where the poor, sick, or diseased are looked at and, usually, rewarded with a bottle. It is an ugly room, drab, and not too clean. The few bright spots in it are the posters warning of disease. Running along the back wall is a bench on which the patients sit while waiting to go in to the Doctor. A shorter bench runs along the wall to the left. Beyond this bench is the entrance door which leads from the waiting-room to the hall, and thence into the street. In the centre of the back wall is a window which looks out into the street. Just to the right of this window, a wooden partition comes down, somewhat diagonally, through nearly two-thirds of the room, and then turns to the right, till it is joined to the side wall on the right. Within this partitioned part of the room are the Surgery and the Dispensary. A door in this partition wall, up towards the back, admits one to the Surgery. Another door in that part of the partition which has turned to the right, near the right side wall, gives entry to the Dispensary. To the left of this door is a small window (shuttered for the moment), with a narrow ledge in front of it, through which the remedies are handed out to the patients. On the Surgery door is the word DOCTOR *in black letters, and on the door of the Dispensary, the word* DISPENSER *also in black. On the back wall, to the left of the window, is a poster on which are the words in black print,* DIPHTHERIA : BEWARE ! *Above the Dispensary window is another one on which are the words in red,* TUBERCULOSIS : BEWARE ! *The Caretaker, Aloysius, nick-named Alleluia, is fixing a third one, to the right of the window at back, on which are the words in green,* CANCER : BEWARE ! *Through the window at back, it can be seen that the weather is bad; hurrying flakes of snow are falling in a zigzag way because of the cold wind blowing. At times through the scene, quick and thick flurries of snow pass by the windows outside.*

The patients are all of one patch, immersed in the same uncertainty and want. The lines of care and weariness on their countenances are the same, save that there are more on the face of the old than on the face of the young. The complexion of the younger is starkly pale; that of Jentree a lemon-yellow; that of the Old Woman, a yellowish-brown; that of Alleluia is pale, with a dot of yellow on the points of the cheeks; that of the Doctor a purplish-white; of the Apothecary a pale one, with a bare hint of struggling ruddiness through the paleness. Though differing in cast of countenance, shape and colour of clothing, they all carry in their faces the lines of conscious, or semi-conscious, uncertainty and resignation.

The face of Aloysius is a rather foolish one; his head is narrow at the top, developing down and out to form a square for a chin. His grey eyebrows gather into turned-up tufts at the corners; his tough nose tilts; and, though he has no moustache, a grey spade beard grows naturally, or has been trained, into a tilting tuft too. His mouth is wide, inclined to grin, and is always slightly agape. Whenever he moves across the room, he does so in a movement, half run, half glide, as if he skated on a surface fit only to glide over in places. As he glides he bends his body over and forward, as a stiff-backed bird might do, holding out his arms from his body as he glides and runs along.

Next to the Doctor (to whom he is subservient and of whom he is very much afraid), he is Lord of the Dispensary, dictating to the out-patients, and making things uncomfortable for them; though they try to please him, and follow his humours as well as they can. He wears a uniform of dark blue, the frock-coat reaching to below his knees. It is ornamented with silver buttons. His trousers are a bit short, coming only to the tops of his boots. His head is covered with a blue-peaked cap, having a wide top, and a narrow strap running along the butt of the peak is fastened on either side by a small silver button. A fussy old fool. He takes off his coat to tackle the job of tacking up the poster. He takes up a hammer, spreads out the poster, and with some difficulty hammers in a tack in one corner. Fixing the opposite one, he drops the tack, and curses, immediately ejaculating, " Mea culpa, mea culpa". He fixes that corner, and, in driving the third tack home, he hits his thumb, exclaims with pain, flings down the hammer, and thrusts the injured thumb under his armpit, first giving vent to a yell of agony.

Alleluia [*pacing about the room, and nursing the injured thumb*]. Ooh ! Sacred Heart ! Me thumb's desthroyed ! May th' curse o'—— [*He checks the profanation by trying to sing in a woeful way*] She's me lady love, she is me baby love. Oooh ! [*He again yells in agony, and bends double to squeeze the injured member tighter under his armpit.*] Curse o'—— [*He checks himself.*] Oh, Holy St. Harmoniumagnus, succour me ! [*He sings woefully again*] I know she likes me, I know she likes me, Because she says so — St. Serenium, ayse th' pain ; ayse it, ayse th' agony ! Preserve me from pain ! Today, tomorrow, an' forever afther ! Right on th' tenderest part !

> [*He goes moaning into the Dispensary, and the clank of bottles is heard.*

> [*Presently, the door leading into the Dispensary waiting-room from the street is cautiously opened, and the shawled head of an Old Woman peers into the room. Then the door is slowly opened, and the Woman enters. Her back is bent. Her boots are broken, and the skirt she wears is old and tattered at the hem. Shawl, skirt, boots, and all, are mud-coloured. She shivers and shudders as she comes in, slowly rubbing her gnarled hands to promote circulation. She goes over to the bench, and sits down stiffly. She coughs, and then wipes her*

*mouth with the corner of her shawl. The clanking of the
bottles stops. She gives another asthmatic cough, and again
wipes her mouth with the end of her shawl. The shutter
of the Dispensary window is pushed up, and Alleluia's head
is thrust out; it looks round the room, and spies the Old
Woman sitting on the bench. The head is withdrawn,
the shutter pulled down, and Alleluia comes out of the
Dispensary, wearing a bandage round the stricken thumb.
He goes over with a glide to the Woman, catches her by
the arm, pulls her from the seat, and guides her to the
door.*

Old Woman [*protesting feebly, but submitting calmly to ejection
as one to whom it is a familiar part of life*]. Ah, now, Mr.
Aloysius, it's only a bare few minutes from the time of
openin'. 'Clare to God, Alleluia, th' weather outside
ud perish a body ; an' I have within me oul' body a
whole kingdom of aches an' pains !

[*Without a word Alleluia opens room door and leads her
out, a look of determined indignation on his face; they can
be heard going down the hall. Shortly after, he returns,
and shuts the door. He cautiously completes the hanging
up of the poster on the wall. He puts on his coat. Then
he hurries into the Dispensary, comes out again with a
sweeping-brush, and slides it over the floor, pushing whatever may be before it under the bench. While he sweeps,
he sings softly, in the rather cracked voice of an old man,
the chorus of " The Rose of Tralee", pausing sometimes,
as he pushes the brush, to do a bit of a waltz with it, and
picking the song up again from where he left off, when its
resumption seems convenient.*

Alleluia [*singing*] :
    She was lovellee an' fayer as ay . . . rosebud of
        summer ;

But it wasn't her beautay aylone . . . that . . .
    won me ;
Aah, no ; 'twas they truth in her . . . eyes . . .
    ever beamin',
That med me lovev Mary . . . they rose of . . .
    Thraa . . . lee !

[*Nearing the end of the chorus, he is near the door of the
Dispensary, and, doing a kind of dancing swirl right
around, as he sings the last line, he glides into the Dispensary and closes the door behind him.*

[*After a moment or two, the entrance door opens and Red
Muffler, a young man of twenty-five, enters the room.
He looks thin and a little careworn. He is very poorly
and thinly dressed ; his muddy-black trousers are
patched with black cloth on one knee. His neck is pro-
tected by a thin, red woollen muffler, and a dark tweed
cap, dotted with snowflakes, is pulled low down over his
eyes. He looks poor, cold, and miserable ; but there
seems to be some element of grit in his standing. He
takes his cap off, and, holding it by the peak, whirls it
round to shake the heavier dampness from it ; then he
replaces it on his head. Between each forefinger and
thumb, he pinches together each leg of his trousers, and
flicks them in an effort to make them feel drier. The Old
Woman's head appears round the edge of the door, peering
nervously into the room. Red Muffler sees her.*

Red Muffler [*to Old Woman*]. Come in, old lady ; here is
more sheltered than th' hall, an' a heaven from th'
sthreet.

Old Woman [*deprecatingly*]. I'll do lovely here. If himself
seen me, it's out into th' sthreet I'd go again, an' a
body pushin' hard to eighty years isn't proof against

th' chill o' th' sleet, an' th' chatther of th' interferin'
wind outside.

Red Muffler [*irritated by her timidity*]. Aw, come in, woman,
for God's sake ! It's this fear of offendin' that keeps
us all so far from th' spice of comfort.

Old Woman [*timidly crossing the threshold*]. I wondher if I
ought to venthure it ? Alleluia 'ill only be shovin' me
out again. [*She crosses herself.*] He's a good Catholic,
an' maybe he won't now.

Red Muffler [*decisively*]. Aw, go and sit down, woman. I'll
know how to deal with this Alleluia of yours when he
shows himself.

Old Woman [*wandering over to the bench*]. Th' docthor
before this one gave us a bad habit, always leavin'
ordhers to let us in before openin' time, if th' weather
was grim, or rain was fallin', or even when the sun
happened to be too boistherous.

Red Muffler. An' what's wrong with th' present docthor ?

Old Woman. Aw, he's one o' th' surly specimens. [*She
rises stiffly, bending double, and groaning, to come close to
him.*] He's partial to th' dhrop. He has th' life
frightened outa poor oul' Alleluia. [*She whispers*] He
can't abide you to come on Mondays, because of his
feelin' frightful afther Sunday's rest.

Red Muffler. Why do you come on Monday, then ?

Old Woman. It's me one free day. I have to work on all
the others.

Red Muffler. Is he doin' yeh anny good ?

Old Woman. Aw, divil a good, so far ; but I'm always
hopeful he may.

Red Muffler. An' is he hopeful ?

Old Woman. Divil a hopeful.   He just says I'm wastin'
his time comin' here ; that me back'll never straighten,
an' th' ache'll never end.   But you can never tell with
God.

Red Muffler [*clapping his cold hands against his sides*].   An' how
much d'ye make outa your work ?

Old Woman. A shillin' a day, son ; five shillin's a week.

Red Muffler. Jasus, that's not much !

Old Woman. It's something, son.   You see, I can do only
rough an' heavy work now.   Me oul' hands is too
shaky for any fancy job.   I don't need much.   I won't
worry if only I can outlast life workin'.   [*Anxiously*]
D'ye know, I don't really think I ought to stay here —
a few more slaps from the flauntin' wind, an' one more
scattherin' of rain over me can't do me much harm.

Red Muffler [*ignoring her anxiety*].   An' have you no-one to
fight for you ; no childhren to stand up for you ?

Old Woman. Fight, is it ?   Fightin' only makes things
worse.   Of course, I've children, but all married, an'
hard set themselves to live.   There's one blessin' — I
can offer everything up to God.

Red Muffler [*venomously*].   Misery isn't much of a gift to
give to God, is it ?

Old Woman [*shocked and staring — after a pause*].   Ah, son,
don't say a thing like that !   We're too poor to take
th' risk of sayin' serious things.   We're told God is
good, an' we need every little help we can get.

Red Muffler. An' th' kind docthor before this fellow come
— where did he go ?

Old Woman. Aw, he went into his grave. Cancer, I'm told. With th' aid o' dhrugs, he kept himself goin' for a year an' a day; then, he was silently seen no more.

Red Muffler [*echoing her*]. Silently seen no more! Will this damned doctor never come! Such as us have barely time to glimpse a gleam that's kind before it hurries to the dark again. It's afther ten, and that damned docthor isn't here!

Old Woman [*anxiously*]. Why, aren't you feelin' well, son?

Red Muffler. Me? Oh, I'm all right. It's our little girl o' nine : our first one. She's been bad a week; she's worse; now, we're afraid she'll soon be something silently seen no more. [*Tensely*] The child is bad; th' child is worse; th' child is chokin'. [*Agonisingly*] Jesus Christ, ha' mercy!

Old Woman [*soothingly*]. I wouldn't be fancyin' death for your little one, son. She'll be all right. God is good. They tell us that God's thought is roomy with anxiety for the very young.

Red Muffler [*impatiently*]. I know what they tell us, I know, woman; but it's past ten; an' ten's th' hour, an' th' blighter should be here. [*The organ is heard playing.*] What music is that?

Old Woman. An organ in the church next door; every Monday someone plays it : practisin', maybe. When th' wind's this way, you can hear it. The caretaker here dances like a fool, and chants an Alleluia ditty whenever it sounds. That's why we call him Alleluia. [*She comes nearer.*] An oul' fool!

Red Muffler. Me feet's numb. It's not good to be left standin' here in these wet things. I'm seepin'.

Old Woman. When you're my age, son, you'll be well used to them things.

    [*He stamps his feet heavily on the floor in an effort to give them the feel of life. The shutter on window in Dispensary is suddenly pulled up, and the head of Alleluia, cap and all, is thrust through it. The head peers around to see who has made the noise, sees Red Muffler, and the head is pulled in again, while the shutter is pulled down with a snap. Then the door of the Dispensary is opened, and Alleluia slides out and over to the Red Muffler. He takes him by the arm and tries to guide him to the entrance door, but he is resisted, and Red Muffler doesn't budge.*

Red Muffler [*shaking off Alleluia's hold*]. Here, you — what's bitin' you?

Alleluia [*a little taken aback by the unexpected resistance*]. You can't stay here. No one's to cross the sthreet door till th' regulation time o' openin'. [*He snatches Red Muffler by the arm again.*] Come on, now — out!

Red Muffler [*violently shaking off Alleluia's hold*]. G'way, you fussy, fiddlin' fool!

    [*A little frightened, and deciding that discretion is needed, Alleluia side-steps away from Red Muffler, spots the Old Woman — now cowering in a corner — and glides over swiftly to where she sits. He catches her arm; she obediently rises, and he begins to guide her over to the entrance.*

Old Woman [*timidly apologetic*]. I musta strayed in be mistake, Mister Alleluia — I mean, Mr. Aloysius.

Th' sleet an' the bullyin' wind has made th' sthreet unkind, sir. Yes, th' wind must ha' blew me in, mister. Without me noticin' either. You'll excuse me, sir ; for I've many burdens of aches an' pains to try to hide from th' blowin' blight of th' weather.

Alleluia [*decisively*]. Yeh can't hide your aches an' pains here, ma'am. You can't expect to have Alleluia hours of comfort at your time o' life, or in your circumstances. Th' last docthor near ruined yous all, so he did, with his scorn of regulations ; with his " make the bareness brighter ", an' his " th' most o' them won't last a lot longer ". Had he lived, he'd ha' wanted cushions for your poor backsides. Th' waste of it ! I'd like to know how we'd fare without th' regulations.

Old Woman [*meditatively*]. Th' last one always had a winsome word for th' sick an' dyin', so he had.

Alleluia. Because he was sick an' dyin' himself — that's why. Out you go, an' don't put your nose in again, till th' docthor arrives.

Old Woman [*half turning to glance at Red Muffler*]. Th' gentleman behind us, sir, advised me to shelther in outa th' weather.

Alleluia [*pushing her out by the door*]. Out you go !
			[*During all this Red Muffler has taken no notice, making no effort to defend the Old Woman; but has turned his back on the other two, and is now staring hard at one of the posters.*

Old Woman [*reaching the door, hesitates, turns suddenly round, and runs across the room till she is half-way to where Red Muffler is standing — bitterly*]. You went before me

when I was comin' in, but you're not before me goin'
out! You keep your courage secret, you do. [*She
makes the motion and the sound of spitting scornfully towards
him*] That's your value to this poor oul' woman, you
poor morsel of a man! [*Alleluia has now got behind her
with a movement that is half a run, half a glide, and hastens
to shoo her out as a drover might a cow, adding an occasional
shove with his hand to her back. As she nears the entrance
door — fervently*] Thanks be to God who spared th' last
poor docthor be givin' him death, an' deliverin' him
from th' lousy lot of us!

[*She disappears out by the door, Alleluia following close on
her heels. Red Muffler turns slowly away from the poster,
and sinks down to sit on the bench, resting with his
elbow on knee, his head on his hand. After a pause, the
Doctor whirls into the room, fussier even than old
Alleluia, followed meekly by the Caretaker. The Doctor
is of middle height, rather plump, and widening per-
ceptibly around the belly. His face — half concealed now
by a thick white wool muffler — is turning to a purplish
tinge by hard drinking. His eyes are small and hard, his
eyebrows thick and shaggy. Had he his black bowler hat
off, it could be seen that he is bald, save for a few reddish-
grey hairs brushed over the crown, in an effort, maybe, to
hide a big expanse of polished skull. He is wearing a
heavy brown topcoat; and his lower legs are encased in
shining black leather leggings; a serviceable umbrella is
in his left hand, a satchel in his right one. As he enters,
he gives a sudden belch, and he ejaculates, as if to himself,
but quite audibly: "Jasus!" He catches sight of Red
Muffler, and turns to Alleluia.*]

Doctor. Who's that fella? What's that fella doin'?

Alleluia. He's waitin' for you, sir.

Doctor. An' how'd he get in before the regulation time ?

Alleluia. He just came in without by your leave from a soul. I expostulated with him, but he wouldn't budge for no-one. Wouldn't budge an inch.

Doctor. Then th' street door must have been open to let him in.

Alleluia [*sliding to the left and to the right of the Doctor, and back again*]. I left it open, sir, for a spessesscific purpose.

Doctor. For a what ? What d'ye mean, man ?

Alleluia [*again sliding to right and left, and around, the Doctor so that the Doctor has to turn to follow what he's saying*]. For you, sir ; I didn't want you to be fouled with the weather an' you fussin' with th' key for th' keyhole.

Doctor [*impatiently*]. Stop that buzzing round me ; you make me giddy, man. I'm quite competent to find the keyhole without a fuss. Don't leave that door open again till the regulation time. If I've forgotten the key, I can ring, can't I ? [*As Alleluia is silent*] Damn it, I can ring, can't I ?

Alleluia. Yis, yis ; of course you can ring ; 'course you can, sir.

Doctor. And you're not deaf, man, as well as bothered, are you ?

Alleluia. Me deaf ? [*With a dancing glide before the Doctor*] I'd hear the cuckoo before it came, sir.

Doctor. Well, hear the surgery bell when it rings, for I'm not in a waiting mood today. How many are outside, d'ye know ?

Alleluia. I seen six or seven or eight, or maybe nine, when I peeped into the street.

Doctor [*sarcastically*]. Are you sure it wasn't ten, now ?

Alleluia. It might ha' well been ten, for the sleet was fallin' between me an' them. More than ten, maybe, sir.

Doctor. Well, you can get them in, and, mind you, no delay when the bell rings. Immediately one enthers, pop another at the edge of the surgery door to be ready when the bell sounds again.

Alleluia [*doing another gliding dance to the right, to the left of the Doctor*]. On their tiptoes ; ears cocked ; tense with listenin', prepared to spring forward when they hear a tinkle.

Doctor [*thrusting the umbrella under his right arm, and gripping the shoulder of Alleluia with his left hand, which he uses to give him a shake*]. Keep still, you rubbered image of desolation ! When the bell gives two quick rings, it's you I want, not a patient. And listen : no gossiping while you're on duty — d'ye hear ?

Alleluia. Gossip, is it ? Me gossip ? An' on duty ? Aw', never ! Th' only words I ever uses is expended on expostulations. Never fear, sir ; I keep well within th' silences of devotion. Gossip on duty is not good company.

Doctor [*explosively*]. Aren't you always at it ! Expostulations ! Give your expostulations a rest today, and just shove them in to me.

Alleluia. You don't know them, doctor ; if you did, you wouldn't wondher any. Not a one o' them'll budge without an expostulation.

Doctor [*wildly*]. Looka here, if you don't learn to quit

yourself better than you do, I'll complain to the Guardians, by God, I will ! [*He gives a more violent and sickly belch.*] Ooh, damn it ! You're making me worse ! If you have me yelling at you today, it'll be th' worse for you. Have you th' Surgery fire going well ?

Alleluia [*cheerfully — and beginning to slide about again*]. Yissir ; oh, ay : it's a beauty ; all aglow, an' most encitin'. I'd hurry in to it, an' get them damp things off you.

Doctor. They're not damp ! [*Near a shout*] I came in a cab !

Alleluia. An' a wise man you were, doctor, to do it.

Doctor [*impatiently*]. Get them in, man, and get them out ! No dallying today.

[*He hurries towards the Surgery ; Red Muffler rises again from the bench to meet him. Alleluia hurries out by the entrance door, and soon returns followed by the patients, sorry-looking men and women from the tenements. Alleluia stands at the entrance door ushering them in, and waving them to the benches. As they troop in, the organ is heard playing again, and the poor patients seem to fall in with the rhythm of the tune as they drag themselves to the benches.*

[*Among them are Black Muffler; the old bent-back woman; a Young Woman of twenty-three, who, behind her hand, gives an occasional dry, hard cough ; Mr. Jentree, a man of forty-five, dressed in a mode of faded respectability — bowler hat, black, somewhat discoloured ; faded brown tweed coat, waistcoat, and trousers ; stiff white collar and black tie ; and a brown mackintosh. As he enters, his head is shaking, a strained look of anxiety disturbs his face which is fortified by a short beard and moustache. He*

*walks uncertainly with the aid of a stick. He sits down
between the Young Woman and the Old Woman. While
seated, first his right leg, and then his left one, gives a
sudden and spasmodic jerk, signifying a nervous disorder.
Among them is Green Muffler, a man of about thirty-five,
clad in the rough clothes of a labourer — corduroy
trousers, old khaki coat from the remains of the first world
war, thick coat of a faded dark blue, and a green muffler
round his neck. When he enters, he looks nervously
around him, as if asking himself if it were well for him
to be there. And when he sits down on the last bit of
bench, he stretches his head forward to look at the posters.
The other patients are but variants of the others in feature
and colour of clothing.*

Red Muffler [*going in front of the Doctor before he gets to the
Surgery door*]. Excuse me, sir ; I want to ask you about
our kid.

Doctor [*brusquely*]. What kid ? Sit down, sit down, man,
and take your turn.

Red Muffler. I'm not ill meself, sir ; I've only come about
our little girl who's very bad.

Doctor [*impatiently*]. Sit down, sit down, till I'm ready
for you.

Red Muffler [*speaking rapidly for fear the Doctor would get
away*]. You seen her a week ago, sir. She's worse, an'
th' missus's afraid for her.

Doctor [*sharply and rapidly*]. Oh, sit down when you're told,
man !

Red Muffler [*submissively complying*]. Yessir.
    [*The Doctor hurries into the Surgery. Alleluia obsequi-
    ously closes door after him. Red Muffler resumes his seat*

*nervously, pulling his coat round him ; buttoning it up,
and then opening it again.*

Young Woman [*coughing behind her hand*]. He's in a bad
mood today.

Old Woman. When's he any other way ? Since the last
doctor's death th' last light left us has gone out.

Black Muffler [*morosely*]. What odds ? Th' fella taken
away done no more for us than this fella that's left.
It's a new doctor, but it's th' old, old treatment. I
dunno that th' last one was fit to be a docthor at all.

Old Woman [*scornfully*]. You dunno ! Who're you to
dunno ? Why wasn't he fit ?

Black Muffler. Well, ma'am, th' last time he saw me, he
said what I needed was betther food, a finer house to
live in, an' a lot more enjoyment. An' when I said
couldn't you give me a bottle, docthor, he laughed at
me, so that I felt ashamed of me life. An' afther what
he had said, d'ye know what he said then ?

Jentree [*impatiently*]. Then what did he say, what did he
say, then ?

Black Muffler. My good young man, he said, you can't
expect to dhrink health into you out of a bottle.
Nobody knows how frightened I felt !

Young Woman. Wouldn't any sensible one be frightened
at th' edge on a remark like that !

Old Woman. Poor innocent man — no wondher th' good
God took him to Himself !

Black Muffler. When he saw th' fright I was in, he put a
hand on me shouldher, and said, Looka, says he,

if health could be got out of a bottle, says he, I'd be
th' healthiest man alive. An' me heart galloped into
th' fear that th' poor man wasn't a docthor at all !
Unless he was beginnin' to go out of his mind. I've
never been th' same since.

Jentree. I dunno how life could be lived without some
kinda bottles.

Old Woman. What if th' poor man did make a slip aself —
it's a wise man doesn't. He just had some kind of a
kink against bottles.

[*Meanwhile, Alleluia has gone into the Dispensary, and
returns with a stick of chalk. With this he draws a
straight line on the floor, half-way between the bench
and the Surgery door. Just outside this door, draws a
circle. Within the circle, he puts a patient facing the
door, and places another patient toeing the line, facing, too,
towards the Surgery door. The Surgery bell rings.
Alleluia hurries the patient in the circle into the Surgery,
shoves the other patient into it, while another one toes the
line. When the first patient comes out, she goes to the
Dispensary, hands in a bottle, gets it back full, and then
she goes away by the entrance door, shivering with antici-
pation at what she will meet outside. This goes on
rapidly till a stream of patients have passed in, come out,
and gone away. Alleluia hurries each in when the bell
tinkles, hurries each to the Dispensary window for the
medicine, and then hurries each out of the place. This is
the common measure of the place, and it goes on rapidly
till Black Muffler passes from the line to the circle, and
from the circle into the Surgery. As each poor patient
comes out to go away, Alleluia waylays him or her, holding
a card out to them, and asking a penny for the Holy Souls,
that Masses may be said for their redemption from Purga-*

*tory. When he gets a penny, he pricks a space in the
card he holds in his hand with a pin. The organ is
heard playing the same tune during the procession of
patients, and Alleluia goes about in a dancing slide to
the tune, chanting, mockingly, " Alleluia, Alleluia,
Alleluia ", waylaying the patients for pennies at
intervals, challenging them with the phrase " Remember
the Holy Souls in Purgatory ". Black Muffler comes
out of the Surgery cautiously and softly shuts the door
behind him.*

Black Muffler [*gesturing back towards the Surgery with his
thumb — in a whisper*]. Hunted me out ! Lyin' down
on a couch, with th' Dispenser givin' him a cordial.
Looks like a cut-down daisy.   We'll be here all day.

Young Woman. Maybe it'll give time for the weather to
clear.

[*Alleluia glides down the room, bends down, hands on
knees, before Green Muffler, and stares at him. The
patients watch the glide, and Black Muffler — again in
the circle — and the rest — except Jentree — turn to
watch and listen.*

Alleluia [*to Green Muffler*]. You're a new customer here,
aren't you ?

Green Muffler [*staring back at him*]. I was never here before,
if that's what you mean.

Alleluia. An' what are you complainin' of, me man ?

Green Muffler. Eh ? [*Stretching out his right arm carefully
and slowly*] Oh, just this arm o' mine — it hurts
terrible when I thry to do anything serious.

Alleluia. Aah, rheumatism !

Green Muffler [*shortly*]. Naw, it's not rheumatism! I know what rheumatism is.

Alleluia [*thoughtfully*]. It might be something goin' against th' blood strame.

Green Muffler [*with sharpness and mockery*]. Are you th' docthor, or wha'?

Alleluia [*importantly*]. I'm next to th' docthor. Where's your bottles?

Green Muffler [*somewhat startled*]. Bottles? What bottles?

Alleluia. There's no use o' you comin' here if you're not thoughtfully and thoroughly supplied with bottles. Every commencer must have three — one for a draught, one for a liniment, and one for a mixture. You can't go into the doctor's presence unless you are in possession of three comely and commodious bottles.

Green Muffler [*impressed*]. I didn' know nothin' about bottles.

Old Woman [*leaning forward as far as she can from the bench towards Green Muffler*]. You might need only one, son; but th' nature of your particular throuble might require two; an' in a diversified complaint, three bottles might be called for; so you have to be prepared. Stands to reason, a patient must be provided with a bottle, or two, or three bottles. As likely as not, son, you'll be a three-bottle man.
  [*The patients are now more interested than ever in the discussion; the one in the circle of chalk moves out of it to be nearer; and the one toeing the line moves nearer too. Jentree is the only one who is occupied with himself, and takes no notice.*

Alleluia [*not liking the interference — turning towards the Old Woman, with his body still bent double and hands on knees*]. If you'll allow me, ma'am, I'd have you notice that this would-be patient is receivin' official attention an' insthruction respectin' any bottles necessary in combination with his ailment.

Young Woman [*coughing behind her hand*]. One ud never know, be th' common look of them, that bottles was so important.   With every patient, bottles there must be.

Black Muffler. Bottles there was, bottles there is, bottles there must be !

Alleluia [*angrily — to the patients in general*]. Are yous goin' to have me expostulatin' all th' day ! Close your gobs, an' cease from shattherin' me explanations to this man !

Green Muffler. Th' whole place seems to be seethin' with bottles.   An' where am I goin' to get them ?
   [*The Surgery bell has been signalling for Alleluia — by giving two quick, consecutive rings — several times ; but all are so excited over, and interested in, the bottles that no-one takes the slightest notice.*

Old Woman [*over to Green Muffler*]. If you've thruppence on you, son, you'll get them in some pub : black porther or green mineral bottles — it doesn't matther, for they're all good of their kind.

Alleluia [*accompanying Green Muffler out by the entrance*]. An' remember, they must be all rinsed clean so as to be in a receptionable condition for th' contention of medicine.
   [*The bell sounds its two quick, consecutive rings again, this time with venomous clarity in the now silent room, startling the patients back into meek and anxious attention.*

Young Woman [*agitated*]. Holy Saint Juniper o' Judea, there's th' docthor callin' a patient !

Old Woman [*to the patient who has been standing in the chalk circle — vigorously*]. Off you go ; in with you !

Black Muffler [*bewildered by the sudden change of topic*]. Who ? Is it me, is it ?

Old Woman [*rapidly*]. You, you ; yes, you. Hop it, man !

Young Woman [*beginning before the Old Woman ends*]. Quick. Yes, you !

Jentree [*beginning before the Young Woman ends*]. Before he's out on top of us, roarin' !
    [*Black Muffler makes a bewildered rush for the Surgery door, which he opens. He goes in, but immediately comes out again, pushed back by the Doctor, who is angry and furious.*

Doctor [*wildly*]. Not you, not you ! Aloysius I rang for ! Good God, that fellow'll drive me mad ! [*Shouting*] Aloysius !

Alleluia [*sliding into the room again — full of hurry and fear*]. Sir, sir ; here, sir !

Doctor [*stormily*]. Where were you, you dolt ! Didn't you hear the bell ? You'll quit this very week-end ! What were you doing, you deaf oul' ditherer ?

Alleluia [*rapidly*]. Explainin' regulations to a patient, sir, about bottles.

Doctor [*furious*]. You fool, what do bottles matter ! My pen — where is it ? Pen, pen, man !

Alleluia [*flustered, but smiling*]. Pen? Oh, the pen, is it? Oh, yes, the pen. Let me think, now. I remember, yes; th' apothecary got a loan of it, sir.

Doctor [*angrily*]. Get it back then, at once. He's no business to touch it! Let him get a pen of his own. This is th' third or fourth time he's pinched it!

Alleluia [*deprecatingly*]. Not pinched, sir; oh, no, not pinched it.

Doctor [*roaring*]. Pinched, I say! [*He gives a half-belch, ending in a sigh — ejaculating as if to himself*] Oh, God! I'm in a shockin' state! [*To Alleluia — angrily*] Why th' hell d'ye let him take it?

Alleluia [*whisperingly*]. Between ourselves, sir, I'm tired expostulatin' with him. You'd want to chain it to your desk, sir.

Doctor. Wish I could chain you where you'd be hidden from view! [*Pushing Alleluia from him*] Go, an' get th' pen! [*To Red Muffler, who has risen, and now takes a step towards him*] Oh, sit down, you; sit down!
[*Crestfallen, Red Muffler does so.*
[*The Apothecary's head is poked out of the Dispensary window; the head is completely bald, except for a tiny web of fringe above the forehead; a thick moustache covers the upper lip, and almost hides the mouth; it juts out aggressively at each side of the face. The head twists round in the direction of the voices.*

Apothecary's Head [*shouting*]. Aloysius; eh, Aloysius!

Alleluia [*running round to the window*]. Yessir.

Apothecary's Head [*thrusting out an arm holding a pen*]. Here's th' damned pen for him!

[*Alleluia snatches the pen, and rushes back to the Doctor,
who snatches it from him.*

Doctor [*indicating with his pen Black Muffler who had stood
within the chalk circle*]. You there — come in. Come on,
come on !   [*He goes into the Surgery.*

Alleluia [*fussy as ever — getting behind the patient, and pushing
him along*]. Go on, go on, go on !
    [*Green Muffler enters by the entrance door. He is damp
and shivery. He carries a porter bottle under an arm,
and the neck and shoulders of mineral-water bottles are
sticking out from the side pockets of his coat. He sits
down, silent and morose, on the end of the bench.*
    [*Alleluia beckons the Young Woman, and places her within
the chalk circle. He takes another patient from the bench
and puts him toeing the line ; bending down to shove back a
foot that ventures over it, arranging the feet so that they
exactly touch the sacred chalk line.*

Alleluia [*petulantly fixing the foot*]. Keep the feet determined toein' the line exact, will you !

Young Woman [*nervously*]. I hope I won't be called on to
stand too long here — I always feel shaky when I
stand for long in th' one place.

Old Woman. He'll take a long time between patients
today ; always does when he's bad from booze.

Jentree [*giving a sudden jerk in his seat*]. You know, if I
don't get some specific attention soon an' sudden, something terrible's bound to happen. I'll fall, paralysed,
from me neck down !

Old Woman [*soothingly*]. You're lettin' it, whatever it is,
play on you too much, son.

Jentree [*testily*]. Aw, for God's sake, woman, talk sense. Can't I feel me legs goin' dead ? D'ye imagine I can go on not noticin' things ? [*A leg gives a spasmodic jerk.*] Oh ! Did yous all see that ? [*To Alleluia*] Eh, misther, I'll have to be let in at oncst !

Alleluia [*with a sweeping glide towards Jentree, and a bend-down to place his face in front of Jentree's*]. You'll wait till th' regulation tinkle of th' bell tells you to go.

Jentree [*as the other leg gives a spasmodic jerk upwards*]. Oh ! There, did yous all see that one go up ? There's no deception, mind yous — I'm really in a desperate condition !

Young Woman [*in the circle*]. Poor man ! An' what gave you them terrible jerks ? What did th' docthor say ?

Jentree [*with scorn*]. Th' docthors ! Th' one before this one, an' this fella, too, said it was because of too much imbibin' of wine.

Old Woman [*startled*]. Wine ? An' where would you come across th' quantity of wine to give you them sharp an' sudden jitters ?

Jentree. I was a wine porther, ma'am, but th' little I lowered through th' years couldn't possibly ha' done it.

Old Woman [*realising the cause, but not willing to hurt*]. Looka that now. I wouldn't say all ; but it might, it only might, mind you, have had a little to do with it.

Jentree [*getting on to his feet with a shivering jerky movement*]. Oh ! Th' bottle I get is doin' me damn all of good ! An' th' wather I have to dhrink's makin' me worse ! Looka, I'm thremblin' all over !

Old Woman [*to the other patients who are now all interested in*

Jentree]. His mind's sthrayin'. [*To Jentree*] Wather? What wather are you dhrinkin', son?

Jentree [*venomously*]. Th' wather them getts o' docthors ordhered me to lower — more'n half a gallon a day. [*He sinks back on to the bench.*] Me left leg's lost its motion. Not in a year, mind you, but in a day! I'd like to see him thryin' it himself. [*He jerks up from the bench again.*] I'll have to be carried home, if this goes on! What manner o' mortal man could swally a tank of wather in a single day?

Old Woman. Indeed, son, th' boyo inside wouldn't like to have to do it himself.

Jentree. I feel close to death when I see the sight of it!

Old Woman. Th' sight of what, son?

Jentree [*explosively*]. Wather, woman; th' wather!

Alleluia [*coming close to the talkers*]. There's only one thing, ma'am, manifested enough to negify th' effects o' wine, an' that's wather; an' th' patient would be well advised to gulp it down, gulp it down with determination, ad lib.

Old Woman [*eagerly — to Jentree*]. Hear that, son? Mr. Aloysius knows what's good for you! Wholesome stuff is wather. Gulp it down, son, an' it's bound to negify any wine that may be ripplin' round in you still: ad lib's th' only way!

Jentree [*to Old Woman — determinedly*]. I'd have you remember, ma'am, that I'm th' custodian of me own ailments, an' am fully endorsed on their concern and their keepin'! [*Indignantly — to Alleluia*] Gulp it down! I wondher would you relish gulpin' cold wather down you till your heart was stunned into stoppin' its beatin' ? Would you like to gulp cold wather down you till every vital organ in your poor body was frightened of what was floodin' into them ? Negify th' effects o' wine ! An' if I go on, what'll I take to negify th' effects of wather ?

Old Woman [to Jentree]. Sure that's the difficulty, son. [To Alleluia] If th' poor man has to negify th' wine with wather, and then has to negify the wather with wine, sure th' poor man'll burst himself thryin' to find a solution for his ailment.

Jentree [to Old Woman]. Sure that's what I'm up against all the time, an' no-one'll listen to me ! [Rising shaking to his feet and sitting down again — a little hysterical] What's keepin' that fella inside ! I'm goin' fast. Th' thremors is mountin' me spine. I'll be gone in a minute, if he doesn't hurry to have a look at me !

Young Woman [from the circle]. Poor man, y'are in a terrible state ! Maybe you'd like to take my turn ? I'm in no hurry, so I'm not. Indeed, I'd rather wait as long as I can in th' hope th' weather ud be betther when I set out for home.

Old Woman [to Jentree — encouragingly]. Yes, do ; go on, son ; take your chance of an earlier overhaul.
[She rises, and, with the help of the Young Woman — coughing with the exertion — planks Jentree in the circle. He is shaky, nervous, and leans heavily on his stick. The Young and the Old Women then return, and sit down on the bench. The Surgery door opens gently, and Black Muffler enters the waiting-room on tiptoe, a frightened look on his face. He closes the Surgery door softly, and

*gives an admonitory and warning gesture with a pre-
scription he is holding in a hand.*

Black Muffler [*with a significant wave of a hand*]. Husssh!
He's in a murtherin' mood today! Can't sit aysy a
second. Went out once, an' I heard him thryin' to
retch. He'll take ages to get through today. Jasus,
we poor have a lot to bear!

Red Muffler [*rising to his feet — angry and fierce*]. An' why do
they bear it! Even with the best docthor in its bosom,
what kind of a kip is this place? I deny that this is
all that God has got to give us! Even with the best
music of a church organ, what betther could we do
here but dance a dance of death! I won't do it; I
won't do it! By God, if that fella inside refuses to
come to our sick kid, I'll know th' reason why!

  [*He sinks down on the bench again, wiping his forehead
  with a soiled rag he has taken from a pocket. After this
  outburst, for a little while, there is a dead silence, the
  patients, standing and sitting, staring at the fiercely-
  spoken Red Muffler.*

  [*Then Black Muffler goes to the window of the Dispensary,
  hands in his prescription and a bottle; waits a moment,
  then gets the bottle back filled with a rich yellow fluid. He
  comes to the middle of the room, and holds the bottle from
  him towards the light.*

Black Muffler [*holding the bottle at arm's length*]. Oh, a
lovely yella, this time; th' last was blue.

Young Woman. Mine was red, so it was.

Old Woman. Show us. [*He hands her the bottle, and she
  holds it out at arm's length.*] So 'tis — a gorgeous yella!
  [*She hands the bottle back to him.*] Be th' look of it, son,
  that should do you a power o' good. This fella thinks

more o' bottles than th' other fella did — I'll say that
of him !

Alleluia [*down at the entrance, beckoning Black Muffler to go*].
Eh, you, with the black muffler, there ; you've been
fully medicamented, an' you've been handed your
documented mixture ; [*he glides up to Black Muffler*]
so no more chit-chat, but go ; but before you go,
remember the Holy Souls.

Black Muffler [*ignoring Alleluia's appeal — pocketing the bottle*].
I'll enther a new lease o' life when I stoke meself up
with this documented stimulant, wha' ? I'll renew
th' bottle, he says. Well, we'll thry it once more,
anyway.
   [*Alleluia slides and glides up to Black Muffler, catches him
   by the arm, and glides down with him to the entrance
   door, ushering him out to the street.*

Jentree [*becoming more nervous*]. What's keepin' him ;
what's th' fella doin' at all ? I'm gettin' worse. I'll
be down prostrate, numb an' nameless, before th' fella
lets me in !

Old Woman [*encouragingly*]. Keep calm, son. Take your
thoughts off yourself.

Jentree [*turning angrily to Old Woman*]. Don't be rattlin'
nonsense into me mind, woman, an' me in agony ! I
need immediate aid to countheract what's comin'. I
can't wait. I want help at once ; now ! [*He totters
rapidly over to the Surgery door ; kicks it below with a foot,
bangs it above with his stick.*] These docthors wouldn't
blink an eyelid if a man passed into oblivion ! [*He
again kicks and hammers on the door.*] Eh, eh, you in there,
does medical discretion always go disregarded in this
place !

[*As Jentree is hammering at the door, it suddenly opens, and the Doctor, furious with anger, appears. Jentree totters back a little, and the patients sit straight and still with respect and a little fear. The patient toeing the line runs off to sit down demurely on the bench.*]

Doctor [*in an agony of rage*]. What's this, my God, what's all this ? [*To Jentree*] Was it you who hammered at the door ?

Jentree [*smilingly*]. Me, sir ? I just gave a few quiet knocks, sir, for I was feelin' fit to die.

Doctor [*yelling*]. Aloysius ! Oh, where's that rambling fool ! Aloysius !
[*Alleluia comes rushing in and over to the Doctor. He grips Jentree and pulls him into the circle again.*]

Alleluia [*to Jentree*]. Stand there ; don't budge !

Doctor [*furiously — to Alleluia*]. I'll budge you, you Poor Law Guardian's gett !

Alleluia [*ignoring the Doctor — pulling the other patient to toe the line again*]. Stand there ; don't budge !

Doctor [*talking rapidly, pulling Alleluia by the coat to a place near the Surgery door*]. You stand there, and don't budge till they're all in and out again ! [*To Jentree*] I told you not to come for a month. I gave you enough bromide mixture for a month. You're not going to die. Be off home.

Jentree. Yessir, nosir. But th' delugin' o' wather y'ordhered's doin' me no good.

Doctor. Take more of it, then, to weaken the wine in you. Now off you go. [*To the Young Woman*] You're Jenny Sullivan, aren't you ?

Young Woman [*with a prologue of a cough*]. Yessir.

Doctor [*to Old Woman*]. What do you want — more liniment ?

Old Woman. Yessir, please.

Doctor. Get it then, and go. [*Indicating Green Muffler*] Who's that man ?

Alleluia [*sliding into a bending position before the Doctor*]. A three-bottle man ; a newcomer.

Doctor [*calling down to him*]. Eh, you, come on in to me.
                              [*He returns to the Surgery.*

Jentree [*as he goes out*]. Weaken th' wine in me ! It's in an ambulance I ought to be, speedin' to a place where a qualified man ud be sacked if he left me out of his sight for a minute ! I'll appeal to the authorities, so I will — this very day !

Old Woman. Arra, be sensible, son ! Let what they give kill or cure us, there's ne'er a one for us to appeal to, bar the good God Himself ! The poor who refuse to be patient, die young.

Red Muffler [*fiercely*]. We've been too patient too long ; too damned long ; too god-damned long, I'm sayin' ! Patience is only th' holy name for suicide !
        [*Alleluia glides along with Green Muffler to the Surgery door, ushers him in, and is about to close the door when the Doctor gives him a note.*

Doctor. Give that to Jenny Sullivan there, and tell her she can go.
        [*Alleluia gives the Young Woman the note. The Old Woman has crossed to the Dispensary window, handed in*

her prescription and bottle; received her liniment, and returned to the back to gaze out of the window at the falling snow.

Old Woman [*tonelessly*]. Th' snowy rain is worse nor what it was even.

Young Woman. Looka what I've got; looka what he's given me!

Old Woman. An' what is it, daughther?

Young Woman [*tonelessly*]. A note to the Consumption Dispensary o' Charles Street. I'm done for now. I feel faint. I'll lose me job an' all, now. It's me death warrant!

Old Woman [*coming over to her*]. Sit still for a few minutes, an' then we'll go home together. You'll have a lot more to go through before you'll be done for. There, sit still, child. I wouldn't say that he wasn't mistaken — th' fellow doesn't know black from white this mornin'. An' anyway, daughther, death's th' last thing th' poor should dhread.

[*A Lad of fifteen years of age comes into the waiting-room, and Alleluia at once glides down to him. The boy is thinly clad in coat and long trousers too big for him. His cap, too, is a size too large. He has the mask-like paleness of the others.*

Alleluia [*to the Lad*]. What d'ye want?

Lad [*handing Alleluia a red ticket*]. For me mother for the docthor to call.

Alleluia [*reprovingly*]. Sir, sir; don't forget th' sir, lad. Are you workin'?

Lad. I deliver th' papers of a mornin'. I get two shillin's a week.

Alleluia. An' how much d'ye keep for yourself?

Lad. Fourpence.

Alleluia. Sir, sir; don't forget th' sir — where were you brought up? Don't you know your catechism?

Lad. Wha'?

Alleluia. Wha'! That's not th' way to addhress a superior. How much o' th' last fourpence have you left?

Lad. Tuppence, sir; only tuppence.

Alleluia. Ah, that's better. [*He shows the Lad the collecting-card.*] Remember th' Holy Souls. Put one o' th' pennies on th' card for th' Holy Souls.
[*After some hesitation, the Lad forks out a penny and gives it to Alleluia, who marks it down by pricking the card with a pin.*

Lad [*earnestly*]. Me mother says, sir, she's very sick an' can't stir in th' bed, an' would th' docthor please hurry to her?

Alleluia [*almost shoving the Lad out*]. Tell your mother that th' docthor'll go full gallop to her!
[*Green Muffler now comes from the Surgery and goes over to the Dispensary window. He planks his three bottles down on the ledge in front of the hand-out window, and then hands in his prescription to the Apothecary. Alleluia glides over to him, in the hope of collecting another penny for the Holy Souls.*

Alleluia [*archly holding collecting-card under* Green Muffler's *nose*]. A penny to help the Holy Souls outa purgatory, kind man o' th' three big bottles.

Apothecary's Voice [*at the window — to* Green Muffler]. Take them bottles away.
[*Alleluia is startled; lowers card, and listens.*

Green Muffler [*startled and puzzled*]. Eh? Wha'? What bottles?

Apothecary's Voice [*impatiently*]. Them on th' ledge. [*Shouting*] Them on th' ledge!
[*Alleluia, scenting danger, glides away, and stands as close as he can get to the Surgery door.*

Green Muffler. I was ordered to bring three bottles. Th' person in authority here said I must have three bottles on me. Bring, says he, three bottles, says he, one for a liniment, one for a mixture, says he, an' one for a draught.

Apothecary's Voice [*impatiently*]. Do what you're told, man! [*Shouting*] Take them outa the way! They're no use here!
[*Green Muffler takes the three bottles from the ledge and deposits them on the floor. After a moment or two, the Apothecary's hand puts a tiny box of pills on the ledge in front of* Green Muffler. *He is shocked, looking at the tiny box, and then at the bottles.*

Green Muffler [*to the patients — who keep a tense silence*]. Did yous see what's after happenin'? Did yous or did yous not? Yous all saw me entherin' burdened with bottles, be strict orders forced to spend me last penny to get them. An' when I present them, as sthrictly ordered be a certain person, I'm shouted at to take them away, an' even th' use of one was denied me. [*He extends his hand with the tiny pill-box on its palm.*] Looka what I got ; just looka what I got ! [*He comes into the centre of the room.*] I'm not dhreamin', mind you. This isn't fairyland either. Yous all seen what happened. After all me huntin' after bottles, looka what's been handed out ! [*He glares towards where Alleluia is busy totting up what he has collected on his card — ostensibly unaware of what is taking place.*] Yous all heard what a certain person said to me. You must have three bottles, he says, one for a mixture, one for a liniment, he says, an' one for a draught. Three, mind you. Yous all sung a song about the necessity for bottles. An' what was the outcome ? Yous all seen it yourselves. Yous all see the bottles scattered about, an' me left with what's shinin' in th' palm of me hand ! I'm not dhreamin', mind you ! Have yous nothin' to say to relieve me feelin's ? [*He moves towards the door to go.*] Jasus, it's a cruel thing to do on anyone. [*He turns to look towards the patients.*] An', mind you, that certain person thried to cadge another penny off me for the Holy Souls ! An' what about th' sufferin' souls here, eh ? [*He goes to the door, and turns again.*] God forbid I'd ever come here again ; but if I have to, I warn that certain person not to mention bottles to me ; for if that certain person does, he'll be a sufferin' soul in Purgatory himself, without a one to help him out !

[*He goes slowly out, leaving the bottles on the floor beside the Dispensary ; and, as he goes, he fixes his gaze on the pill-box.*

[*The Doctor comes from the Surgery, dressed for the street as he was when we first saw him. He sees the patients sitting on the bench.*

Doctor [*calling*]. Aloysius ! [*Alleluia comes gliding up to him.*] Why are these still here ? Why haven't they gone home ?

Old Woman [*apologetically — to the doctor*]. The Young Woman here felt faint, an' we were restin' till she got a bit betther.

Doctor. She can't rest here. It's nearly closing time. The best place for her is home. [*To Old Woman*] Do you live near her ?

Old Woman. Only a sthreet away, sir.

Doctor. Well, see her safe home, like a good woman. [*To Alleluia*] Close the house up, Aloysius. [*To Red Muffler who has come close to him*] What is it you want, and speak quick, for I'm in a hurry.

Red Muffler. It's me child, sir ; me little girl, sir, only just nine years old.

Doctor. Yes, yes ; what about her ?

Red Muffler. We're afraid for her. You saw her four days ago ; top room, hundhred an' one Hill Sthreet, sir. We want you to come at once.

Doctor. I know, I know ; everyone wants the doctor to come at once. I'll come sometime tomorrow.

[*The Doctor makes a step forward towards the entrance door, but Red Muffler makes one too, so that he stands some-what in the way of the Doctor's passage to the door. At the same time, the Apothecary comes out of the Dispensary. He is dressed for the street — long mackintosh, thick white and red muffler, and a grey trilby hat pulled well down on his forehead. He carries an attaché-case and a walking-stick. He stands outside the Dispensary door and watches what is going on.*

Red Muffler [*blocking the Doctor's way to the door*]. No, today sir, please ; now. She needs you now. Have a look at her, at least. Last night was one of agony to th' missus an' me, listenin' to her losin' her breath. We're afraid soon she'll silently be seen no more. She's bad ; she's worse ; she's chokin' !

Doctor. I'll go tomorrow ; I can't go sooner. There are others needing attention, you know.

> [*He goes to go, but Red Muffler catches his arm.*

Red Muffler [*desperately*]. Nine years isn't long enough for a life to live ! Damn it, man, if you've none for me, have some thought for th' mother watchin' th' child's rash sthruggles to live !

Doctor [*chucking his arm from Red Muffler's hold*]. Oh, man alive, there are thousands of kids like yours gasping for life in the city today.

Red Muffler [*fiercely*]. An' no-one seems to care a coloured damn about them !

Doctor. No living doctor can give them what they need, man. To worry about them would send me to the grave, too.

> [*A young woman appears at the entrance door. Her head and half her body are covered by a grey shawl; her thin skirt is black, fading now to a rusty brown ; her boots are old, and are sodden with the slush of the streets.*

Doctor [*seeing Grey Shawl — angrily to Alleluia*]. Don't let any more in — put that one out !

> [*Alleluia goes gliding down and tries to turn Grey Shawl back, but she pushes him roughly aside and hastens up to Red Muffler.*
> [*The Doctor is now half-way down to the door; Red Muffler*

*beside him, a little to his front ; Grey Shawl in front of
Red Muffler ; the Old Woman and the Young Woman have
risen from the bench, and stand behind to the left, almost
directly in front of the poster warning of Diphtheria.
The Old Woman has an arm around the young one,
though she needs support herself. The Apothecary stands
a little in front of his Dispensary door.*

Red Muffler [*to Grey Shawl — frightened at seeing her*].
What'r you doin' here ? I had to wait to thry to get
th' docthor. Who's with th' child ? Why th' hell
did you leave her ?

Grey Shawl [*very quietly*]. You needn't throuble th'
docthor further, Frank. An' I didn't leave little Sheila,
it was her who left me.
  [*Her hand steals forward to cling to a hand of Red Muffler's,
  and there is a silence for some moments.*

Red Muffler [*quietly*]. Well, we've got all we could get
here, so we'd betther go. [*To the Doctor*] You might have
safely said you'd come, an' kept hope danglin' still in
front of us that healin' still was here, an' common
goodness. Our little one has had th' charity to save
you from a cold an' tirin' journey in th' mornin'.
[*Fiercely*] Oh, you blasted fomenter of medicine, you
might have listened to what I thried to say !

Grey Shawl [*frightened*]. Frank ! Do come home, an'
don't make a show of us an' little Sheila. I'm
frightened she's feelin' lonely wherever she may be
now.

Old Woman [*coaxingly*]. Ay, do, son, go home. Ah, it's
curious how th' old is left to wither on, while th'
young often go before they've time to bloom. It

doesn't seem right to me. I could ha' gladly gone in
the little one's place; for head down an' back bent,
what's for me to thry to tarry here a minute longer!
God Almighty does odd things at times.

Grey Shawl [*coaxingly*]. Come on, Frank, till you see her.
She's got all her old good looks back again. [*Brokenly*]
Oh, me little one'll be runnin' round frightened,
lookin' for her mammy, among the spirits of the blest!

Red Muffler [*to the Doctor*]. D'ye hear that? She's got her
old good looks all back again. Death has sometimes a
kindlier touch than many a human hand.

> [*Red Muffler and Grey Shawl go out followed by the Old
> Woman and the Young Woman, who pass Red Muffler
> and Grey Shawl by as Red Muffler turns around at the
> door with a parting shot at the Doctor.*

Red Muffler [*turning back at the door*]. The pair of yous can
go home now, an' snore away some other buddin' life!
Yous are afraid to fight these things. That's what's th'
matther — we're all afraid to fight!

Apothecary [*after a pause*]. Cheeky boyo, that! Not a
grain of gratitude in one of them for all we thry to do
for them. Well, I'll be off — good day. It would
almost make a man despair of humanity! See you in
th' morning.

Doctor. Good day. I hope so.

> [*The Apothecary goes off. Alleluia comes gliding down to
> the Doctor and holds out the red ticket given to him by the
> young Lad.*

Alleluia [*holding out the ticket*]. Another visitin' ticket, sir.

Doctor [*impatiently*]. Put it on my desk, put it on my desk,
man! [*Alleluia glides off swiftly, with hand extended holding*

*the red ticket; dives into the Surgery; comes out again, and
watches the Doctor go. The Doctor pulls the white muffler
closer around his neck, settles his hat more firmly on his head,
giving a few thick coughs as he does so, and goes out of the
waiting-room. Giving a richer belch as he goes out by the
door.]* Jasus, I'm in a terrible state !

*[Alleluia shuts the Surgery door and locks it, putting the
key in his pocket. He goes to the Dispensary door and
locks that too. He sees the three bottles on the floor that
Green Muffler left behind him. He takes them up and
shoves them under the bench, singing the chorus of " The
Rose of Tralee " as he does these things. The organ is
heard softly playing its old tune; it comes faintly into
the room, as if to counterpoint the song sung by Alleluia.*

*Alleluia [singing, and breaking off at times, resuming again
when his breathing finds it convenient]* :
She was lovellee an' fayer as ay . . . rose . . . bud
    in summer,
But it was not . . . her beau . . . tee aylone that
    won . . . me ;
Ah, no, 'twas they trewth in her . . . eyes fondly
    beam . . . in',
That mayed me love Mary, they rose of

*[He is now at the entrance door; he gives a last look round,
then goes out, closing the door behind him. Outside the
door]*

Traaa . . . leee !

AS THE CURTAIN FALLS

THE ROSE OF TRALEE

She was love-ly and fair as a rose-bud in summer But 'twas not her beau-ty a-lone that won me, Ah, no, 'twas the truth in her eyes fond-ly beam-ing, that made me love Ma-ry the rose of Tra-lee!

ALLELUIA
Caretaker's Chant

All-all-e-*lui*-á all-e-all-e-*lui*-á.

All-all-e-*lui*-á all-e-all-e-*lui*-á.

END OF VOL. III

PRINTED BY R. & R. CLARK, LTD., EDINBURGH

CAERLEON COLLEGE
OF EDUCATION, LIBRARY